W0254263

Rogues, Widows and Orphans

Also by Rebecca Lee and available from Profile Books

How Words Get Good: The Story of Making a Book

Rogues, Widows and Orphans

Mischief and Misadventures in the World of Books

Rebecca Lee

Profile Books

First published in Great Britain in 2026 by
Profile Books Ltd
29 Cloth Fair
London
EC1A 7JQ

www.profilebooks.com

Grateful acknowledgement is made to Cambridge University Press via PLSclear to quote from *An Experiment in Criticism* by C. S. Lewis

Illustrations throughout by Steve Coventry-Panton

SRD

Typeset in Doves Type by CC Book Production

Printed and bound in India by
Manipal Technologies Limited, Manipal

A CIP catalogue record for this book is available from the British Library.

Our product safety representative in the EU is BGC Sustainability & Compliance, 7 avenue du Général Leclerc, Paris, 75014, France https://baldwinglobalconsulting.com

ISBN 978 1 80522 118 0
eISBN 978 1 80522 119 7

For G. P. S.

Still the best writer in our household

Contents

Introduction 1

1. Bad Times: A Short History of the Typo 9
2. Bad Taste: Welcome to Ick Lit 43
3. Bad Takes: Censorship and Sensibility 85
4. Bad Apples: Plagiarism, Plunder, Pretence and Pranks 131
5. Bad Blood: Veins to Pick 171
6. Bad Endings: Old Stories, New Chapters 211

Acknowledgements 257
Selected Bibliography 259
Notes 261
Index 287

Introduction

'Words are, of course, the most powerful drug used by mankind.'

Rudyard Kipling

Mark Twain was barely thirteen when he discovered the intoxicating power of words to wreak havoc. Working as a printer's apprentice – a role aptly known as the 'printer's devil' for the chaos these young ink-stained workers sometimes caused – Twain found himself temporarily in charge of his brother's newspaper, the *Hannibal Journal.* Left unsupervised, he couldn't resist the temptation to stir up trouble. He decided to run a series of scandalous stories: one about a rival newspaper editor who had been jilted and left heartbroken, another lampooning two prominent citizens of the town, and a third mocking 'the "loudest" dressed man in the state . . . an inveterate woman-killer'.

The response to these stories was swift and, quite literally, explosive: 'While setting up the piece I was suddenly riven from head to heel by what I regarded as a perfect thunderbolt of humor . . . the paper came out, and I never knew any little thing attract so much attention as those playful trifles of mine . . . Higgins [the rival, heartbroken editor] dropped in with a double-barreled shotgun early in the forenoon,' reported Twain, with some sangfroid. Fortunately for literature, and Twain, Higgins ultimately chose humiliation over homicide. 'When he found that it was an infant (as he called me) that had done him the damage, he simply pulled my ears and went away; but he threw up his situation that night and left town.'

Twain's experience reveals something fundamental about the power of words: one writer's 'perfect thunderbolt of humor' can be another person's instant flash of fury. Words can be simultaneously 'right' (if you are Twain, sniping in type) and 'wrong' if you are Shotgun Higgins. Moving house might seem like a bit of an overreaction, but that's words for you; they have power far beyond the confines of the page, and sometimes consequences beyond their authors' intentions. They can have afterlives that destroy reputations, end careers, start wars, topple governments, or simply make someone so furious that they reach for their weapon. For a printer's devil to discover this power so young must have been both intoxicating and dangerous – a perfect metaphor for the stories we'll explore in these pages.

As someone who loves books, it might seem counter-intuitive that I'm writing one dedicated to all the ways words can go wrong. After all, I've spent my entire career trying to round up and eliminate errors for a major publisher. But as anyone who has gleefully spotted a typo in a prestigious publication, felt a flicker of schadenfreude at a pompous critic's downfall, or secretly enjoyed a literary scandal knows, it is possible to love books while delighting in their disasters. In fact, a love of books is profoundly *enhanced* by the stories behind the stories.

This paradoxical relationship is part of any book lover's experience. Books have the power not just to surprise, delight and transport, but to shock, annoy and provoke. They can earn vaulting plaudits and damning contempt – often simultaneously – for the *exact same* collection of words. I see no contradiction in loving books while also enjoying it when things spiral into calamity. You can't have the former without allowing the possibility for the latter. *Nihil sine toto.*

This book explores the myriad ways words can go wrong – sometimes comically, sometimes catastrophically – revealing the hidden side of writing, reading, publishing and literature, along with the surprising ripple effects and far-reaching consequences these mistakes can have on readers, culture and wider history.

Beyond the entertainment value of literary disasters, there's a more serious purpose, and understanding these failures shines a spotlight on how profoundly words shape our world. When the 1631 'Wicked Bible' accidentally commanded readers to commit adultery by omitting a crucial 'not' from the seventh commandment, it wasn't just an error – it was a scandal that cost the printers their licence and created a moral and social controversy that lasted decades. In 1989, when the publication of Salman Rushdie's *The Satanic Verses* sparked global protests and death threats, it demonstrated how words can literally become matters of life and death. The Japanese translator of *The Satanic Verses* was murdered in 1991, and Rushdie himself was attacked following the same threat more than thirty years later. These words, like many others before them, cast a long and bloody shadow.

Words can fail in predictable ways: misspellings, grammatical errors, plagiarism or simple incompetence. But they can also fail in unpredictable ways that change the course of history. These 'rogue words' escape authorial control and develop a life of their own, with consequences no one intended or anticipated. Sometimes this happens through error, as with the Wicked Bible. Sometimes the provocation is deliberate, as with Rushdie, or, as we'll find out, two Australians mischievously deciding to prank an entire literary movement with an elaborate poetry hoax. Either way, these rogue words remind us that once language is unleashed, there is always a chance it might become uncontrollable. Rogue words and their unforeseen consequences are the literary equivalent of detonating a bomb in a typewriter and running away.

The stakes here are genuinely high. Words are how we convey our most profound thoughts and ideas from one person to another. They're the foundation of law, religion, science and culture. When they go wrong, the consequences persist, refract and echo, sometimes for centuries. They start revolutions, destroy reputations, create moral panics, and occasionally lead to shotgun-wielding newspaper editors pursuing thirteen-year-old printer's devils.

Understanding how and why words go wrong also reveals the mechanics of how they go right. We'll explore the efforts of editors, publishers, translators and censors to control language – and why despite their best efforts, they so often fail.

We're going to start small, looking at the terror of the error: those tiny slips, hitches and hiccups (hiccoughs?) with big ambitions and even bigger consequences that can cause blood to boil, run cold or – for a certain type of reader – pulse with excitement. Once warmed up, we'll graduate to more substantive literary misdemeanours: the unwieldy sentences, purple prose and unlikely plot permutations that cause bookworms to shake their heads, grit their teeth and – most damning of all – arch an eyebrow. Before, of course, jumping online to share their disbelief at just how *bad* some writing can *be*. From plot holes and flowery language to Mary Sues and *deus ex machinas*, this book offers a lick of every flavour of ick lit, as well as celebrating the surprising pleasures it can offer the discerning connoisseur. 'People do not deserve to have good writing, they are so pleased with bad,' opined Ralph Waldo Emerson, unfairly choosing to blame readers themselves for the bad writing they must sometimes endure.

Hermann Hesse described words as 'the history of the human spirit', and this noble calling, plus industrialisation, meant that from the fifteenth century onwards, words could generate literary chaos at scale. When books were handwritten, errors might have been awkward and embarrassing, but there was a decent possibility of controlling them. Or, at least, having them only affect your immediate neighbours. Print runs and readerships were limited, and words could only travel at the speed of a horse and cart, which restricted their capacity to do damage. But with the advent of Gutenberg's moveable type, the printed word got a passport to everyone, everywhere, all the time (the printing press also supercharged literacy, and had a hand in developing a new, middle class). Bestriding the world, moving rapidly through centuries and across continents, conquering hundreds of new and impressionable minds a day – all without so much as a basic spellcheck function. The reign of error had truly begun.

Powerful as they are, though, words rarely have it all their own way. Even the best of them. In fact, usually the best of them when it comes to humanity's predilection for waging war on books. Heresy! Blasphemy! Obscenity! There have always been attempts to censor, control and corral words in a largely futile rearguard action against that most insidious of contagions: independent thought. This history of restriction tells us a lot more about the power of words and the trouble they can cause than might be first apparent, so we'll spend some time exploring the suppression of expression.

There's also the toxic relationship between writers and their own words to consider. Even the most skilled authors can be destroyed by their craft – driven mad by writer's block, crushed by rejection, or consumed by the kind of long-term literary feuds that make flash-in-the-pan social media spats look civilised. History reveals a problematic and sometimes downright unhealthy relationship between words and the authors who try their hardest to herd them. While we try and keep them in line, words have a way of homing in on and ruthlessly exploiting the weakest points of the human psyche. Whether it's destroying a writer's sanity by refusing to show up when most desperately needed, conspiring to pummel an author's fragile ego with a cavalcade of rejections, or dragging their progenitor into an inexorable spiral of bad reviews and bitter rivalry, words always want to have the final say.

It's not just authors who are destroyed by their own love of language. Book lovers, bookworms, and bibliophiles are in danger of stepping over the line to become total bibliomaniacs with an all-consuming desire for paper and ink. Obsessives, collectors, frauds and hoaxers; some people will do anything for a good story, including making themselves the centre of it.

Despite its long record of glorious blunders, the book has endured – dog-eared, typo-ridden, riotous – and it looks like it's not done causing trouble just yet. So our last stop will be to peer into the future to see how technology is creating new ways for words to go wrong. From the impact of e-books and social media to the existential challenge posed by AI, does the humble human-authored book still have a future after hundreds of years successfully seeing off all-comers?

This is ultimately a book about resilience. Despite everything – typos, scandals, censorship, technological disruption – books have survived largely unchanged for centuries. They've adapted, evolved, and continued causing trouble in new and creative ways. Like young Mark Twain discovering that his 'playful trifles' could drive a man to homicidal rage, every generation of writers (and readers) learns anew that words are not safe toys. They're volatile, unpredictable forces that, despite careful handling, often explode.

But that's exactly why we love them. As we'll see, the history of print is the history of error, but in among the printers' terms for disaster – the 'pie' (jumbled type in a heap), 'choke' (type filled up with dirt) and 'squabble' (letters running amok in the wrong line) – we find words like 'Pearl', 'Diamond' and 'Ruby' used to describe different sizes of type. Even in chaos, the letters glint like jewels. And Twain, despite nearly getting shot for his teenage journalism, wasn't put off. The printer's devil had learned his lesson about the power of words – but rather than being chastened, he was inspired. The boy who once made a rival editor flee town would grow up to become one of America's greatest writers, wielding words with the same mischievous precision that once had a man reaching for his shotgun. It just goes to show: there's a beautiful and compelling story in every precious pica.

1.

Bad Times: A Short History of the Typo

'Every time you make a typo, the errorists win.'

Anon.

A comedy of errors

In the beginning was the Word, and hot on its heels was the typo.

It's 1599, or perhaps 1598, and you're sitting in a busy, noisy, hot print shop, composing some text by a writer called William Shakespeare. You've probably heard of him – after all, he's one of the most well-known playwrights of the time, and his name on the title page already means 'big seller'. The play you're working on is called *Romeo and Juliet*, and although you don't know it, more than 400 years later it will still be being performed, read, discussed and critiqued. You're also unaware that a tiny slip you're about to make will be immortalised in print to confuse, bemuse and intrigue Shakespeare fans for the next four centuries.

You're stood in front of a wooden-framed typecase, which, in the half-century or so since Johannes Gutenberg invented moveable type, has already been streamlined and refined to make working at it as smooth, accurate and fast as possible. You're benefitting from the experience of all those compositors (the people who assemble type) who have gone before you: the height of the frame that holds your 'sorts' of types has been adjusted so that your right elbow 'may just clear the front of the lower case by the *a* box, without the smallest elevation of the shoulder', according to a late nineteenth-century description. Nobody wants shoulder strain from hours of picking out letters.

The boxes of type you work with are stacked one above the other in rows, at a slight angle to make them easier for you to reach. Each box is filled with small metal letters, all cast backwards, so that, when printed, they appear the right way round. You live in a mirror-word world. But you've been doing this so long you don't even look at the boxes; you know exactly where each letter is, so you can pick by memory. But today, one of the upper case 'N's has been jostled out of its box, and is now out of place in the box below – a cuckoo in the nest of the upper case 'V's. That's how you end up typesetting the line 'Nerona's ancient Citizens', instead of *Verona's*.

Presumably, you don't notice. Neither does anyone else: proofreaders don't yet exist. The error escapes to be printed, bound and distributed, puzzling the earliest readers of *Romeo and Juliet*. And a puzzle is all this typo is – it's not especially embarrassing, and it doesn't ruin the experience of the play. It's pretty obviously an error. But this small slip, seemingly insignificant in isolation, is a microcosm of the countless errors that have peppered print since Gutenberg, each telling its own story about the creation process.

Mistakes are a fundamental part of literary life. There can be a certain wonder for readers in typos and errors – 'how did *that* happen?!' – perhaps not appreciated quite so much by authors. As Oscar Wilde bemoaned, 'A poet can survive everything but a misprint.' But these slips allow us a peek behind the curtain of how books are made, and what happens when it goes wrong. And because we all make mistakes, they are a portal allowing us to share in emotions that, though we might be separated by hundreds of years or miles, by language or background, are common to anyone who has ever hit 'print' (or, more likely now, 'send') and immediately, or in the dead of night three days later, tasted regret. That's most of us, and it's why we're starting with a look at the humble word, and the trouble it can cause.

Though it might not take up much space on the page, a word has immense power. Especially when it's wrong. As we're going to discover, some of the smallest typos can lead to the biggest problems. You know the ones – embarrassment, lawsuits, changing the course of history.

Fortunately, it's rare that a moment of inattention leads to that kind of outsize reaction, but while mistakes have always haunted books (and the souls of those responsible), attitudes towards error have fluctuated. Initially seen as something beyond a writer's or printer's control, to be embraced as an integral part of the chaos of literary life, increasingly we've attempted to find ways to corral and confine mistakes, and in recent years attempted to drive them out of books altogether, in a task both Sisyphean and Herculean. These misspelt words might get far more than their fair share of attention, but then they have a habit of revealing more than you'd think. Of course, if you're the person responsible for the error, then 'regret' is always the overriding taste in the back of the throat. But for the rest of us, mistakes have a happy way of providing an entertaining extra depth to a story. There's not much to say about things going right, and plenty to enjoy in things going wrong.

Galley slave

The constant struggle with imperfection, the inherent 'wrongness' embedded in the very process of print, has inevitably led us to a yearning for flawless production, a dream of perfection only available in the realms of fiction. So now let's imagine that it's 2057, and instead of being an inattentive compositor, you're a 7-foot robot with glowing red eyes called EZ-27, or 'Easy' to your friends. Someone who has seen you work describes how:

> 'In the short time it took him to turn those pages, he caught every mistake in spelling, grammar and punctuation. He has noted errors in word order and detected inconsistencies. And he will retain the information, letter-perfect, indefinitely.'

That's right. You're a proofreading robot. You'd have homed in on 'Nerona's' like, well, a reader who can fire lasers from their eyes. Then you'd have automatically corrected it to 'Verona's' and filed the mistake away, so future scholars had a record of it for eternity. Easy was created by Isaac Asimov in a 1957 story called 'Galley Slave'. It's a courtroom drama – and yes, Easy takes the stand. All seven feet of him. Easy is the twentieth-century ideal of a proofreader: one that in less than a quarter of an hour can catch every type of mistake in a book (this one is called

Social Tensions Involved in Space-Flight and Their Resolution), correct them, and store the information, forever. While not needing sleep, food, remuneration or decent working conditions. Oh, brave new word-world.

Asimov's story title is a play on the word 'galley', used to describe a type of proof printed on a galley press (which takes its name from the long, low ships called 'galleys'; the enslaved unfortunates who were forced to row them were known as 'galley slaves') – they've been around since the 1650s – while 'proofs' have been with us since the 1600s – just a little too late to catch our compositor's Shakespearean error. Printers came up with 'proofs' to test what they were going to print; recognition of how since we began writing, composing and typing, writers, readers and book producers have spent a lot of time and energy fretting about eliminating mistakes: errors, typos, misprints, slips, inconsistencies, blunders. Likely as not, the printer would get the blame and have to take the time and trouble to fix what had gone wrong; the 'proof' was a way to try and manage and mitigate these risks.

Whatever we call them, mistakes have been there since books were first produced: history shows that you can't have one without the other. The story of the printing press is one of human ingenuity and brilliance, but it has a parallel story showing up our endless capacity to get things wrong. Books are our record both of things going right – and of when it all goes *very* wrong. Statistically, for every millions of lines of text that were perfectly put together, there will be thousands that weren't. The durability of the book, and the numbers it has been produced in, mean that these errors are still with us, causing havoc down the years. And our shared humanity means that we can find these slips fascinating and amusing, while simultaneously feeling empathetic schadenfreude for those held responsible. We've literally all been there.

Copycats

Gutenberg invented the printing press, but not the mistake. Let me introduce you to Titivillus, who's been causing mayhem since 1285, when he was first namechecked in a text by the theologian John of Wales. Titivillus was a 'patron-demon' (a demon that people would have an intimate relationship with), and his original brief was a watching one: he kept a close eye on priests and parishioners to make sure they didn't gossip, talk out of turn, or let their minds wander during church services. If they did err, Titivillus collected these 'neglygences in syllables and wordes' into a big sack each day, and took them down to Hell to be tallied up against the offenders, making him the world's most irritating micromanager.

In a typical case of mission creep, Titivillus went all in and morphed from a mere recorder of error to an instigator of it. There is a beautiful illustration from the fifteenth century of John the Evangelist sitting peacefully writing his gospel, while next to him a manically grinning Titivillus pours John's ink away. As the 'patron-demon' of scribes, over time he began to be blamed for anything that might blot a copybook: ink running out, smudges, textual errors. Titivillus was a useful scapegoat for those scribes who worked shoddily – a convenient way to excuse your very human failings. And he was much needed. Mistakes on vellum were a nightmare – almost impossible to erase without starting again – in a time when the cost of labour and materials meant that manuscripts were luxury products. No wonder these men of God could only get out of bed every morning to face down yesterday's errors by creating a devil to take responsibility for them.

Scribes also had to get creative with erasing mistakes. In one thirteenth-century Book of Hours the penman must have been horrified to discover a page where he had skipped a line entirely. Thinking on his feet, he wrote the missing text in at the bottom of the page, then, imaginatively, drew a little figure, a rope and a ladder – a sketch of the sentence being hauled into the right place. Other manuscripts show forgotten words being lassoed by rope and 'pulled' from the margins to the right place on the page, or hands with pointing fingers and sometimes elaborate cuffs showing how a reader should mentally pick up and lift a line to a different spot. These charming nods to the relationship between reader and book scribe are in-jokes that indicate how common it was for error to creep in. The writers were asking for the reader's forbearance – for them to play along in fixing their slips. Correction was a team effort.

The conditions the scribes worked under, in dim light and through all seasons, and the method of having to read a line from their copy, hold it in their mind and then write it out again, while needing to keep their train of thought as they re-dipped their pen in ink, were not conducive to accuracy. Errors were so common that they had their own very specific names: metathesis (transposing words, or letters), homeoteleuton (repetition at the end of words), homeoarchy (skipping a line), haplography (missing a word), dittography (repetition again, but this time of the whole word) and contamination (copying the wrong text into the wrong place). As well as avoiding all that, scribes had to write in *scriptio continua*, which meant there were no spaces between the words – they all ran merrily into each other. No wonder mistakes were made.

In 2014, a manuscript from the thirteenth century was discovered to have been written on top of a much older text. Digital imaging revealed several marginal marks from a beleaguered scribe: 'I am very tired, with a heavy head, and what I write I do not know!'; 'The one who writes tends towards errors'; 'Very drowsy and foolish'. These heartfelt asides give us a glimpse into these copyists as real people just like us today: doing their best, up against deadlines and distractions, trying to power through with a headache or hangover.

Scribes were usually copying out religious books – words of the greatest significance, the literal word of God. What they were writing wasn't open to interpretation; this was the word as truth. It wasn't as if God was prone to typos, although because so many of the earliest books were Bibles, produced by fallible humans, it could certainly seem that way. From the 'Fool's Bible' ('the fool hath said in his heart there is a God', which got the printer fined £3,000) to the 'Cannibal's Bible' ('If the latter husband ate her'), even the big man couldn't escape the trickster Titivillus. My favourite is in a 1944 edition of the King James Bible, where a damaged piece of type meant that female readers were urged to 'submit yourselves to your owl husbands' (it should have read 'own husbands'). Sometimes a subtle biblical error caused controversy over centuries, with plenty of academics and clergy making entire careers out of studying and arguing over variations in Bibles.

Fortunately for those of us who don't have owl husbands, as time went on, scribes became more accurate. They were better trained and more skilful, which leaves us with both fewer errors, and insights into them as people. It's a devilish trade-off: perfection tells us nothing. But while Titivillus might have given the beleaguered scribes a break from his meddling, he was still alive in the imagination of copyists (if not on the page), and found a new calling. Next, he became a useful focal point for their fears about the dramatic invention that threatened to make them obsolete – the printing press.

The corrections

By the early 1600s, scribes were an endangered species, threatened by the power and reach of mechanised print unleashed by Johannes Gutenberg in the mid-fifteenth century. But while typo types might have morphed from manual to mechanical, the continuing human craving for an explanation of error meant that Titivillus wasn't going to disappear with the scribes. Having proved his value as a folkloric scapegoat, he simply moved from the scriptorium to the print shop, embraced the new technology of moveable type, and started getting up to all sorts of pranks. He could now have almost limitless fun: printing was mechanical and complicated in ways that manuscript production wasn't, and the opportunities for things to go wrong had exponentially multiplied. Not only that, while a mistake in a manuscript might have been embarrassing, it was thankfully contained in just one copy. Now, however, the little devil could replicate mistakes in hundreds of books at once – the dawn of a golden era for him.

From the very start of mass-producing books, things went wrong. And then, with a sigh that echoed down the centuries, it became clear they would *continue* to go wrong, and a whole new vocabulary for mistakes would be needed. The sheer volume and variety of ways things could spin out of control in the bustling, mechanical environment of the print shop demanded its own specialised, often colourful, language. From a 'bodkin' (a steel instrument used to pick out incorrect letters from type) to 'bottle-arsed' type (wider at the bottom than the top) and 'bottle-necked' (yep, you guessed it: type that's thicker at the top than the bottom), the language of print is the language of error. From botched work to battered type, these evocative words all meant something very specific. And speaking of evocative words, how about widows and orphans? In typesetting these are words that are left alone at the beginning or end of a paragraph, words cast out and doomed to a life of permanent isolation from the other characters on the page.

Apparently, our inky devil doesn't just have all the best tunes. Like Granny with the festive selection box, he also grabbed all the best words from the publishing lexicon. Aptly enough, every print shop had a corner called 'hell', which was where broken, 'inferior' type got sent. A 'pie' wasn't just dinner, but a soul-crushingly muddled mess of metal type that had fallen on the shop floor. At the end of the day, 'clearing pie' would happen in every reputable print shop – an attempt to battle back against the rogues and have the words in line again before the next shift.

Lines of text could 'choke' (be clogged with dirt) or, my favourite, 'squabble', with letters running amok into the wrong lines. Squabbling letters have a hint of unruly toddlers at bedtime refusing to go to their rooms. A letter could be 'on its feet' or, if it didn't stand upright, 'off its feet', making it sound slightly tipsy. And it wasn't just the letters that went rogue, squabbling among themselves, falling off their feet, bottled-arsed. 'Blocked up' described text that was ready to go but that, crucially, couldn't be printed because, variously, the author hadn't returned their proofs, or the text hadn't been proofread, or the compositors had gone AWOL, or were on strike. 'Blocked up' type describes words in a traffic jam or holding pattern, waiting for everyone else to get their acts together before they could be freed.

This vibrant and visceral lexicon reveals just how central errors were to the daily life and language of the print shop. Beyond simply naming these frustrating glitches and gremlins of the composing room, however, printers also sought explanations – or perhaps scapegoats – for the constant battle against textual corruption. It wasn't enough to clear the 'pie' or un-'choke' the lines at the end of each day; blame needed to be assigned.

So, when he wasn't misspelling words, inverting words or causing entire lines of text to disappear, Titivillus was encouraging the youngest members of a printer's staff – the office apprentices – to do his work for him. Eventually, these apprentices became known as 'printer's devils', due both to their ink-stained appearance, and their association with the mischievous mistake-maker. These young devils were Titivillus come alive. And printers weren't averse to joining forces with the devil; they had a symbiotic relationship with him. Print shops were often signposted with a red devil outside them; one can still be seen today in York.

Sometimes a printer's edits could change the course of history, or, at least, science. In 1543 a German printer published an edition of Nicolaus Copernicus's *On the Revolutions of the Heavenly Spheres*, his famous contribution to science demonstrating that the universe was heliocentric: that the Earth orbited the Sun, rather than being the centre of the universe. While his book was being prepared for print, Copernicus was ill, and unable to check the proofs – he left everything to his printer and the correctors and learned men who worked for him. This was usual in the early days of print – printers weren't just responsible for producing a book, but for typesetting, checking the accuracy of the work, and correcting proofs, too. A printer's colophon – his name and address on the title page – meant that legally he, not the author, was responsible for making sure that what he printed didn't fall foul of the law.

It was only in the nineteenth century when the original manuscript of *Heavenly Spheres* came to light that scholars realised that as well as making corrections to the text, the printer had added in an entire anonymous Preface, which watered down the claims of the book. The Preface stated that Copernicus's theory about the universe wasn't necessarily the *truth*, but just one possible hypothesis, an argument that fundamentally undermined Copernicus's intentions. We might not agree with this way of working now, but the earliest text correctors were interventionist in all sorts of ways, and a book was a true collaboration of minds. The printer and author were equal in importance in the gestation of a book.

Although later scholars were outraged by the behaviour of Copernicus's printer, in the long run, this cuckoo Preface helped to dilute the message of the book in a beneficial way. It meant that *Heavenly Spheres* was able to evade censorship and reach a far wider audience. All because of the intervention of the cautious printer and his correctors.

While early print was a collaboration when it came to words, printers took on enormous financial risk, and this they carried alone. There was the cost of the printing press, the metal type, paper, ink and labour. This outlay had no guaranteed return: printers had to try and predict what their readers wanted (as difficult then as it is for publishers now) to make any money at all. While scribes had learned the hard way to take great care over the accuracy of their product, the opposite was true with print. In a new and competitive marketplace, it was vital to get words in front of readers as quickly as possible. So, the first printers were pragmatists, desperate to get something out there and start making a return on their investment.

That haste meant that books evolved from the 'ideal' form of the manuscript – accurate, beautiful, rare and luxurious – to an everyday object – democratic, abundant and error-strewn. Texts were no longer produced in secluded cloisters by men and women of God but instead churned out in their thousands in bustling centres of commerce. The limited number of manuscripts in circulation had meant they were prized, but the flood of books unleashed by mechanised printing meant that they quickly became devalued. The explosion of print in the Middle Ages brought with it a whole new world of reading – and of error.

This shoddy work by these new arrivals didn't go unnoticed. In 1521 Martin Luther wrote a letter commenting on the work of his printer, Johann Grunenberg: 'It is printed so poorly, so carelessly and confusedly, to say nothing of the bad typefaces and paper. Johann the printer is always the same old Johann and does not improve.' By 1525, Luther wasn't just irritated with his own printer, but with all of them. In an essay called 'Admonition to the Printers in Nurnberg', Luther complained about: 'my dear printers, who thus steal and rob' by sending out copies of his work where 'bits are left out, here they are displaced, there falsified, and other parts not corrected'.

Twenty years later, in 1545, Luther wrote in the Preface to his Bible yet another warning to printers. That's right. For two decades, Luther couldn't stop banging on about the failings of printers. The guy was obsessed with ink errors. This time he described how 'They just print it off quickly, as there's money to be made. Whereas (if they were true printers) they surely ought to know from experience that one can't be careful enough when it comes to such work as printing.'

Despite his complaints, Luther believed that 'Printing is the ultimate gift of God and the greatest one' – he was quick to recognise that mechanised printing could be harnessed to spread his message efficiently. But bad printing remained the ultimate sin. Luther believed in

Sola scriptura – 'scripture alone' – which meant that he felt that the printed Bible was the final source of religious truth, to be trusted more than even the Pope. 'I deny that he is above scripture,' was Luther's response to the idea of papal infallibility: the printed word triumphed over *any* man. That's why it was vital that printers got it right.

Luther was not the only writer to hold a grudge against printers. As soon as mass book production began, it was followed by lawsuits between writers and printers about accuracy and reputation. One legal tussle of 1499 stated that the author was responsible for proofreading their work – already, printers were fed up with being blamed not just for mechanical issues, but for every little typo, and were pushing back. But gradually, and perhaps needled by Luther's complaints, printers began to realise that accuracy, not just speed, could help their reputations. In this competitive new world, speed was good, but speed plus *accuracy* was something to shout about. Printers began to boast on the title pages of their books that 'learned men' had 'diligently amended' their texts. There was a shift away from publishing any old words, towards trying instead to ensure that what ended up in front of readers were the right words and, most importantly, made *sense*. This change, which happened in the fifteenth century in Europe and a little later in England, saw printers start to employ a new type of worker: a middle manager whose job it was to correct the pages they produced and who, usefully, could be blamed for mistakes.

These 'correctors' were a new managerial class and would have attracted a certain type of personality: pedantic, academic, careful, happy to live off glue, ink and free reading material in lieu of a liveable wage. People like me. Their days were spent reviewing the work of the compositors – the workers who laid out the type – by poring over galley proofs. They had to understand the mechanics of printing, as well as spelling, grammar and punctuation. They would be expected to read Greek and Latin and as many other languages as possible. We know quite a lot about them through a book called *Orthotypographia*, written in 1608 by a corrector from Thuringia (in modern-day Germany) called Hieronymus Hornschuch. HH (please, let's call him that – his name is catnip to Titivillus) was scathing about printers, complaining that 'They do everything solely for the use of money', and that they 'debase their material . . . with so many shameful mistakes . . . one cannot find even one page completely free of errors'. HH griped that some printers tried to save money by doing the job of the corrector themselves, but, as in his opinion 'they understand nothing', their texts remained as error-strewn as ever.

As someone who works as a twenty-first-century corrector, *Orthotypographia* is a fun read. No, really. Trust me. It's the shared frustrations that have lasted over 400-plus years of book production that are the most entertaining and revealing. HH shakes his metaphorical head (he probably did it literally, too) at authors handing in shoddy texts: 'It is particularly bothersome for them if someone submits his writings to their press not neatly written,' he states, going on to describe how 'even though they convene a meeting of the entire printing house and try to form pictures of nearly every word there is, yet they can guess very little.' Tell me about it. I've lost too many hours of my working life to deciphering cramped handwriting scrawled over margins, trying to work out exactly what's meant.

HH lays the blame for shoddy work firmly at the door of the author: 'The faults that remain as a result of incorrect, unintelligible, badly produced manuscripts, should not be considered typographical errors, but should be attributed to the authors of the books themselves.' Things were evolving from the (mostly) good-natured collaborative efforts of early printers and authors, and the battle lines of blame were emerging and hardening. These skirmishes still happen today: mistakes in print are the real orphans, with no one wanting to take responsibility.

HH also had views on the attributes necessary to be a good corrector: 'Conscientious approach, good eyesight and sobriety.' It's likely that this triumvirate was hard to come by in a time when universal optical care wasn't available, but drink was. It's rare to see an illustration of a printer's workshop without a small boy delivering flagons of ale to the thirsty printers; drunkenness was an occupational hazard, which was no doubt why HH warned against it.

HH believed that 'correct punctuation produces great elegance . . . whereas inconsistent punctuation seems to be the product of a disorderly mind'. You get the feeling he'd come across quite a few disorderly minds in his career (me too). But despite the prevalence of drunkenness, poor handwriting and inconsistent punctuation that plagued early printing, *Orthotypographia* shows how once print had established itself as the market leader, it then turned to the fight against inaccuracy and error. To do so, it created an entire new class of Titivilluses: eagle-eyed, punctuation-obsessed teetotallers, to use as scapegoats.

Much ado about nothing

Even as the role of the corrector became established, the legacy of earlier printing practices and the complex transmission of texts meant that errors – sometimes concerning the most fundamental aspects of print, like the spelling of the author's name – remained stubbornly embedded. Everything we think we know about Shakespeare has come through 400 years of interpretation and editing, and even the spelling of his name is probably down to a typo. He signed himself 'Shakspear' – and of the six signatures of his that survive, none of them has an 'e' between the 'ks' in his name. The 'ks' of Shakspear was a problem for printers: in the sixteenth century their type used a long 's' (ſ), and when set in italics (as author names usually were) that '*k*' and the '*ſ*' nestled next to it would overlap, chipping the metal type and sometimes breaking it – so-called 'botched' type. So, the compositors came up with a creative workaround: they stuck an 'e' in between the two letters. Problem solved. Well, sort of. Problem solved in the short term, conundrum over the correct way of spelling the name of the most famous playwright in the world set for eternity. Perhaps this was Titivillus's plan all along, to hitch his name to Shakespeare's forever.

In his lifetime, Shakespeare's plays were sold to theatre companies, who would make changes to the text as they used it. Additions, deletions, minor improvements. The manuscript was a living thing, in a state of flux. And as the GOAT, Shakespeare had an extensive back catalogue of 'bad' versions of his plays: 'bad' *Hamlet*, 'bad' *Romeo and Juliet* – early versions of his manuscripts that showed him developing his craft. Texts of his plays were sometimes constructed from members of the audience of a performance scribbling it down, or by a group of actors reassembling the text from memory as they rehearsed (actors would pass round a draft of the play and copy out their own lines, which was also a good way of helping them remember them). It's almost impossible for us to know what Shakespeare *really* intended for his plays – they have been interpreted and 'improved' by so many different editors – and printers.

The complexities of writing, composing and typesetting Shakespeare's work inevitably led to errors which stayed in print for centuries.

'And when I lived, I was your mother's wife,' reads a line in *Much Ado About Nothing* – probably a printer's error for 'And when I lived, I was your other wife.' Correcting such obvious errors, likely made by an overburdened compositor, is uncontentious, but not all mistakes are the same.

There's a difference between 'true' typos – introduced by the compositor or printer – and errors that Shakespeare himself might have made. In *The Two Gentlemen of Verona* Shakespeare doesn't seem to have a clue where Verona is, or that you can't get to it by ship from Milan. Later in the play, he's confused about whether the action is happening in Milan, Padua or Verona. This scholarly problem was recognised by Alexander Pope – poet, critic, hack-for-hire and one of the first writers to revise Shakespeare's work. In 1725 he produced a new edition of *The Two Gentlemen of Verona* which 'corrected' Shakespeare's mistake, and all editions afterwards followed his. But is this right? Don't the mistakes that Shakespeare made tell us something about him (that although he might have been educated and well-travelled in some senses, he hadn't been to Verona) – that we lose by having Pope stand between us and the text?

Pope was one of the first editors of Shakespeare to bother to go back and compare all the versions of his plays against each other ('Beauties and Faults of all sorts', as he described Shakespeare's words in his Preface). He was at pains to be as accurate and thorough as he could. But he wasn't averse to playing fast and loose with updating the text for eighteenth-century readers. He removed some lines and made them into footnotes. He refined Shakespeare's style. He kicked quite a few puns to the kerb. You get the feeling he felt he sometimes knew better. And unsurprisingly, not everyone agreed with his interpretation. In 1726 a book was published called *Shakespeare Restored: Or, a*

Specimen of the Many Errors as well Committed, as Unamended, by Mr Pope in his Late Edition of this Poet; Designed Not only to correct the said Edition, but to restore the True Reading of Shakespeare in all the Editions ever yet publish'd – a title (and subtitle) that issued a pretty comprehensive slapdown. It was by editor and author Lewis Theobald, who was incensed by Pope's 'smoothed' Shakespeare text. On the one hand, Theobald believed that an editor's duty was simply to preserve the original text, not to 'improve' on it (as Pope believed he had done), while on the other he criticised Pope for his 'religious abhorrence of all Innovation', whereby Pope refused to change obviously corrupted text.

All these interventions over the centuries (and Pope and Theobald were just the first), even if done with the best of intentions, diluted Shakespeare's original words in ways he could never have imagined. And Pope wasn't going to go quietly. Quibbling over the minutiae of Shakespeare was just too important. He responded to Theobald with a rebuke of his own in 1728, in a mock-heroic poem called *The Dunciad*, with Tibbald as the 'King of the Dunces' – a living representation of bad taste and dullness. This was how seriously the question of textual integrity was taken – the argument rumbled on for decades. Pope could perhaps have taken a little more of his own advice from *An Essay on Criticism*, published in 1711, where he advised readers that 'To err is human; to forgive, divine.'

Words fall apart, the binding cannot hold

'The kingdom of error in early modern Europe was as vividly real as the Kingdom of Satan. It was located not in the bowels of the earth but on its surface, in the shops of printers,' writes historian Anthony

Grafton in the 2023 book *Printing and Misprinting*. The earliest print houses were hot, noisy and chaotic – print was complicated, and there was much that could go wrong. So much, in fact, that there was a widespread belief that Satan's kingdom had a physical home right in the middle of the print shop, with printers churning out inaccurate and false information to lead readers astray. 'Error' wasn't just an ephemeral idea. The kingdom of error was an expansion of the realm of Titivillus, now working directly with the devil himself.

That might be why from the sixteenth century onwards error was celebrated as an integral part of a book's life. Instead of being ashamed of it, stories were made from it. Books were a revolutionary new product, and a certain amount of inaccuracy was accepted and tolerated from these upstart disrupters. Readers began to scribble in the margins of books with their responses, and as books were routinely passed around among many readers, unruly marginalia gradually gave way to more orderly footnotes and textual ornaments that allowed bookworms to duke it out on the page and follow each other's critiques.

When print goes wrong it's difficult to undo, which is why there were so many ways of trying to fix errors. Unlike the monk who could haul his missing line into place with a cartoon stepladder, printers were soon getting inventive with pasting in correction slips, printing new leaves to go into finished books, and drawing up extensive errata lists. One of the most well-known is the 'Judas Bible' where 'Judas' had been printed instead of 'Jesus'. The printer created a tiny slip of paper with the correct name to be pasted over it. And spare a thought for the publishers of Winston Churchill's *The Gathering Storm*, the first volume of his epic history of the Second World War. In 1948 they were on the receiving end of a midnight phone call from the irate author after he spotted – on page 56 of the finished copy – a description of the French Army as 'the poop of the French nation'. Of course, Churchill had meant to write 'prop', not 'poop', and demanded that the publishers print an errata slip, which they duly did.

Like the printers boasting on their title pages about the accuracy of their texts, errata lists, far from being a negative, were a positive sign to a reader that a printer had truly *cared* for a book. They had made the effort to highlight (and own) their mistakes, a job done presumably through gritted teeth, but in a spirit of absolute transparency for writer and reader alike. Best to get ahead of them, like author, politician and historian Hilaire Belloc, who had to shamefacedly agree to this errata slip appearing in his 1916 *The Last Days of the French Monarchy*:

> The author very much regrets to say that since the first edition of this book was printed off and bound, he discovered its title was identical with one written on the same subject . . . he trusts that this errata slip will correct any confusion between the two works.

Along with errata slips, one of the reasons we're able to see errors in action is that every scrap of paper used in early printing was valuable, even when something went wrong. From the earliest times that words were put down on parchment for posterity, they were also at risk of being lost. There's even a word for it: a palimpsest. This is a text that has had the original text scraped or washed off for another text to be put on top of it, in the interests of economy. Some ancient writings only survive in palimpsest form. These shadow texts are often of intense interest to scholars: many original liturgical texts were overwritten with new versions. Some palimpsest texts were overwritten because the original was heretical or dangerous, but more prosaically, the dearth of writing materials available meant that everything had to be reused and recycled.

Early printers had the same problem: a lack of materials with which to print. If you had that awful moment of seeing a page come off the printing press with a big mistake in it, you didn't throw it away. Instead, the paper was used as binding for another book – error included. Offprints and offcuts were still useful – and the error survived for posterity.

As print production and publishing steadily developed, the responsibility for catching errors broadened further. Now as well as the corrector, there was the proofreader. The correctors – the people we met in *Orthotypographia* – were employed in-house by a printer, double checking the work of the compositor – before text was set as a galley proof. After that, it went to a proofreader, usually employed directly by the author, as an extra third-party bulwark against error. The first reference to proofreading in the UK didn't come until 1683, too late for Shakespeare, in a book called *Mechanick Exercises*, where proofreaders were described as needing 'a quick Eye to espy the smallest fault'.

By the seventeenth and eighteenth centuries, authors were generally responsible for proofreading their own books, a responsibility which printers probably passed over gladly. Many authors farmed out the job to their friends (they still do); Samuel Johnson was a noted and in-demand proofreader, not least because of his dedication to standardising spelling through his *Dictionary*.

The evolution of responsibility for mistakes in a text from the printer, to the author, and then over time outsourced to the professionals – copy-editors and proofreaders – reflects the shady patches that mistakes dwell in. As Anthony Grafton describes in *Inky Fingers* (2020), 'Every time authors become enraged at copy editors, professors, editors, or agents – and every time editors complain that authors do not appreciate their work – they are replaying a scene that is deeply embedded in the classical tradition.' In *Orthotypographia* Hornschuch described the corrector's trade as like working in a 'sweatshop'. Earning your living as a corrector was no noble undertaking; authors viewed you with disdain and blamed you for every mistake, whether you were responsible or not. An integral part of the story of print is the eternal argument about who takes responsibility for error: from individual scribes, to printers or authors, or correctors, proofreaders and publishing houses.

By the middle of the nineteenth century there were about 300 'correctors' working in London. And moving through the centuries, the number of specialists who began to be involved in working on a book grew. Initially it was restricted to a printer and his staff – a compositor and a corrector, if he had one. But as professional publishers began to emerge in the early seventeenth century, they took on more responsibility for text checking. The printer's colophon, which saw them take official responsibility for a book's contents, began to be replaced by the publisher's colophon. That led to copy-editing and proofreading becoming commonplace, outsourced and professionalised. Publishers stepped into the role of collaborators, working closely with authors as co-creators of a book. Invariably, this led to higher expectations from authors, and readers. Charles Dickens wrote that: 'I must gratefully acknowledge that I have never gone through the sheets of any book I have written without having had presented to me . . . some unquestionable indication that I had been closely followed in my work by a patient and trained mind, and not merely by a skilful eye' – a ringing endorsement of the usefulness of a professional text checker. But not all authors agreed. Mark Twain was having none of it: 'Yesterday [my publisher] wrote that the printer's proof-reader was improving my punctuation for me, & I telegraphed orders to have him shot without giving him time to pray' – tongue-in-cheek (and what was it with Twain, firearms and words?), but an indication that the battle between author and producer over who was responsible for what continued.

As well as seeing the role of a text corrector become more clearly defined, the nineteenth century also saw greater formalisation in spelling and language. Samuel Johnson's 1755 *Dictionary* had kicked things off, with subsequent works such as Noah Webster's 1828 *American Dictionary of the English Language* leading to improved standardisation among the chaos of variant spellings and punctuation rules. Proofreaders also began to use universal standard symbols to mark up proofs – a common language between corrector, printer and typesetter that made it easier for everyone to understand what changes needed to be made. These symbols are still widely used today, including 'Stet', an abbreviation for the handy Latin phrase 'let it stand', used when proofreaders make a mistake in their proof correction that they wish the corrector to ignore. 'Stet' was first used back in 1755 – a quick but scholarly way of acknowledging that Titivillus had got to you and you'd made a mistake. Perhaps using fancy Latin was a distraction from a proofreader being wrong.

Efforts were made in the nineteenth century to untangle the chaos that had gone before: words were nailed down (as much as they could be) in meaning, usage and spelling, to create uniformity and a better reading experience – which also meant everyone's expectations about errors began to change. Once there were concrete rules in place about grammar and word usage, there were inevitably more complaints about it, too. The late nineteenth and early twentieth century saw the development of 'Letters to the Editor' for newsprint, where irate readers could vent their spleen about errors in their daily paper. The speed at which newspapers were produced of course meant there were usually more errors to be found, but at least readers have the joy of pointing them out. The *Guardian* (affectionately nicknamed the *Grauniad* for its propensity for typos) once misnamed Vikram Seth's *A Suitable Boy* as *A Suitable Buy*, and reviewed a performance of Shakespeare's *The Taming of the Screw*; these are recent examples, but Titivillus was showing his hand as early as 1838 when an article on Poor Law protests claimed they were instigated by 'writers', not rioters.

Proofreading and errors continued to find ways to evade the increased ranks of correctors lined up to catch them. As well as straightforward typos, in the twentieth century new errors sprang up from the 'line o' type' machine, which cast an entire line of type in one go. While the sixteenth-century compositor had a slow and laborious job, being able to make an entire line of text without break sped up typesetting hugely. But at the same time, it introduced new types of errors: line and word break issues, along with typesetting ones. Some types of errors became infamous: the letters on type-casting machines were lined up in order of usage, to help speed up the casting. The nonsense line *etaoin shrdlu* (the twelve most-used letters in the alphabet) would sometimes accidentally appear in print, a result of lines of type being filled out and discarded – or not. A 1978 documentary about the last issue of *The New York Times* composed with hot metal type was called *Farewell, Etaoin Shrdlu* – another nod to the hand of Titivillus and the world of error.

Even as proofreading and correcting was professionalised, however, writers were becoming ever more inventive in how they wrote. They were as likely to ignore the established rules of spelling and grammar as they were to use them – because doing so allowed them to break new literary ground and grab the attention of their readers. In the early twentieth century, the emergence of Modernism, which encouraged writers to move away from the confines of the traditional structure of the poem or narrative novel, meant that creativity was unleashed in ways that the original correctors could never have foreseen. In the original French edition of *Sodom and Gomorrah* (1922), the fourth volume of *In Search of Lost Time*, Marcel Proust wrote a sentence that had 847 words before you got to a full stop, while William Faulkner was prone to punctuation-less writing like this, from *The Sound and the Fury* (1929): 'My God the cigar what would your mother say if she found a blister on her mantel just in time too look here Quentin we're about to do something we'll both regret I like you liked you as soon as I saw you I says he must be . . .' These were words that revelled in not conforming to any sort of expectations – a delight for readers, perhaps, but a monumental headache for editors and proofreaders.

The high (or low, depending on your view) point of Modernism might be James Joyce's *Ulysses*, one of the most complicated texts in the history of publishing. Joyce's novel uses stream of consciousness, differing narrative styles between and across chapters, experiments with language, a non-linear structure, wordplay, puns, parody, ambiguity, allusions and the absurd to expand the boundaries of writing. But what to make of it if you were Joyce's proofreader? How to impose order on language when the *disorder* of language is a fundamental part of the writing style – when sentences are cut off and trail away, or when words are forced together in new portmanteaus that no reader would have encountered before?

We can see this confusion in the first edition of *Ulysses*, published in Paris in 1922. There were more than 2,000 typos in the first edition.

In America the text was even more ambiguous and uncertain because it was set from a pirated edition, rather than an official one. One paragraph has the protagonist Leopold Bloom coming across a misspelling of his name ('L. Boom') in a newspaper article. This was an intentional mistake on Joyce's part, but his first publishers decided to go ahead and correct it, believing it to be a true error. How could they have known? Joyce was not an easy author to work with: bigger publishers were wary of such controversial work, so his first publishers tended to be small and inexperienced. Joyce was also often in self-imposed exile in different parts of Europe, and that physical distance between him and his publishers would have made a back-and-forwards about his literary intentions challenging. As well as being physically difficult to pin down, Joyce was demanding and viewed publishers with suspicion. No wonder they often preferred to keep their heads below the parapet and just get the book out.*

So how does a proofreader tackle a sentence like 'Bronze by gold heard the hoofirons, steelyringing', or respect how Joyce used words to mimic spoken language, with words running together with no punctuation? In *Ulysses* typos aren't necessarily mistakes, just another example of Joycean genius, much as in *Finnegans Wake*, where Joyce left the phrase 'Come In', which Samuel Beckett had helpfully included in the text. Beckett was taking down Joyce's words as he dictated them, and someone had knocked at the door. Joyce liked the addition to the text so much that he insisted it was kept. Keeping up with the text of

* This was a family trait. For many years, Joyce's copyright was guarded ferociously by his grandson, Stephen Joyce. He claimed that 'Every artist's born right is to have their work . . . reproduced as they want it to be reproduced.' All well and good, but not if you can't reach the author to find out exactly what they intended.

Ulysses or *Finnegans Wake* is like trying to navigate Dublin – you're never quite sure if you're lost, or if it's all part of the journey.

The future perfect

Five hundred years ago, or 300 years ago, or possibly even fifty years ago, you might have worked as a printer or known someone who did. You might have passed one, or several, on your way to work, and could hear, see and feel the industry and labour that went into producing a book. Print shops and their workers were part of the community. They were visible, vital and shaped entire areas of towns and cities, like Fleet Street in London. The language of print was so ubiquitous that it became embedded into language: cliché, stereotype and upper and lower case are all everyday phrases that have reached us from the print shop.

Perhaps because we're now so physically divorced from the business of book production, we find it difficult to understand why and how things can go wrong. We're all so familiar with spellcheck that we can't imagine how typos can still make it through – but of course, they do. In 2010 American author Jonathan Franzen discussed in front of an audience how his forthcoming novel *Freedom* had been disrupted by the spirit of Titivillus. Franzen described how the first printing of the book was made not from the final, corrected text, but from an earlier draft of the manuscript, which still contained many errors. As if having to acknowledge this publicly wasn't enough, *Freedom* had been labelled 'the book of the century' by its publishers, HarperCollins, which is why 80,000 hardbacks had been printed – an enormous print run. The hyperbolic tagline was presumably what drew Titivillus's interest.

In the end, readers were able to exchange their faulty copies for corrected ones. The mistake was caused by the book's typesetter – the appropriately named Palimpsest – sending the wrong file to the printer. The size of the print run was simultaneously a headache for HarperCollins, and the reason why the error-strewn book wouldn't even become a collector's item. There were simply too many copies of it in print.

Mistakes like *Freedom* cost a publisher time, money and reputation to fix. But generally, errors in books don't lead either to having to pulp thousands of copies, or an uplift in the value of a book. Misprints can be significant in demonstrating that a book is a first edition or an early print run, but the book is valuable in *spite* of them, not because of them. The first edition of Ernest Hemingway's 1926 novel *The Sun Also Rises* misspells 'stopped' as 'stoppped' – significant only because the initial print run was limited to a little over 5,000 copies, which means that a century after publication, the number of copies surviving to be collected is minuscule, and because *The Sun Also Rises* is now acknowledged as one of the most important texts of early twentieth-century literature. While typos are a useful way of working out if a book is an early edition or not, since as time goes on they are routinely spotted and corrected, in and of themselves they generally don't make a book more valuable.

The wrong words will always find a way. The printer's devil didn't disappear; his tools simply changed. 'With automatic spell checkers running unleashed over what we compose, our era is that of correctly spelled typos,' says astrophysicist Neil deGrasse Tyson. The danger of automation – from spellcheck to autocorrect – is complacency. Titivillus thrives on it. Complacency makes us believe that all is safe and well with the spelling of our words, and we fail to recognise the danger of 'form' instead of 'from' and 'Untied' instead of 'United'. These sorts of typos, emerging from our fingers as they fly on autopilot across our keyboards, weren't something medieval scribes had to worry about. Technology only helps when we understand its limitations and find ways to compensate for it.

The dream of harnessing technology to eliminate error has a longer history than we might think. In the early twentieth century, a physicist developed a machine that could read letters and convert them into telegraph code. And in 1935 a patent was granted to an Austrian, Gustav Tauschek, for a 'reading machine'. These were early examples of optical character recognition (OCR) – a way of taking printed text and making it readable by machine. Scanning text removes the need to have a person sit inputting it letter by letter, which makes typesetting faster and cheaper – and reduces human error. But scanners struggle with their own very particular types of mistakes: reading 'burn' as 'bum', for example, or as I recently came across, a character being described as very 'modem' instead of 'modern'. While OCR can use technology to speed up text production, there still needs to be a human at the coalface.

As automation has encroached, we've had to find ways of working in tandem with it, to get the best from both the human eye and the digital scanner. In the early 2000s, Project Gutenberg, which works to digitise books, established Distributed Proofreaders. Project Gutenberg scans books in the public domain using OCR, but that can still leave many mistakes in a text, as we have seen. The human eye can also make mistakes, or fail to spot them, but the concept of Distributed Proofreaders is that the scanned text is uploaded next to the original, and humans complete the proofreading process by comparing the two.

The more eyes involved the better the chance of producing the perfect, error-free text.

Meanwhile, some e-book platforms already allow readers to submit typos or errors directly, meaning a book can be continuously improved in real time. This echoes when errors in a text were part of a two-way conversation between author and reader, defining their relationship. Of course, this process is a double-edged sword for a writer: it's hard to stomach your mistakes being pointed out to you, no matter how polite and well-meaning the messenger (and presumably they aren't always polite, or well-meaning). Perhaps we'll have to wheel out Titivillus again to provide cover. Unlike a print version, where a typo has first to be spotted, then wait for a reprint to be corrected, technology now means that as soon as an error peeks above a line, it can be eliminated, immediately. Publishing may in future look to harness the blockchain technology used by cryptocurrencies: imagine a world where you could track and verify every version of a manuscript, and then every edition of a book, so that you would always know who made which change, and when. Isaac Asimov probably did.

What we would gain in textual accuracy, however, would be lost in the joy of seeing how a book comes to *be*. The processes of revision, editing, re-thinking, revising and yes, correcting, that plays across the pages of an author's text are more meaningful when we know they are made in the writer's own hand. We can literally see, and feel, the work unfolding, which gives us a far greater understanding of, and closeness to, the text and its author.

At the start of this chapter, we met Easy the proofreading robot. Easy (and his manufacturers) end the story in court, accused of destroying the career of an academic called Simon Ninheimer by deliberately rewording parts of his book in galley proof, in a way which, according to Ninheimer, made him appear to be 'an incompetent scholar . . . a believer of ridiculous and outmoded viewpoints'. As the case unfolds, it turns out that Ninheimer secretly ordered the robot to make the changes to his book, so that he could attempt to highlight the dangers of automating proofreading and so destroy the reputation of mechanical text readers forever. He defends his decision by explaining that:

> A book should take shape in the hands of the writer. One must actually see the chapters grow and develop. One must work and rework and watch the changes take place beyond the original concept even. There is taking the galleys in hand and seeing how the sentences look in print and molding them again. There are a hundred contacts between a man and his work at every stage of the game – and the contact itself is pleasurable and repays a man for the work he puts into his creation more than anything else could. Your robot would take all that away.

While the concept of an infallible proofreading robot is a tempting one, Ninheimer has a point. Writing *is* all about individual human creativity – the hundreds of 'pleasurable' contacts between a writer and their work, followed by those between a reader and the text – mistakes and all. And the risk of automating book production is that this creativity becomes even further subsumed by technology. Are our spellcheckers capable of understanding that writers *play* with language – intentionally using variations in spelling, grammar and syntax to produce unique, thrilling and novel stories? Storytelling has grown more complex as time has gone on – we've seen profound shifts in language and style since the debut of the linear novel – as writers seek to push through the boundaries of what has been written before. The subversion of language – using it in unexpected ways – is what makes a book remarkable. Computers can't possibly understand the endlessly flexible, mercurial ways that writers might choose to make use of words.

We've progressed from a time when errors were never hidden away but were an accepted part of a book, and a writer's story, to imagining a future where a reader might never have to encounter a rogue word in the wild. But advances in digital technology mean that if an error is made in programming, a mistake can be disseminated far and wide, possibly without being noticed, until it has proliferated, well, everywhere.

Ultimately, readers, publishers and authors will want to balance the gains of technology with traditional methods of scrutinising text. Only humans read books for pleasure, so we must rely on humans to read books for errors, too. While one of the many joys of reading is in seeing when things go wrong, only humans can untangle and make sense of what they are looking at. *Is* it an error? Is it intentional? Does it matter? It's all part of the story. As Ninheimer laments at the end of 'Galley Slave':

> Your robot takes over the galleys. Soon it, or other robots, would take over the original writing, the searching of the sources, the checking and cross-checking of passages, perhaps even the deduction of conclusions. What would that leave the scholar? One thing only – the barren decisions concerning what orders to give the robot next! I want to save the future generations of the world of scholarship from such a final hell.

We're far less tolerant of mistakes than we have ever been. But being wrong is a shared human experience. Typos are a part of life; they have shaped our world more than we realise. Perhaps next time we spot one, we should pause to wonder what might have been. It's futile to try and aim for perfection when humans are so imperfect – and while an error tells us so much about a book's story. And who doesn't have a sneaking admiration for those typos that make it through? They're storytellers, and survivors, just like Titivillus. And be warned, he's still causing mayhem: for fifty years, if you'd looked him up in the *Oxford English Dictionary*, you'd have found the wrong page number for a footnote about him.* But given that errors look set to stay with us for as long as we write books, for writers, printers and editors, we probably want to keep him close.

* Of course, this could have just been an intentional and obscure in-joke by the compilers of the *OED* to try and placate Titivillus. I guess we'll never know.

2.

Bad Taste: Welcome to Ick Lit

'Easy reading is damn hard writing.'
Nathaniel Hawthorne (attrib.)

It is a truth universally acknowledged that the next best thing to reading a book is broadcasting your opinions of it. There's a reason that literary salons and dinner parties abounded in the nineteenth century to discuss good and, more entertainingly, bad writers. Nowadays we join a book club, log on to message boards and discussion forums, listen avidly to a podcast or scroll BookTok for hours to talk, judge and argue ferociously about writing.

This chapter is an addition to those celebrations of non-cerebration: an examination of the ways in which words can be wonderfully bad, and how that makes them still feel wonderfully pleasurable, and memorable. Of course, one person's masterpiece is another's 'I've-never-got-further-than-chapter-three-and-never-will-and-anyone-who-does-is-intellectually-suspect' – the polarity of experience when we talk about reading is what makes books so exceptional. Books bring out stronger opinions than almost any other form of entertainment. Perhaps it's because while not all books are intellectual, original or well written – in fact, in this chapter we'll revel in plenty that enjoy pure rule-breaking chaos – even bad words still take us away from ourselves and, crucially, closer to each other, to share in the tragedy and triumph of being human. This chapter delves into the joyous, messy realm of 'bad taste', exploring why we love to hate certain writing, whether objective rules for 'good' writing exist, and what delights, if any, can be found when authors throw the rulebook out the window.

Writers, critics and readers have all, in different ways and at different times, addressed the question of how to write, and what makes writing good or bad. It's an eternal fascination for other writers, and for readers like you and me. After the admittedly bigger topic of 'how do I live?', comes 'how do I write – and write well?' No two answers on how to write (or live) are the same, of course, and each can only be a personal response: ultimately, what's good or bad about a piece of writing is decided by you alone. It's one of the few areas in life where we're allowed complete autonomy. In a world where it can sometimes feel as if we have no control over anything, it's a relief that inside the few inches of brain that we call our own, we are unchallenged masters of our very own literary kingdom, free to like what we damn well like, without apology or mitigation, at least privately.

And enjoyment of bad writing brings its own very specific pleasures: mindless entertainment is a great way to relax, and a pacy thriller with no hidden meaning or symbolism can give hours of delight.

Deep down, do you crave re-reading all of *Sweet Valley High*? Or find yourself longing for a lightly plotted but compelling romance, knowing all the while that, despite what you might claim to your book group, you absolutely DON'T want to read anything in translation, or that's been shortlisted for a literary prize? That's fine – you don't need to out yourself. We're all anonymous here.

So, while there are plenty of sacred cows in storytelling that critics and the literary establishment at large like to bang on about – the three-act structure and shibboleths like 'show, don't tell!' – ultimately, what's good or bad about a piece of writing is decided by each reader for themselves. That might be why judging writing is so much fun, and so vital to our lives. When we're struggling with the 'how to live' part of life, we can escape for a few hours with a book, and then – sometimes – extend that pleasure by discussing all the things we didn't like about it with an understanding friend. Bad writing brings common ground – and good times. The words we love – and those we can't bear – tell us a lot about each other. It's hard not to feel disappointed if a friend or someone we think we know well recommends a book or an author to us and we don't like it; worse, we can't understand why on earth *they* liked it, and thought we might, too. And who hasn't tried to spare the feelings of a fellow reader when they ask what you thought of something they loved, or had to psych themselves up to find a tactful way of communicating what you honestly think about your reading group's latest choice and why it wasn't for you, or violently disagreeing with the endless 'Top 100 books of this year/decade/all time' lists?

While some words are considered unreadable, that doesn't mean they are unenjoyable. I know that sounds like an oxymoron but stick with me here. Enjoyment isn't, and shouldn't be, confined to perfection. Enjoyment can be found in the struggle, in the bad choices a writer makes, and in a shared realisation that we might not be able to do any better, and that writing is difficult – practically and emotionally. Writing anything takes a certain amount of courage; showing it to even one person doubles the bravery needed, while publishing quadruples it, requiring nerves of steel and the ability to take criticism not so much on the chin as, well, all over your body. Secretly, we can take great comfort in the joys of 'bad' writing: sometimes we just want something mind-numbing, straightforward, that gives us a story that we've read a thousand times before, with characterisation and language that we don't have to sweat over. There's also the hope it brings that, yes, we too could be a writer! If this girl has all the confidence and none of the skills but goes ahead and does it, so can I!

Speaking of confidence, I can't promise that I will never go looking online for things that my readers have said about me, but whatever your opinions, I hope you all have a great dinner party, date or day out opining on my words. If you hate them, at least you can use your ick about my lit to help you locate your reading tribe. What a terrible sentence. Judge away!

Free for all, or rules for all?

One of the joys of being a writer is being as contrary as you like with your arguments, finding novel ways to justify contradicting yourself. After all, these are MY words, and I'll do what I want with them, thanks for asking. All this is to say: having argued that readers make the rules about what is good and bad in writing, I must acknowledge that I'm an unreliable narrator. While personal taste reigns supreme in our private reading lives, the history of literature is also the history of attempting to define quality, leading to a long tradition of rules – we could call them constraints – in writing. 'The more constraints one imposes, the more one frees one's self of the chains that shackle the spirit,' said the composer Igor Stravinsky, in one of those useful bon mots I keep on hand to make me sound like Yoda when faced with a casual enquiry about how to write a book.

A story is made of a list of basic ingredients: plot, character, style and language – but it's the ratio of each that can be a problem, so constraint, or knowing when (and where) to stop, is vital. As Orson Welles said, 'If you want a happy ending, that depends, of course, on where you stop your story.' I'm not going to over-egg the cookery metaphor and start talking about decorative icing finishes atop the basic ingredients. Instead, I'll note that traditionally writers have tried to deal with the five elements of plot (exposition, rising action, climax, falling action and resolution),* while simultaneously wrestling with the challenge of writing fleshed-out characters with enough flaws to be believable, all liberally dusted with the icing sugar of sparkling language and style. Easy.

But despite the constraints our paragraphs must submit to, the 'rules' of writing are so ephemeral, personal and slippery that if you asked ten different writers for their view, you'd get ten different answers. Margaret Atwood tells us that we need 'a thesaurus, a rudimentary grammar book, and a grip on reality', while Kurt Vonnegut advised that writers need to 'Be a sadist. No matter how sweet and innocent your leading characters, make awful things happen to them – in order

* Nineteenth-century German novelist Gustav Freytag displayed these traditional elements of storytelling in a pyramid structure, often used today to demonstrate them visually.

that the reader may see what they are made of.' Fine, a sadist with a firm grip on reality, then – I'm halfway there already.

Literary criticism has been a hobby, passion and industry since Longinus in the first century, and probably before then, too. Critic Vincent B. Leitch described how Longinus believed that the purpose of great writing was to expose the reader to nothing less than the sublime, via 'great thoughts, strong emotions, certain figures of thought and speech, noble diction, and dignified word arrangement' (I love the phrase 'dignified word arrangement' – we should use it more in literary praise). Longinus was following in the footsteps of Aristotle, who as well as being known as a snappy dresser and believing that the sex of goats could be determined by which way the wind was blowing, also found time to establish his own rules for 'good' writing. In Aristotle's view, that was writing capable of producing fear and pity in the reader, via characters that were moral, realistic, consistent and appropriate, and with a cliff-hanger plot that incorporated the two Ds: discovery and denouement.

In the slipstream of Aristotle was Horace, whose *Ars Poetica* is one of the most important texts in the history of literary criticism – the study of what makes a text good. *Ars Poetica* had rules on plot, prose, and the virtue of 'decorum', which word Horace used to describe writing done in a style that suited its subject matter – 'A comick incident loaths tragic strains.' For Horace, the aim of writing was that it should instruct, or delight: 'The poet wishes to benefit or please, or to be pleasant and helpful at the same time.' I'd add that over and above being pleasant and helpful, being a well-reviewed best-seller would be nice, but Horace was a bigger and better person than me.

Of course, it's not only the ancients who had something to say about rules for writing. George Orwell was right about pretty much everything, including what questions to ask yourself when putting pen to parchment. He would begin by interrogating his words with these queries:

> *What am I trying to say?*
> *What words will express it?*
> *What image or idiom will make it clearer?*
> *Is this image fresh enough to have an effect?*

And then he developed these rules further, landing on these beauties, still beloved by writers everywhere:

> *Never use a metaphor, simile, or other figure of speech which you are used to seeing in print.*
> *Never use a long word where a short one will do.*
> *If it is possible to cut a word out, always cut it out.*
> *Never use the passive where you can use the active.*
> *Never use a foreign phrase, a scientific word, or a jargon word if you can think of an everyday English equivalent.*
> *Break any of these rules sooner than say anything outright barbarous.*

These seemingly straightforward rules provide a useful benchmark against which we can measure the joyful 'barbarism' of writing that ignores them entirely. But before that, we should add one more rule, to keep our study of constraint useful, but constrained. This final one is summarised by Martin Amis in his 2001 book *The War Against Cliché*, which title helps us understand the serious threat of the platitude when it comes to words. It's war, I tell you. Well, Martin does:

'All writing is a campaign against cliché. Not just clichés of the pen but clichés of the mind and clichés of the heart. When I dispraise, I am usually quoting clichés. When I praise, I am usually quoting the opposed qualities of freshness, energy and reverberation of voice.'

Freshness, energy, reverberation of voice – a wish list for all writers. But as William S. Burroughs noted: 'You do an awful lot of bad writing in order to do any good writing. Incredibly bad. I think it would be very interesting to make a collection of some of the worst writing by good writers.' It would, wouldn't it? Because it's only by looking at bad writing that we can appreciate a little more how the good comes to be, and happily for us, bad writing is good entertainment.

Before we take up Burroughs' challenge, we should remind ourselves of Horace's very simple summary for aspiring writers: 'Choose a subject that is suited to your abilities . . . give long thought to what you are capable of undertaking, and what is beyond you. A man who chooses a subject within his powers will never be at a loss for words, and his thoughts will be clear and orderly.' This makes writing sound so easy – but I think we've all sensed that sometimes an author has bitten off a little more than their pen can comfortably chew. So, now that we have established what the rules *are*, let's find out who makes them, and indulge ourselves in finding out what happens when you ignore them.

Rule-makers

The value of literature and the rules it should adhere to have been debated since we first started telling stories to each other. The rules of writing and what literature stood for weren't just of interest to other writers and readers: the ancient Greeks considered them fundamental to what society stood for. Opinions varied on the importance of words and writers in the world: in *The Republic* Plato argued that poets and poetry were mere copies of reality and hence led readers away from truth; he didn't place much value on literature. But as we've seen, any Greek thinker worth his salt had an opinion on how words should be used. And the way the Greeks thought about the rules of writing cast a long shadow. As late on as the Renaissance, translations of Aristotle's works into Latin and Italian and the post-Middle Ages rediscovery of ancient texts meant that writers were relying once more on the Greek theorists to tell them how to write.

George Gascoigne's 'Certayne Notes of Instruction in English Verse', written in 1575, was one of the earliest poetry-writing manuals in English, and had a profound influence on the Elizabethan poets. But any time one writer tried to establish 'the rules', along came another one to break them. Philip Sidney's *Defence of Poesie*, published in 1595, emphasised that the poetic mind could make its own rules – a have-your-cake-and-eat-it approach that I certainly can work with. So could the Romantics. For these nineteenth-century poets, rules simply did not exist: poetry was transcendental, driven by overflowing and intense feeling. Poetry, said Shelley, 'strips the veil of familiarity from the world, and lays bare the naked and sleeping beauty, which is the spirit of its forms'. There's no rule that helps with *that*.

By the twentieth century, literary study had become a discipline all its own; one that attracted the attention not just of critics, academics and theorists, but of writers themselves. And this study combined analysis of both bad, and good, art. As author Mark O'Connell says, 'There is nothing uniquely contemporary, or even modern, about the ironic enjoyment of bad art. It's been a popular diversion for centuries.' Indeed. We're used to endless lists of 'best' and 'worst' books appearing online. In fact, the first 'best' books list was drawn up in 1886 by polymath Sir John Lubbock, who noted that 'The choice of books, like that of friends, is a serious duty.' His list was not one of personal favourites, but instead books that were 'must-reads' for readers wanting to educate themselves. 'Our ancestors had a difficulty in procuring them. Our difficulty now is what to select,' said Lubbock of books, but he was happy to have a go at narrowing the field for readers – just perhaps a little too much in his own image. There was only one woman on the list (George Eliot), though he did apparently *consider* having Jane Austen on there.

Although Lubbock's list of 'bests' might have had noble aims, it's far more fun to consider the worst books, and in 1909 a writer called Samuel McChord Crothers did just that, pointing out that 'there is nothing better than the thorough analysis of a book which has no redeeming qualities'. His article 'The Hundred Worst Books' was published in *The Atlantic*, an indication that serious analysis of bad books was moving away from the literary establishment and out into a wider readership. McChord Crothers bemoaned writers with no originality ('The thoroughly bad writer is one who in three hundred and fifty pages tells you exactly what you expected, in precisely the way you expected him to tell it'), and books that committed the ultimate sin: 'The chief end of a book is to be read, and the lowest depth into which it can fall is to be unreadable.'

McChord Crothers was just one of many literary critics who have attempted to define 'bad' writing, and he saw it as an essential public service. 'For purposes of instruction in literature, the reefs and shoals should be properly marked,' he wrote, meaning that readers deserved to be warned about bad writing they might stumble across; the shock could be too much for them otherwise. But intrepid readers, like you, me and the reviewers, theorists and writers that have gone before, will want to go and explore these dangerous reefs and shoals for ourselves. You don't need to be a professional critic to enjoy a thorough analysis of a book which has 'no redeeming qualities'. That, after all, is why we're here.

'No plot, just vibes'

In *The Big Sleep*, Raymond Chandler's first outing for detective Philip Marlowe, the story begins with a murder that is ultimately never solved. When it came to the film adaptation the filmmakers wrote to Chandler to ask him to clarify who killed chauffeur Owen Taylor. 'Damned if I know,' came the laconic response. Chandler was fabulously relaxed about the lack of plot resolution in *The Big Sleep*, but our earliest reading experiences tend to lean heavily on plot for satisfaction: would *The Very Hungry Caterpillar* succeed if the caterpillar didn't eventually become a butterfly, thereby hitting Aristotle's brief that all stories should have a denouement? What would be the *point* of the Famous Five if they never solved the mystery? Plot – the very human urge to know *what happens next* – is the driving force of all the big classics: the *Odyssey*, *Great Expectations*, *War and Peace* – it pulls along the connecting thread of universal themes (that question of 'how to live' again) that keeps us turning the (many) pages.

It's not just having a plot that the critics thought was important: so were the mechanics of how it functioned. Cheating your way to plot resolution was not on. But the temptation of an easy solution to a plotting issue has proven too much for plenty of writers over the centuries. In Euripides' *Medea* it's a chariot drawn by dragons that saves the day, in William Golding's *Lord of the Flies* it's a passing ship, and in L. Frank Baum's *The Wonderful Wizard of Oz*, it's the most unearned plot manipulation in literature: 'It was all a dream.' But you've got to feel for these guys. Sometimes you write yourself into a corner, and passing ships or vivid dreams seem like the only way out.

The Greeks were shameless about plot hacks. They often made use of a *deus ex machina* – literally, 'god from the machine' – so-called as the deity in question would be lowered onto the stage (or raised from a trapdoor) via a mechanical device to tidy up the loose ends of a play. Aristotle argued in his *Poetics* that a *deus ex machina* indicated a weak, lazy writer – that if a plot was strong enough, no such device was necessary. As Antiphanes said: 'When they don't know what to say and have completely given up on the play' – out pops a god.

Conversely, professional overthinker Friedrich Nietzsche believed that a device such as a *deus ex machina* should be avoided because it was unrealistic. The world was messy, and that mess should not be artificially resolved; to do so would create a false sense of consolation that a story could always neatly square things away. He's not wrong, but what a mood-hoover. Of course, Nietzsche's point of view has the potential to create some tension between the author and audience: one of the pesky annoyances about readers is that they mostly enjoy a plot with resolution. But not *all* readers. BookTok, a TikTok subcommunity that focuses on books and literature, is currently alive with enjoyment of stories that have 'no plot, just vibes' – books like Ottessa Moshfegh's *My Year of Rest and Relaxation*, or anything by Sally Rooney, where the characters just sort of *exist*; lying around for weeks on end not doing much, or living lives of intense introspection where they ponder one thing for hours, then perhaps switch to thinking about another, before contemplating folding their laundry. BookTokers have also pinpointed plot-free-but-vibing authors from previous eras – writers like Sylvia Plath and Virgina Woolf (after all, Mrs Dalloway is a woman just spending the day preparing for a party), whose characters might also be said to inhabit largely plot-free pages.

A plot-free narrative is restful for a reader. You can meditate along with the protagonist, giving yourself up to the whims of the author, floating along on the flotsam and jetsam of their language without having to keep track of where you are in time and space. And plot-free is a breeze compared with reading a book where there *is* a plot, but it's perhaps more plot than the author can handle. While critics like McChord Crothers sought to define and warn against 'bad' writing, other authors seemed to revel in defying expectations entirely, creating works memorable precisely *because* they ignore every conceivable rule of plot, character and, sometimes, basic common sense. Let's look at the work of Harry Stephen Keeler, one of the strangest writers imaginable, to see what happens when the plot/vibes ratio gets wildly out of whack.

Keeler was born in 1890 in Chicago (which he always referred to as 'the London of the West'), and his entire (prolific) literary output was based on a theory he called 'web-work', which he carefully expanded on in a paper titled 'The Mechanics (and Kinematics) of Web-Work Plot Construction, with Diagrams'. Keeler loved an explanatory diagram – strange, as his plots were so random they should have been unmappable. In his paper, Keeler attempts to define what a plot is and comes up with the following: 'Plot is the relationship between a number of incidents that shall permit, by its intersection with a particular character, a dramatic story.' 'Web-Work Plot Construction' suggests that Keeler wanted to establish ground rules for what plot is, but despite his attempts to nail it to the wall, plot proved to be a slippery opponent.

Part of the problem might have been his working methods. These included producing a huge, overlong manuscript, which he would then go through, cutting out extraneous plots and subplots, of which there were many. That spare material would then be kept (he called it 'the chunk', which makes it sound quite characterful; like an overfed literary house pet) until he wrote a second manuscript – at which point he would reuse 'the chunk' and fold it into the second story. In turn that would then be cut, producing another . . . chunk. It's a sort of virtuous circle of literary recycling, in which nothing goes to waste, or, presumably, bears any relation to the plot it's meant to be supporting. 'Keeler is the master of the ludicrous but internally consistent coincidence, used both for creating situations and solving them,' wrote one reviewer. Oh – he was also obsessed with skulls and featured them in all his stories (he often included a little light trepanning, too) – sometimes shoehorned in as part of the action, or just as an extraneous and indulgent detail.

Apparently, Keeler collected newspaper clippings of strange and bizarre events (me too, although mine are all virtual), and to start a story would grab a handful of clippings, then try to work out how to link them together. It's a tragedy that he never got to use a web browser; imagine the number of open tabs. Rather than that of a traditional thriller writer, his working method has been described as like the Dadaists (these early twentieth-century disrupters embraced chaos and absurdity, challenging the established rules of writing) or, conversely, the Oulipo (they enjoyed actively constrained writing; for them, sticking to the rules was more important than the end result. You could say that, really, they wrote for themselves, not their readers). In an essay on Keeler, author William Poundstone writes that 'The perfect Keeler character is a clockwork automaton; the perfect Keeler plot is a pinball machine.' In his appreciation of Keeler, 'The Wild and Woolly World of Harry Stephen Keeler', Francis M. Nevins Jr writes that 'every absurd complication turns out to make blissfully perfect sense within the author's zany terms of reference . . . his most famous and most characteristic ploy is the system of interlocked backbreaking coincidences.' Coincidence is the enemy of plot, but coincidence plus constraint and a dash of chaos led to Keeler creating something truly unique.

G. K. Chesterton explained that in a good detective story, 'A footprint, a strange flower, a cipher telegram and a smashed top-hat – these do not excite us because they are disconnected, but because the author is under an implied contract to connect them. It is not the inexplicable that thrills us; it is the explanation we have not heard.' Keeler's plotting was as inexplicable and disconnected as a cipher telegram is to a strange flower, and he gleefully smashed up the top hats and the contract with the reader that said he was duty-bound to connect the parts of his plots to each other.

In a 1936 novel called *X. Jones of Scotland Yard* (the X. stood for 'Xenius', a name due a revival), the story is told through a series of documents – letters, diagrams, family trees, even eerie black-and-white photographs. The plot revolves around a tycoon found dead on a croquet lawn, surrounded by tiny footprints. And in *The Spectacles of Mr Cagliostro*, the eponymous protagonist must wear a pair of blue glasses for a year. Eventually, he can see a secret message, visible only to him via the glasses. Why? Oh, a clause in a will, somewhere. In *The Face of the Man from Saturn* someone kills an antique dealer, so they can steal the face (only the face!) from a surrealist painting. The blurb for this one reads: 'Only Harry Stephen Keeler could tell such a tale, while inserting one of his most famous short stories, "The Strange

Story of John Jones' Dollar". You won't forget it!' This leads us to another of Keeler's unorthodox methods of writing.

Along with the genius of recycling 'the chunk', Keeler was also prone to padding out his manuscripts with the words of his wife, Hazel Goodwin. Handily, she was a short story writer, so Keeler would, especially towards the end of his career, expand his own work with spare bits of hers. He would have one of his characters start browsing a story as part of the plot. They would open up a book or magazine at random, and start reading. But what they would read was one of his wife's stories (or sometimes, one of his own, as in *The Face of the Man from Saturn*). This could go on for hundreds of pages. Did these stories contain anything relevant to the main plot of the novel? Of course not – how on earth could they? But they were an efficient way of bumping up his word count. And Keeler's novels were long, some more than 700 pages; one enthusiast I found online described them as being like *Waiting for Godot*, drawn out to the length of *Finnegans Wake*, if you can imagine such a thing.

Most readers pick up a mystery or suspense novel expecting to be able to hazard a guess as to who the murderer is. It's part of the joy of reading these types of books, and of writing them. The challenge for the author is in laying a trail with hopefully just enough clues for the alert reader to puzzle out who did it, and why. The plot is a pact, a deal between reader and writer, an integral part of why we read. But the pact crumbles to dust with Keeler. In *The Ace of Spades Murder* the killer makes his first appearance on the third to last page of the book; there has been not a single mention of him previously. But that seems positively generous compared to the denouement of *X. Jones*. It's 448 pages long, but to find out who the murderer is, you either need to wade through the entire thing (don't; I did it for you) or turn to the last page. No, sorry, to a footnote on the last page. There, you will discover that the killer (who, naturally, is a man dressed as a baby who travels by helicopter to kill his victims) 'was, of course, Napoleon Bonaparte, Emperor of France!' It's the ultimate deus ex helicopter machina.

Keeler's American publishers, Dutton, embraced and encouraged this plotting chaos. They published a series of books as 'Dutton Clue Mystery' titles, whereby each novel was published

> with a special page inserted in each book at a point where all the characters and necessary clues have been presented to make it possible for you to determine the guilty person or persons. At this point, without reading further, you make your decision, write the name of the person or persons you believe to be guilty on the coupon of the page, and send it to us. If you are right, we will send you a card of award.

That might have worked with traditional thriller writers, but not so with Keeler. For example, 1931's *The Matilda Hunter Murder* included the coupon, but it was inserted in the book at a point where it was followed by another 200 pages of plot – so presumably you'd have had to have guessed wildly at the guilty party. To be honest, reading on for the rest of the book would probably have led to the same outcome.

Speaking of publishers, in 1941 Keeler wrote *The Peacock Fan*, a satire on the publishing industry, featuring two characters (publishers Simon and Tolliver Vinnedge) who collude to get one of their authors sent to the gallows. This was the final straw for Dutton, and they dropped him soon after. While Keeler achieved modest success in the 1930s, by the 1950s his career was in freefall. What happened next is best told in the words of Nevins, who single-handedly resurrected Keeler's work from obscurity:

> In his own wacko way he worked desperately to adapt to new markets and new styles. Seeing that science fiction was enjoying boom times, he tried his hand at that genre. The result was a series of commercially impossible novels whose protagonist is a house. [Yes, you read that right. A house.] Seeing that the police procedural represented the new wave in detective fiction, he tried his hand at that genre too. The result was another string of commercially impossible novels, each featuring a different Chicago police detective as the main character but having about as much relation to, say, Ed McBain's 87th Precinct series as a toad has to grand opera.

Although his writings are undoubtedly at the sharp end of the weird writing spectrum, Keeler made a steady living from them. He was published, he edited a pulp magazine, and he had a cult following, then, and now. And it feels as if he had a whale of a time constructing his stories. He's all vibes AND outlandish plot. Neil Gaiman said: 'My guiltiest pleasure is Harry Stephen Keeler. He may have been the greatest bad writer America has ever produced. Or perhaps the worst great writer. I do not know. There are few faults you can accuse him of that he is not guilty of. But I love him.'

A year after he was dropped by Dutton, *The New York Times* wrote that 'We are drawn to the unescapable conclusion that Mr Keeler writes his peculiar novels merely to satisfy his own undisciplined urge for creative joy.' And that undisciplined creative joy is still inspiring others today. Keeler has his own fan club, and his books are back in print, including many that were unpublished when he died. There's even an X account which posts as him: 'A million stories are trembling to be crystallized on the black ribbon of the typewriter'; proof that even the craziest of writers can inspire a truly beautiful line. In some ways, Keeler was made for social media and it's a real shame he missed out: 'And comparisons – comparisons odious! – were rearing themselves like impenetrable granite ghosts lined starkly along the fence of reason', and other gems inspired by his words can be found at @HarrySKeeler. The skulls are waiting.

Real characters

Harry Keeler's 'characters' are nothing of the sort – instead, they are ciphers – lightly sketched, predictable (or unpredictable in ways that haven't been earned), with no discernible backstory to explain their actions. There's Penelope Periwinkle, a kleptomaniac librarian who only steals books bound in a specific shade of puce; she lives in constant fear of Barnaby Gundelfinger (owner of a chamber of horrors), who she is convinced wants her collection for a sinister display. Or Professor Algernon Fogg, an inventor who wears mismatched socks as a matter of principle and has dreamt up a 'Reverse Weather Machine' designed to create highly localised, brief showers of lukewarm tapioca pudding. Fogg insists this is the key to solving world hunger, but only uses it to inconvenience his neighbour, Mrs Higgins, who runs a rival pigeon-fancying club.

It seems unlikely that Keeler was troubled by Heraclitus' maxim that 'Character is fate', but think of Michael Henchard's drunken decision to sell his wife and child in *The Mayor of Casterbridge*, or how Hamlet's downfall is due entirely to his own character flaws, rather than any external events. Character is the emotional centre of good writing. Plot gets busy getting stuff done, and you certainly couldn't travel from Preface to Epilogue without it, but character is what makes us *feel* stuff along the way.

A well-drawn character in a book is someone we can empathise with, because despite being entirely fictional, they are just like us – or, at least, they have certain characteristics that we recognise as human. From Sherlock Holmes to Holden Caulfield, and Atticus Finch to Jane Eyre, we might struggle many years later to recall the precise details of a book's plot, but we retain an emotional snapshot of a protagonist's character. The fictional characters we recall can be good, or bad (murderous serial killers like Hannibal Lecter, Patrick Bateman or Tom Ripley) – that bit doesn't matter. It's more important that they are whole, human and relatable. Well, okay – they can also be Grand High Witch, as in Roald Dahl's *The Witches*. Who could forget 'the most evil woman in the entire world' and her bald head and blue spittle?

As you'll have picked up on by now, there are exceptions to every writerly rule. From first publication in 1925 onwards F. Scott Fitzgerald copped some criticism for his characterisation of Jay Gatsby, with Edith Wharton writing to him to say that 'My present quarrel with you is only this: that to make Gatsby really great, you ought to have given us his early career (not from the cradle – but from his visit to the yacht, if not before) instead of a short résumé of it. That would have situated him, and made his final tragedy a tragedy instead of a *fait divers* for the morning papers.' H. L. Mencken wrote in the *Chicago Tribune* that 'Fitzgerald seems to be far more interested in maintaining its suspense than in getting under the skins of its people', a response perhaps to the one-dimensional nature of Jay Gatsby's character. After all, he really only has one interest in life: winning back Daisy Buchanan.

In our time we've all come across recognisable character tropes while happily curled up in a chair reading – the damsel in distress (Gothic literature famously went to town on this); the wisecracking sidekick (a sidekick is very much okay, of course. Dr John Watson is Sherlock Holmes's – but Watson is also a fleshed-out and believable character himself – for those reasons almost as beloved as his friend and mentor); the evil villain with no credible backstory. This last one was a trap that Arthur Conan Doyle eventually toppled into: just what *was* Moriarty's motivation for wanting to destroy Holmes?

Anthony Burgess said that 'A character, to be acceptable as more than a chess piece, has to be ignorant of the future, unsure about the past, and not at all sure what he's supposed to be doing.' Fictional characters, just like us, need room to evolve, and their uncertainty about their place in the world helps us relate. There's not much mileage in a character starting off Chapter One in their final form. *Pride and Prejudice* begins with Lizzie Bennet as a close-minded young woman who must evolve into a more thoughtful one; in *Emma* the heroine undergoes a similar, and sometimes painful, transformation. Thomas Hardy was the master of character evolution – Michael Henchard, Bathsheba Everdene and Jude Fawley must all grapple with social constraints, their own nature and the influence of fate before they can reach their final representations.

When asked what he thought was the best way to start a novel, William Faulkner said, 'I would say to get the character in your mind. Once he is in your mind, and he is right, and he's true, then he does the work himself. All you need to do then is to trot along behind him and put down what he does and what he says.' This suggests that a truly great character is one imbued with such humanity that they evolve organically, seemingly separately from their creator. Ultimately, memorable characters like Hamlet, Jane Eyre or Jude Fawley last in our mind's eye because of their complexity and relatability, however dark or flawed they may be. They feel *real* because their actions, motivations and internal lives are rendered with depth, consistency and believability, and that allows readers to form a lasting emotional connection to them that transcends the intricacies of plot.

All this stands in stark contrast to the pitfalls of lazy characterisation, where figures remain mere ciphers (like those found in Keeler's work), lacking the ability to evolve, or to evoke genuine empathy or interest. Even worse, perhaps, is the trope of the 'Mary Sue' – the impossibly perfect, universally beloved character devoid of meaningful flaws or struggles. Such creations – often a sign of authorial wish fulfilment and which generally inhabit fan fiction – fail to resonate because they lack essential human imperfections and vulnerabilities. Crafting memorable, impactful fiction hinges not just on *what* happens, but crucially on *who* it happens to, demanding characters that are whole and human, not simply sketched outlines, or out-there oddities like Keeler's. Though I do want to know more about the tapioca weather machine.

Language at the limits

It wasn't just Harry Keeler's plots that were impenetrable. His style was, too. In *The Riddle of the Traveling Skull* (one of his most popular works, republished in 2005), readers need to work their way through paragraphs like this:

> For it must be remembered that at the time I knew quite nothing, naturally, concerning Milo Payne, the mysterious

> Cockney-talking Englishman with the checkered long-beaked Sherlockholmsian cap; nor of the latter's 'Barr-Bag' which was as like my own bag as one Milwaukee wienerwurst is like another; nor of Legga, the Human Spider, with her four legs and her six arms; nor of Ichabod Chang, ex-convict, and son of Dong Chang; nor of the elusive poetess, Abigail Sprigge; nor of the Great Simon, with his 2,163 pearl buttons . . .

Keeler's language is pure purple prose – a phrase that our friend Horace coined back in the day. He brought to writers' attention the fact that 'Weighty openings and grand declarations often/ Have one or two purple patches tacked on, that gleam/ Far and wide . . .'

'Purple prose' is now used to denote flowery, overwritten, overwrought language – gleaming 'far and wide' over a page. According to Horace, purple prose stood in direct opposition to decorum – used to describe writing that was done in a style suitable to its subject matter. Purple prose is indulgent, showy and in-your-face – it does everything it can to get a reader's attention while simultaneously concealing the point of a story.

Purple prose does nothing for a reader. It doesn't move the story on, or provide clarity, or do anything other than make you feel a bit befuddled. But it too had its day in the sun: the Victorians loved it. Take a look at this sentence by Jerome K. Jerome in *Three Men in a Boat*, published in 1889:

> The river – with the sunlight flashing from its dancing wavelets, gilding gold the grey-green beech-trunks, glinting through the dark, cool wood paths, chasing shadows o'er the shallows, flinging diamonds from the mill-wheels, throwing kisses to the lilies, wantoning with the weirs' white waters, silvering

> moss-grown walls and bridges, brightening every tiny townlet, making sweet each lane and meadow, lying tangled in the rushes, peeping, laughing, from each inlet, gleaming gay on many a far sail, making soft the air with glory – is a golden fairy stream.

Today we're urged to 'show, don't tell', but the Victorians were way more in to 'tell, then tell a bit more, and just a little bit more after that'. They prized and praised *authenticity*, so everything needed to be described as fulsomely as possible. That's why writers like Dickens, Hardy and the Brontës are often accused of writing in purple prose – you know, those long, unwieldy sentences that go on and on with subclause after subclause, tacked together with semicolons and ellipses that mean you lose the thread halfway through a sentence, and must start again.

Writers can also fall from grace (as I have just done with that phrase) and allow themselves to be tempted by cliché – using lazy language or a phrase that we've read a million times before. In defence of writers today, we live in a post-Shakespearean world, where anything that could be written about the human experience has already been penned by the Bard, passed into language and popular culture, then embedded itself into our collective consciousness. It's almost impossible to write about being human without using a cliché that's been in use for the last 400 years. If all writing is built on the accretion of words that have gone before, should we even worry about it? And cliché has its fans, and uses. In *An Experiment in Criticism* (1961), C. S. Lewis attempted to tackle the question of whether books could be categorised as 'good' or 'bad', depending not on what was in them, but how they were read. A 'literary' reader might read the same book over and over, to extract as much meaning from the writing as possible – as critic Cyril Connolly said, 'Literature is the art of writing something that will be read twice';

an 'unliterary' one was more likely to read a book once, enjoy it, and move on. Lewis was keen to discover the appeal of what might be considered 'bad' writing for the 'unliterary' reader, noting that there is a very good reason we might enjoy reading a hackneyed and clichéd phrase: 'because it is immediately recognisable'. He explains:

> 'My blood ran cold' is a hieroglyph for fear. Any attempt, such as a great writer might make, to render this fear concrete in its full particularity, is doubly a chokepear to the unliterary reader. For it offers him what he doesn't want, and offers it only on the condition of his giving to the words a kind and degree of attention which he does not intend to give. It is like trying to sell him something he has no use for at a price he does not wish to pay.

Moving on from Lewis's unexpected use of the word 'chokepear' (a medieval torture instrument; not a word I was expecting to use in this paragraph), this is an important point: we're always told that cliché in writing is bad, but, in truth (to use a cliché) it has its uses. It's a shortcut for both reader and writer, a bridge to mutual understanding. As Lewis explains, an 'unliterary' reader appreciates cliché, as without too much intellectual heavy lifting, it provides a handy background for plot – which is ultimately what they are looking for. Indeed, says Lewis, 'good' writing, for an unliterary reader, 'may offend him', by 'being either too spare for his purpose or too full. A woodland scene by D. H. Lawrence or a mountain valley by Ruskin gives him far more than he knows what to do with.' Cliché gets straight to it: it gives a reader exactly what they need (and no more) to enjoy the story, and exactly when they need it. When you think of it like that, what's not to enjoy?

The opposite of Lewis's 'unliterary' reader is the 'stylemonger', a term he uses to describe readers who: 'On taking up a book . . . concentrate on what they call its "style" or its "English". They judge this neither by its sound nor by its power to communicate but by its conformity to certain arbitrary rules.' These are the people, says Lewis, who think writing 'bad' if it uses:

> Americanisms, Gallicisms, split infinitives, and sentences that end with a preposition. They do not inquire whether the Americanism or Gallicism in question increases or impoverishes the expressiveness of our language. It is nothing to them that the best English speakers and writers have been ending sentences with prepositions for over a thousand years.

These 'stylemongers' are, essentially, pedants: incapable of enjoying prose while they read. 'Their reading is a perpetual witch hunt,' says Lewis, rather than a pleasurable experience. These are not people who read for comfort – in fact, the more stylistic tics they find to take issue with, the happier they are. What critics might consider 'bad' writing, says Lewis, provides readers with what they want: 'imminent dangers and hair-breadth escapes', 'they like to have inquisitiveness aroused' and stories that enable readers to participate in 'pleasure or happiness'. Unsurprisingly from the man who wrote *The Chronicles of Narnia* and was a friend of J. R. R. Tolkien, *An Experiment in Criticism* is also a defence of what we now call 'genre' fiction – romance, fantasy, thriller, science fiction – writing often disparaged for its plot-driven and 'unliterary' style.

When we think about big-selling and attention-grabbing genre books like *The Da Vinci Code* or *Fifty Shades of Grey*, we might be puzzled (even offended) at their popularity. But if we apply Lewis's rules about what readers *want,* we can see that they provide danger and escape, arouse our inquisitiveness, and allow us to participate in pleasure or happiness. They fulfil the brief. That's why despite sentences like 'The fond memory caused Sophie a pang of sadness as the harsh reality of the murder gripped her again' from Dan Brown and 'The elevator whisks me with terminal velocity to the twentieth floor' from E. L. James, these two writers between them have sold about 400 million copies worldwide. Like the salt-fat-sugar combination that fast food retailers have perfected to make us want to keep coming back for more, a writer who can crack the inquisitiveness-danger-escape formula will never want for customers. As one reviewer said of Dan Brown's most recent book, 2025's *The Secret of Secrets,* 'It's weapons-grade bollocks from beginning to end, none of it makes a lick of sense, and you'll roar through it with entire enjoyment if you like this sort of thing.'

Ultimately, Lewis argues, we should move away from categorising writing as 'lowbrow', or 'highbrow', but instead ask: will reading this change my world? Will I want to read it again, because it brings me satisfaction? If so, it doesn't matter how clichéd the writing, or whether critics might call the style or language bad: for millions of readers, it works. So, let's satisfy our inquisitiveness, hopefully escape danger unscathed, and allow ourselves just a little pleasure as we meet a writer who revels in the dark triad of bad plot, language and character.

The ultimate drive-thru of bad writing

It's not difficult to find lists of books considered badly written, or unreadable. We've established that this is personal to each of us, but critical opinion does tend to coalesce round the same old titles: any of the Twilight series, Liz Truss's *Ten Years to Save the West*, anything by Morrissey. These authors do of course have readers who enjoy and champion their work, some perhaps even without irony – but there is one author whom everyone can seem to agree is a terrible writer – possibly, in fact, the worst – a penner of terrible prose matched with unconnected plots and unbelievable characters, all magnificently enhanced by her total failure to recognise her literary limits.

Her name is Amanda McKittrick Ros, and she was born in 1860 in Ireland, beginning her literary escapades in 1897, when her husband agreed to finance the publication of her first novel, *Irene Iddesleigh*. From the start of her writing career McKittrick Ros had a keen yet unearned sense of herself as a writer of renown; she described her readers as 'the million and one who thirst for aught that drops from my pen' and felt that she would be 'talked about at the end of a thousand years'. As we'll see, on the latter claim, she hasn't so far been proved wrong.

So how did McKittrick Ros become so well known for her (bad) writing – why do so many critics point to her as an example of the worst? Mark O'Connell explains in *Epic Fail: Bad Art, Viral Fame, and the History of the Worst Thing Ever* that the tipping point, the moment that McKittrick Ros would have been described as 'going viral', came early in her career, with a review in 1898 of *Irene Iddesleigh* by Barry Pain,* 'the mock-reverential spirit of which more or less set the tone for Ros' entire career'. Pain had been sent a copy of *Irene* by some friends who thought he might find it enjoyable; initially he did,

* Pain was a writer and journalist who became associated at the turn of the twentieth century with the 'new humour' – used to describe humorous working-class writers like Jerome K. Jerome.

but by the time he had finished reading it, he 'shrank before it in tears and terror'. This was presumably hyperbole, followed up with a dash of sarcasm – the review went on to call *Irene* 'The Book of the Century', which it might have been, but not in ways anticipated by the author.

Following Pain's lead, Aldous Huxley compared McKittrick Ros's writing to the Elizabethan Euphuists:* 'the result of the discovery of art by an unsophisticated mind' (she took this as a compliment, remarking to a friend that Huxley was 'the only critic who understands my writings'), while reviewer Thomas Beer opined that her writing 'has the final merit of concealing thought and plot. Your mind rocks along in an amiable delirium.' When Mark Twain was sent a copy of *Irene* in 1905, he replied to the gifter, saying 'Many years ago I began to collect "hogwash" literature, and I am glad of the chance to add to it the extraordinary book which you have sent me.'

So, Pain's review, and those that followed, established from the off the 'so bad, it's good' spirit that also encouraged later readers to investigate McKittrick Ros's work. And her unconventional way of dealing with criticism also kept her name in the spotlight. McKittrick Ros's writing might not have been admirable, but her sangfroid in the face of negative reviews was. She was a dedicated letter-writer and litigant, describing herself as 'the notorious boil on the tip of critics' tongues', and she certainly delivered with Pain, calling him 'a clay crab of corruption' and a 'cancerous irritant wart' who was clearly secretly in love with her. Her second novel, *Delina Delaney*, published a year after *Irene Iddesleigh*, kicked off with a twenty-page criticism directed

* Described as a 'peculiarly mannered style of English prose', the Euphuists prized classical learning and an ornate style, and had no use for plots at all. Early proponents of 'no plot, just vibes'.

squarely at Pain, in which she retaliated with vigour: 'This so-called Barry Pain . . . I care not for the opinion of half-starved upstarts.'

What the reviewers started and McKittrick Ros consolidated, other readers ran with. 'Delina Delaney' dinners sprang up, where diners took part in 'the Amanda game', with one guest asking a question, and another answering 'in keeping with the mood and spirit' of McKittrick Ros's writing. By 1907 there was an Amanda McKittrick Ros Society hosting weekly readings of her work. As well as trying to track down copies of her books, which were hard to come by (unsurprisingly, they weren't often reprinted), members also wrote to her in the hope of receiving a reply – and sometimes, she obliged. One correspondent wrote to her in 1910 to congratulate her on her response to Barry Pain's review: 'The wit and humour embodied in this preface is subtle and evasive, requiring deep and concentrated thought on the part of the reader' – an early example of trolling that she was presumably completely unaware of; she cheerfully replied 'I feel I am a great favourite as a writer. My fame is established, which is the chief point of success.' That she was happy to engage with her public presumably added to her notoriety. And the fascination with her work was sustained into the mid-twentieth century. Between the 1930s and 1940s the Oxford University literary group The Inklings held meetings where they would read aloud from her books to each other; the last man standing, whoever could read the longest without laughing, was the winner.

Had *Irene Iddesleigh* not found its way to Barry Pain by happenstance, it's likely that McKittrick Ros would have suffered much the same fate as hundreds of authors over the years: a quick descent to immediate literary obscurity. Instead, she became a poster girl for the maxim that there is no such thing as bad publicity. But what, exactly, was the problem? As O'Connell explains: 'Ros's writing is not just bad . . . its badness is so potent that it seems to undermine the very *idea* of literature, to expose the whole endeavour of making art out of language as essentially and irredeemably fraudulent – and, even worse, silly.' There's something in this – trying to read McKittrick Ros might start out as an ironic dinner-party joke, but eventually, she grinds you down so that the very words and sentences start to lose all shape, and you find yourself wondering what the point is of reading, or writing – or living. Let's take a look. The entire text of *Irene Iddesleigh* can be found online, but really, any sentence will stand for the whole. We might as well go for the first one:

> Sympathise with me, indeed! Ah, no! Cast your sympathy on the chill waves of troubled waters; fling it on the oases of futurity; dash it against the rock of gossip; or, better still, allow it to remain within the false and faithless bosom of buried scorn.

Scrolling through the text of *Irene Iddesleigh* has a hypnotic and sedating effect. Every line, every paragraph, appears on the face of it reasonable – consists of recognisable words, makes (mostly) grammatical sense – but the overall experience is one of deadening confusion. It's almost impossible to understand what conclusion the sentence is meant to lead you to, or how it moves the plot along. There is no respite from the overworked metaphor, and while Horace talks of 'one or two' patches of purple prose, McKittrick Ros inverts this by producing an entire book of it, with relief coming in just the occasional patch scribbled in lilac.

And while the language is bad, it isn't for the plots, either, that people read McKittrick Ros's novels. Perhaps she felt the same as

American short story writer Grace Paley, who considered that plot was 'the absolute line between two points which I've always despised. Not for literary reasons, but because it takes all hope away. Everyone, real or invented, deserves the open destiny of life.' This sentiment wasn't shared by Albert Camus, who noted that 'We call a writer bad when he expresses himself in reference to an inner context the reader cannot know. The mediocre writer is thus led to say anything he pleases.'

'Saying anything [s]he pleases' is one way to describe McKittrick Ros's writing. People read her books, notes O'Connell, 'for the masochistic pleasures of translating them into something like sense' – and he is right. There is a can't-look-away fascination in trying to untangle her – a sort of sadistic wonder that writing, which should be able to convey thoughts, feelings and emotions, to attempt to unlock the mystery of being human, can lead instead to such baffled confusion:

> Our hopes when elevated to that standard of ambition which demands unison may fall asunder like an ancient ruin. They are no longer fit for construction unless on an approved principle. They smoulder away like the ashes of burnt embers, and are cast outwardly from their confined abode, never more to be found where once they existed only as smouldering serpents of scorned pride.

Alongside the non-existent plots, McKittrick Ros's novels have no coherent chronology: long-lost characters bump into each other in unlikely places, while one novel begins with a character who then disappears completely from the story. And McKittrick Ros had a love for alliteration in her book titles (*Irene Iddesleigh*, *Delina Delaney* and

Helen Huddleson) and for her characters – Barney Bloater, Mabel Moab and Marjory Mason; other characters revelled in names like Lord Raspberry, Lady Pear and the Earl of Grape. She also wrote in 'an extraordinary manner of beginning a sentence with a phrase that belongs to the previous sentence and is unrelated to the subject it governs', as described by her biographer Jack Loudan in his 1954 book *O Rare Amanda!* And that's before you get to her habit of never calling a spade a spade. Eyes were 'globes of glare', legs 'bony supports' and trousers 'the southern necessity'.

Barry Pain had established early on that the fundamental problem with McKittrick Ros's writing was her complete lack of a sense of humour. 'Never was any absence so essentially and intrinsically absential, as the absence of the sense of humour in this book,' he wrote about *Irene Iddesleigh*. And Jack Loudan agreed, explaining that 'Amanda's most stupendous characteristic is the absence of a sense of humour: but it should be emphasised that with that absence there went an equally stupendous belief in herself.' As Charles Bukowski said: 'Bad writers tend to have the self-confidence, while the good ones tend to have self-doubt.' For McKittrick Ros, this lack of perspective in regard to her own talents meant that she took *any* interest from readers – whether positive, negative, sarcastic or ironic – as proof of her brilliance.

Of course, perhaps as time went by, McKittrick Ros noticed the joke and decided to lean into it as a way of enhancing her notoriety and her book sales. In a 2024 article on McKittrick Ros in the *Washington Post* Andrew Doyle comments: 'Is it not possible that once her reputation was established, she learned to play along, making those who mocked her the butt of the joke?' It certainly *is* possible, but her letters suggest her belief in her genius was genuine: 'Lords, Ladies, Earls, Countesses and Ambassadors are my chief patronisers. In fact I hold letters concerning my works from all crowned heads except the Czar of Russia and the Emperor of Austria,' she wrote.

Jack Loudan notes in *O Rare Amanda!* that 'poetry and nonsense have a close alliance', so it's not a surprise that McKittrick Ros was also a poet, publishing collections called *Poems of Puncture* and *Fumes of Formation*. *PoP* includes 'Mickey Monkeyface McBlear', 'Rev. Goliath Ginbottle' and 'To Those Whom the Shoe Fits' ('There's nothing in the world I hate/ Like a drunken woman,/ She drags herself so very low/ You couldn't call her human'). *FoF* contains an infamous poem called 'Visiting Westminster Abbey', which begins:

Holy Moses! Take a look!
Flesh decayed in every nook!
Some rare bits of brain lie here,
Mortal loads of beef and beer.

Here McKittrick Ros shows herself as a poet in the same style as William McGonagall, known as 'the worst poet in the English language'. McGonagall had one guiding poetic principle: if it rhymed, it was fine. His poetic apogee, or perhaps nadir, was reached with his verses on the Tay Bridge Disaster, a fatal train accident in Scotland in 1879:

Beautiful Railway Bridge of the Silv'ry Tay!
Alas! I am very sorry to say
That ninety lives have been taken away
On the last Sabbath day of 1879,
Which will be remember'd for a very long time.

As well as sharing a love of rhyming, like McKittrick Ros, McGonagall had an unshakeable belief in his destiny as a writer. Here he is describing the moment he decided to be a poet – invoking Lord Byron, no less:

> I seemed to feel as it were a strange kind of feeling stealing over me, and remained so for about five minutes. A flame, as Lord Byron has said, seemed to kindle up my entire frame, along with a strong desire to write poetry; and I felt so happy, so happy, that I was inclined to dance, then I began to pace backwards and forwards in the room, trying to shake off all thought of writing poetry; but the more I tried, the more strong the sensation became. It was so strong, I imagined that a pen was in my right hand, and a voice crying, 'Write! Write!'

In fact, it's the kind of paragraph you can imagine McKittrick Ros penning in one of her novels.

While it's easy to poke fun at McKittrick Ros's writing (and McGonagall's), it's worth acknowledging that when it came to it, she was clearly a woman who had serious ambition, even if it wasn't in any way matched by her skill. Her writing wasn't necessarily worse than other Victorian prose stylists, it's just that her style never varied: it was always terrible. Remember that Charles Dickens wrote this sentence in *Great Expectations*: 'I had seen the damp lying outside of my little window, as if some goblin had been crying there all night, and using the window for a pocket-handkerchief' – and his friend and fellow writer Wilkie Collins said (after Dickens's death, admittedly), of the latter half of *Dombey and Sons*, that 'No intelligent person can have read without astonishment at the badness of it.' Collins really enjoyed sticking the literary boot into his collaborator (they worked together several times), writing on his copy of *The Life of Charles Dickens* by John Forster that Dickens was only 'after Walter Scott' the most popular novelist of the nineteenth century. Ouch.

Most writers go through periods of hesitation and a lack of confidence. Uncertainty about whether what they write is of any value runs constantly through their minds. It's the capacity for reflection, the willingness to listen to others, to be edited, to listen to feedback, that means that what initially emerges from the pen or keyboard can be improved in some way. But not so with McKittrick Ros. In 1930, she wrote to her publisher, asking him what he thought about the Nobel Prize in Literature: 'What do you think of this prize? Do you think I should make a "dart" for it?' Even a solitary line by her in a letter manages to upend the reader. How does one make a 'dart' for a prize awarded by committee? Did she truly believe she could take the grandest literary prize? If anyone could have done it by sheer force of will, McKittrick Ros could. Let's hope her publisher didn't try to dissuade her – if only for the story. Well, and because she'd never have listened.

McKittrick Ros's complete lack of a sense of humour, or her top-level trolling of readers and reviewers, carried her undaunted through her writing career, until in 1939 she joined 'the boundless battalion of the breathless', as she described the dead, who weren't safe from her alliterative tendencies. At the conclusion of his study of her, Loudan reflects that 'Amanda's world is subjectively her own. She is nearer to the automatic writing of surrealism, which André Breton . . . describes as being created with "an absence of all control exercised by reason and all aesthetic or moral preoccupation".' How else to explain the first line of her poem 'Ode to Easter'?

Dear Lord, the day of eggs is here.

Dear Lord, indeed. As Barry Pain wrote when he kicked this all off in his review of *Irene Iddesleigh*, it 'is a thing which happens once in a million years. There is no one above it and no one beside it, and it sits alone as the nightingale sings. The words that would attempt to give any clear idea of it have still to be invented.'

Banging up to date

In a very alternate universe, if Amanda McKittrick Ros had been an academic, she might have written something just like this:

> The move from a structuralist account in which capital is understood to structure social relations in relatively homologous ways to a view of hegemony in which power relations are subject to repetition, convergence, and rearticulation brought the question of temporality into the thinking of structure, and marked a shift from a form of Althusserian theory that takes structural totalities as theoretical objects to one in which the insights into the contingent possibility of structure inaugurate a renewed conception of hegemony as bound up with the contingent sites and strategies of the rearticulation of power.

Actually, it was written by feminist philosopher Judith Butler. In the late 1990s, the academic journal *Philosophy and Literature* held a 'Bad Writing Contest', to spotlight the very worst examples of academic prose. The editor of the journal explained that the competition 'celebrates the most stylistically lamentable passages found in scholarly books and articles published in the last few years. Entries must be non-ironic, from serious, published academic journals or books. Deliberate parody cannot be allowed in a field where unintended self-parody is so widespread.' This niche topic spiralled out into the wider world when Butler was awarded the prize in 1998.

But this type of bad writing award is inherently unfair. To be sure, Butler's sentence is not a great reading experience, but it's just one of many thousands written by her over the course of a long, influential and lauded career. Her undoubted academic prowess coupled with the award led to opinion pieces in *The New York Times*, and across mainstream media, arguing back and forwards on both what bad writing was, and whether there was any point in highlighting it in this way. After all, the idea of a 'Bad Writing Contest' is essentially a gimmick – a snapshot of a wider career taken out of context, to drum up headlines for the sake of novelty.

But while C. S. Lewis defends one type of 'bad' writing on the grounds that it gives readers what they want, contemporary culture also finds humour and stories in celebrating other kinds of literary failure. We readers can't get enough of 'bad' writing, which is why it routinely makes the headlines. The Bad Sex Award, established in 1993, aimed to 'draw attention to the crude, tasteless, often perfunctory use of redundant passages of sexual description in the modern novel, and to discourage it'. Illustrious winners include Philip Roth, Nick Cave, John Updike and Norman Mailer.

Until 2019, when the decision was made to end the competition, the Bad Sex Award was a news story, which certainly fulfils the 'draw attention' part of the brief. But does it discourage it? After all, no writer *truly* believes as they sit at their desk that someday, their laboured-over words are going to be held up to ridicule – you just couldn't carry on, otherwise. But although the Bad Sex Award is ostensibly for bad writing on a very specific topic, it can also be a useful proxy award for bad writing in general – a suggestion that actually, we still don't have enough official ways to recognise and celebrate bad writing.

The 2015 winner of the Bad Sex Award was Mancunian musician Steven Patrick Morrissey for his debut novel *List of the Lost*. But it wasn't just the words Morrissey used for his sex scenes that were judged to be bad (though they were).* Reviewers of *List of the Lost* were united in their condemnation of the entire enterprise. In the *Guardian* Michael Hann wrote that 'Every character in *List of the Lost* speaks like a parody of Morrissey at his most florid and self-indulgent: bad puns, hopeless "quickfire" dialogue, and desperate self-pity: "I suffer greatly in painful silence and I speak to you, now, with servitude whilst also pleading for your understanding. I am alone and I agonize in an exasperated state."'

Others described *List of the Lost* as 'more self-indulgent and tedious than its slender dimensions would suggest possible' and 'a leaden festival of self-pity'.† But as with Judith Butler, the wider context of the author is what drove much of the criticism of his writing: it's the juxtaposition between this 'bad sixth-form James Joyce impersonation' as one reviewer described it, and the brilliance of Morrissey's lyrics for the Smiths in his original career. The gap between Morrissey's good

* '. . . one giggling snowball of full-figured copulation, screaming and shouting as they playfully bit and pulled at each other in a dangerous and clamorous roller-coaster coil of sexually violent rotation . . .'

† I can imagine Morrissey flogging tickets to this.

stuff and his bad stuff is a yawning chasm readers struggle to traverse, hence the attention, and the outrage.

As we have seen with Amanda McKittrick Ros's fan club meetups, readers have always found ways to share in the hilarity and humour of bad writing. After all, where's the fun in guffawing silently to yourself when you come across an overblown metaphor or unconvincing leading man? The whole point of this stuff is to be able to make other people laugh along with you, and share the emotion. That might explain the existence of bad writing contests, which have proliferated over the years, and the internet has helped them to become known worldwide.

The granddaddy of them all is the Bulwer-Lytton Fiction Contest, a prize awarded for the worst possible opening line of an imaginary novel. Named after Victorian novelist Edward George Bulwer-Lytton, whose novel *Paul Clifford* begins with the infamous line 'It was a dark and stormy night', for forty years (the competition was recently retired) aspiring entrants could compete in a half-dozen categories. Your winning sentence could be in science fiction,* or 'Vile Puns',† or it could take home the big one, the Grand Prize. In 2024 that was won by these few words: 'She had a body that reached out and slapped my face like a five-pound ham-hock tossed from a speeding truck.' Glorious, though not a patch on my favourite entry, from 2011: 'Cheryl's mind turned like the vanes of a wind-powered turbine, chopping her sparrow-like

* 'The professor had constantly warned his protégé about the time travel related risks of meeting a past version of yourself or killing your grandfather, but unfortunately he'd never mentioned the worst time machine risk of all – sticking your head out of the window' won in this category in 2018.

† '"I do enjoy turning a prophet," said Torquemada, as he roasted the heretic seer on a spit' scooped this prize in 2024.

thoughts into bloody pieces that fell onto a growing pile of forgotten memories.' Beautiful.

While the BLFC is awarded for imaginary books, there is also recognition out there for actual, published books, such as the Diagram Prize for Oddest Book Title (first awarded in 1978 for *Proceedings of the Second International Workshop on Nude Mice*), and the International Imitation Hemingway Competition (not to be confused with the Hemingway Look-Alike Contest, or the PEN/Hemingway Award for Debut Novel), which encouraged readers to submit a 'really good page of really bad Hemingway' for consideration. The titles alone deserve appreciation: previous winners include *The Old Man and the Flea* and *The Bug Count Also Rises*. But Hemingway had the last word about all this unseemly noise. 'Parody', he wrote, is 'the last refuge of the frustrated writer . . . The greater the work of literature, the easier the parody.' So while readers can fill a few hours enjoying ranking 'bad' writing, authors can reassure themselves with the thought that it simply acknowledges their greatness.

But why dedicate attention to 'bad' writing when, as this chapter demonstrates, aesthetic judgement varies so widely? The answer to that lies in the *nature* of a writer's perceived failures and the reactions they provoke. Bad writing is a unique lens with which to examine the realm of words. It can illustrate the dramatic breaking of established literary conventions, or push stylistic choices to an absurdity that, paradoxically, helps illuminate the rules for the rest of us. And we shouldn't discount the joy of tapping into the communal 'ick' factor, generating a shared negative aesthetic response. As observers like Mark Twain and Mark O'Connell have highlighted, there is often an inherent, magnetic fascination in dissecting spectacular failure – in understanding *how* and *why* something misses the mark so profoundly. Engaging with comedic transgression, the shared revulsion, and the captivating nature of artistic failure helps us move beyond simple dismissal. 'Bad taste' is not a monolithic judgement, but a complex, multi-faceted phenomenon, and understanding its mechanics is as pleasurable and informative as any other lens we might analyse literature through.

So, where does that leave us, amid the wreckage of bad puns, unfortunate sex scenes, and novels plotted by pulling newspaper clippings out of a hat? Perhaps back at the start: happily ensconced in our own literary kingdoms, free to decide for ourselves what delights, what instructs, and what makes us want to throw a book across the room (before picking it up again to read the worst bits aloud to a friend, naturally). Forget the rules, the critics, the earnestly compiled lists of 'must-reads': the real joy is in the shared experience, the fervent discussion in the book club, the late-night texting about that truly atrocious metaphor, the unifying power of a collective ick.

After all, whether it's high art or gloriously unrepentant trash, words are simply pathways – sometimes scenic, sometimes bewilderingly indirect – leading us closer to understanding ourselves, and each other. So go forth, read bravely, judge mercilessly (or mercifully, as the mood takes you), and never, ever apologise for finding delight and pleasure in the peculiar, the imperfect, or the downright perplexing. The best stories, like the best gossip, are always the ones that leave you saying: 'You won't *believe* what I just read . . .'

3.

Bad Takes: Censorship and Sensibility

'I sometimes think that bad books are worse, far worse, than bad companions . . . the book is a perfectly decent-looking thing and steals subtly into the imagination.'

E. M. Forster

We think of words as the ultimate tool of communication – a way for us to speak to each other across centuries and continents. But their history is inextricably linked to the story of restriction. From the dawn of writing, recognition of just how powerful and troublesome words could be meant there were constant attempts by those wanting to retain the status quo to prevent words finding readers. The ways words are restricted have varied: some are censored – a book remains available to read or buy, but with parts of it altered or redacted – while others are banned by law-makers, making it difficult or impossible to access them.

Censoring suspect words is nothing new: expurgation in England was sometimes known as 'bowdlerisation' after Thomas Bowdler, who in 1807 published twenty of Shakespeare's plays in editions 'suitable for women and children' – removing anything he considered blasphemous or too racy. Initially, the idea of a sanitised Shakespeare went down well with readers, and there were soon numerous other similar editions in print.

After Bowdler's second edition of *The Family Shakespeare* was published in 1818, his name began to be used as a verb: 'to bowdlerise' means to remove parts of a work that are considered offensive or unsuitable. With one critic noting that Bowdler's editorial cuts were like 'a baby playing with a pair of shears', his sanitised syllables fell out of fashion in the early part of the twentieth century, but the initial wide readership of these truncated texts demonstrates that censorship is a complicated topic. Not all cuts are unwelcome.

Vandalism of books, censorship and legal challenges have been used throughout literary history to disrupt words and stop them reaching an audience – and interference continues to this day. The big censorship cases of the twentieth century, like *Lady Chatterley's Lover*, which reflected a loosening of legal restrictions following the Obscene Publications Act of 1959, were watersheds in pushing back against restriction, and an acknowledgement that the state had no place in censoring people's reading material. But those involved in the *Lady Chatterley* trial might be surprised to know that in the twenty-first century words are being restricted in new and significant ways. An Index on Censorship poll in 2024 revealed that 53 per cent of British school librarians had been asked to remove books from their shelves, mostly titles covering LGBTQIA+ topics (this trend mirrors the US, where restrictions in school libraries grew by 33 per cent in 2022–23).

Given who has historically been restricting words – religious institutions and states – we shouldn't be surprised that sex, sexuality and politics have most often been the reason for censorship or book banning, and that pressure has now reached public and school libraries, too. Those who feel they have something to lose from allowing words to circulate freely – be it power, influence or social control – will go to almost any lengths to intercept them, so high are the stakes.

Counter-intuitively, publishers and writers themselves have also sometimes chosen to restrict words: perhaps to make sure that at least *something* of what they want to say can be published, or because they fear unintended consequences. The ways we constrain words might have changed, but they remain under as much scrutiny and surveillance as ever.

'I thank God,' wrote William Berkeley in 1671, 'there are no free schools nor printing, and I hope we shall not have these [for a] hundred years; for learning has brought disobedience, and heresy.' Berkeley was the governor of Virginia, and with the first authorised printing press arriving there in 1730, he didn't get close to his hundred-year hope. His sentiment expresses how censorship of words was often justified under the guise of 'protecting' readers: not all eyes are equal. Restricting words allows those in power to protect *themselves*, under the pretence of protecting readers. Nowadays it might not be readers who need shielding, but instead book subjects. Modern laws on privacy and libel have constructed a tightrope between an author's right to write what they want, and the right to privacy of the people they write about.

Given how many ways in which words can be a threat, and the ramifications of setting them free to be read, it's not surprising that those with responsibility for words have had to think carefully before unleashing them. As censors throughout history have discovered, books are particularly difficult to neutralise. Their potentially dangerous messages come respectably dressed in a celebrated and revered medium, one that on the whole, people are encouraged to engage with. Whether author, printer, publisher or bookseller, words can often feel like hostages to fortune. While they might delight one group, they may scandalise another; words can be divisive, damaging, disruptive and unwelcome. And although it's *possible* to anticipate how readers might respond to published words, sometimes the size of the furore caused, or the power of the audience upset, can come as a complete surprise.

Setting words free has always involved questions of taste, propriety, social norms, outrage and compromise. Do sensitivity readers – increasingly employed by publishers to assess whether a manuscript contains writing that might be considered insensitive or harmful to some readers – now play the role of censors, as some critics suggest? Or do they provide a valuable service in opening literature up to perspectives that the author might have missed? What about the tension between an author's freedom to choose the words they want, and a publisher's responsibility to its audience? Words that were acceptable 200 years ago are being read by audiences today with wildly different expectations, standards and experiences from those of the past. Not only that, twenty-first-century readers can turn in a moment to social media to share and amplify their views – positive and negative – worldwide.

Everything about literary censorship is paradoxical. The Sibylline Books were being consulted by the Roman Senate in 399 BC, but were burned and destroyed in 405 AD. *Uncle Tom's Cabin* was shunned in the Southern United States in the mid-nineteenth century, with one bookseller who sold copies of it forced out of their hometown of Mobile, Alabama. *The Catcher in the Rye* is simultaneously one of the most restricted and most taught novels in the United States. As audiences change (partly in response to what is being written and published), what might have once been outrageous to read can come to be widely accepted.

We might think that book bans and censorship are firmly in the past, that we've learned that burning writers (William Tyndale was strangled, then burned at the stake, with copies of his Bible translation burned in front of him) and books (in 1933 the Nazis began burning books: the destruction of 25,000 volumes in Berlin on the night of 10 May presaged the destruction of millions over the next decade) never works – and often has the opposite effect to that which is intended. Yet in the United States in 2022, there were over 1,200 attempts to censor books, and the fight has evolved from restricting the words that readers might have in their homes, to managing those in the public sphere, with centralised attempts to control what libraries and schools can stock on their shelves. There's a difference in the words that are tolerated on a personal bookshelf, and those in mass circulation that some groups feel need to be watched closely. What books are banned, and why, is an ever-changing landscape that demonstrates what we revere, and fear. The history and controversy of banned words is testament to the power of them.

Perpetual prohibition

Books are portable, accessible and durable, which means they can survive over centuries. Just because one era deals with their potential for upset, it doesn't mean the next can forget about them. Disruptive words have a way of always getting through to threaten some, and liberate others.

Book destruction began at almost the same time as book production – in fact, even earlier, with 'dangerous' manuscripts being destroyed. Ovid claimed that he was forced from Rome after he wrote *The Art of Love*, poetically describing the reasons for his exile as 'a song and a mistake'; while he may have been displaying creative licence in this story, we do know that copies were later burned by the preacher Savonarola in his 'bonfire of the vanities' for their 'corrupting' erotic content. Later still, at the end of the sixteenth century, *The Art of Love* was destroyed again in England by the Bishops of London and Canterbury; in the 1930s it was still causing trouble and was banned in the United States. *The Art of Love* has endured censorship and destruction on different continents for over 2,000 years, demonstrating how difficult it is for words to escape their reputation.

As more and more books were printed and published, physically destroying copies of them became impractical. Controlling what people read, and therefore thought, became increasingly difficult in the flood of printed material unleashed by Gutenberg's printing press. At the same time, the printing press was instrumental in spreading new ideas and helping the Protestant Reformation challenge the foundations of the Catholic Church.

This dual threat – an exponential rise in the number of books and readers alongside Protestant writings that the Church believed were heretical or blasphemous – required a new and organised form of control. The Church resorted to compiling lists of the most dangerous books out there as a warning to both writers and readers that words had consequences. The *Index Librorum Prohibitorum* (Index of Forbidden Books), first drawn up in 1560 and lasting until 1966, famously listed works by Copernicus, Galileo and Kepler (all accused of promoting a heliocentric view of the universe). These ideas were too dangerous to be printed in any form. But the Church somewhat undermined its own aim of discouraging certain words by instead providing a handy checklist of those books which for a mind hungry for knowledge might be worth tracking down. And the Index provides a useful checklist for us today: book banning tells us what was most important to people at different times. Those words worth restricting held the most power and potential danger. In this way, the Index is a shortcut that points directly to what was of greatest concern. What didn't make the list is just as useful for us to know as what did.

This bureaucratic gatekeeping was an unwinnable war. As early as the seventeenth century, the Church found itself unable to match the pace of books being published. It might ban a writer, but copies of their books could always be found by those who *really* wanted them. And plenty of suspect words found loopholes. *Uncle Tom's Cabin* escaped because it had only been published in English, which the Vatican viewed as a 'Protestant' language, and therefore not something that concerned them. The Index never listed Marx, Freud or Darwin – or Hitler. For three years the Church contemplated placing *Mein Kampf* on the list, but never did so.

Of course, the Index of Forbidden Books demonstrates more about the Catholic Church than it does about the individual writers it took issue with. The criteria were heresy, blasphemy and anti-clericalism, which is why it didn't include works by D. H. Lawrence or James Joyce. Like the biggest of oil tankers, the Church couldn't move fast enough to react to early twentieth-century obscenity. But as the years wore on, the list hoovered up more and more writers – Graham Greene, André Gide, Simone de Beauvoir – for obscenity, rather than because they were against Catholic dogma.

Eventually, the unsustainable Index consumed itself, banning

Church theologians who had fallen foul of it (including some of the original censors who compiled early lists) in a vicious and unending circle of eternal censorship. The final published list, in 1948, attracted attention in *The New York Times* for banning all Jean-Paul Sartre's works, and by the time of the Second Vatican Council in 1966 the Church had to concede defeat. Responsibility for reading material was now left to an individual's conscience. While the books on the list remained forbidden for Catholics to read – 'the Index retains its moral force despite its dissolution' – the tides of modernity and the globalisation of ideas meant that in the end, the Index had to quietly censor itself.

Turning pages red

The most common reason for a book to be censored was because it challenged established religions and rulers. These early troublesome texts were an existential threat to those who held the power, so it's not surprising that they dedicated so much time and effort to restricting them. Initially, books were more likely to be redacted and amended (that is, censored) than banned outright: the investment in time and money that went into producing a manuscript or early book was enormous, which meant that those in charge often preferred to remove certain words or passages and allow the physical copy to continue to exist. In a turbulent world of fluctuating rulers and religions, it was easier to retroactively amend, say, a Bible or other religious text, than it was to produce a new one.

Blotting out text that fell out of favour with ink or pasting over it using scraps of paper means that these physical books can trace the seesaw of history for us. In England, on 9 June 1535, Henry VIII issued a statute requiring all references to the Pope to be removed from books. These redactions had to be done physically, and overnight, meaning they were done imperfectly, highlighting for historians exactly what Henry was at such pains to destroy. In *Portable Magic* (2022), literary scholar Emma Smith writes that 'Censorship becomes . . . an attempt to enable rather than suppress the book. It is a creative process that makes a new book, better fitted to and more expressive of its own content.' Every attempt to censor written material highlights for a reader something that is missing and, human nature being what it is, makes it more intriguing. And while we usually view censors negatively, as the people who block words from our view, as Smith says, we could also see them as enabling: without their work in removing *some* words, the others would never reach us.

'Sondry contentious and sinyster opiniones, have by wrong teachynge and naughtye bokes increaced and growen within this his realme of England,' noted Henry VIII in 1538. In fact, Henry had spotted the proliferation of naughtye bokes with their sinyster opiniones almost a decade earlier. In 1529, he issued a list of banned books, becoming one of the first rulers in Europe to enact restrictions. The list had been drawn up by Thomas More, his chancellor, although ironically (of course) More had been granted special dispensation to read suspect Protestant books, to better understand the mind of the enemy.

In 1538 Henry went further and decreed that all books printed in England must first be approved by his body of advisors, known as the Privy Council. In some form or other, this requirement remained until 1694. The state could now control words before they were ever set free, rather than having to hunt them down and retrospectively ban them. His mechanism for doing this was through the Stationers' Company, established as a guild in 1403 and receiving a Royal Charter in 1557. The Company could seize any book it considered offensive (backed up by laws passed in 1586, 1637 and 1622 that required an official licence to print books in England) and had the power to bring offenders before the ecclesiastical authorities; it also decided who could have a licence to print. The Company was a monopoly, and controlled copyright, which wasn't, as it is now, held by the author, but by the printer of a book. Authors didn't get a look-in: they weren't even allowed to be members of the Company. In a way, this was fair enough: it was the printer of a book who could be punished (harshly – up to and including death) if they produced something out of step with the guidelines of the time. Between 1662 and 1694 in England, and even earlier on the Continent, a printed book had to have an 'imprimatur', a declaration authorising its publication (from the Latin 'let it be printed') on its pages. Imprimaturs in England were issued by the Lord Chamberlain (or, if concerning plays, which accounted for a large number of printed books, it fell to the Master of the Revels – a cheery-sounding job title for a censor), or the Archbishops of Canterbury or London. These imprimaturs were a physical acknowledgement that a book was certified officially not naughtye.

As the social landscape changed, there were increasing calls for government control of words to be ended. 'He who destroys a good book kills reason itself,' wrote John Milton in *Areopagitica*, his defence of free speech, published in 1644. Milton, John Locke and others agitated against the Stationers' Company, which they felt restricted the flow of education and ideas, alongside denying authors control over their work, or any income from it. While the Licensing of the Press Act, first passed in 1662, was meant to be renewed every two years by Parliament, in 1694 it declined to do so. This was in line with a changing public mood: the trickle-down of Milton and Locke's arguments, and the rise of a new, bourgeois class, interested in reading and discussing literature in the coffee shops that were springing up. In effect, this removed the ability of the government to censor words, and the Stationers' monopoly over the copyright of texts.

For the first 350 or so years after the arrival of Gutenberg's printing press, being 'an author' was a made-up job description. Writers might supply words, but printers and governments had the control. Unsurprisingly, by the early years of the eighteenth century authors were demanding a bit more respect and began agitating for a new form of licensing: one that rewarded them fairly. 'One Man Studies Seven Year, to bring a finish'd Peice into the World, and a Pyrate Printer, Reprints his Copy immediately, and Sells it for a quarter of the Price . . . these things call for an Act of Parliament,' wrote Daniel Defoe in 1705. Not only did authors not control copyright, they were also at the mercy of illegal and unscrupulous printers making a quick buck by producing unauthorised editions. The problem was especially acute in America, where books were constantly pirated from Europe. Charles Dickens's immense popularity in the nineteenth-century United States came with significant frustration at rampant book piracy there: 'The exquisite justice of never deriving sixpence from an enormous American sale of all my books,' he complained with heavy irony.

Because no international copyright agreement existed between Great Britain and the United States, American publishers were legally free to reprint Dickens's novels without permission and, crucially, without paying him any royalties. As soon as instalments of works like *The Pickwick Papers* or *Oliver Twist* arrived by ship from Britain, publishers would rush out cheap American editions, selling them in vast numbers across the country. While this made his work widely accessible and his name known, Dickens naturally felt robbed of legitimate earnings.

During his first tour of the United States in 1842, Dickens became a vocal advocate for international copyright law, using his celebrity status to argue passionately that authors deserved payment for their work regardless of national borders, and that protecting foreign authors would ultimately benefit American literature, too. However, his campaign met with considerable hostility from powerful American publishing interests and segments of the press, who profited from the status quo and retaliated by portraying Dickens as greedy. Despite his determined efforts, Dickens saw no change in American copyright law during his lifetime, continuing to lose substantial income to these unauthorised editions.

Dickens, and many other authors, had been concerned about the *lack* of restrictions on who could own, print and publish their words; some form of control, or censorship, they believed, would be a *good* thing. In England, pressure from authors had led to the Statute of Anne, the first copyright law in the world, being passed in 1710. It was an attempt to bring order from the chaos of unlicensed and unregulated words, to protect authors, printers, booksellers and readers. This was a win for the words, and for their authors, too, and unleashed a revived age of literature. Between 1750 and 1775 there was a 50 per cent increase in the number of books printed, jumping to 170 per cent between 1775 and 1800. Much of this ink explosion was centred on a new type of writing – the novel. This novel form (ahem) was fictional but realistic, which made it an ideal way to explore people's emotions and desires, and it proved wildly popular, quickly overtaking other forms of storytelling. In England, the novel emerged as a counterpoint to Augustan literature – dry and philosophical works concerned with politics, satire and history. In contrast, the novel focused on characterisation and what we might today call vibes, with the 'sentimental' hero or heroine going on a journey of self-discovery (a sort of self-help through story), and the plot being incidental – or least only there to advance the emotions of the protagonist. Novels with titles such as *Pamela; or, Virtue Rewarded* (Samuel Richardson) or *A Sentimental Journey* (Laurence Sterne) had a focus on virtue, fine feeling and sensibility, shared by both characters and readers.

As is often the way, the startling success of a breakthrough product creating a new audience led quickly to parody. Books began to be written with a reversal of the usual sentimental plot; instead of an emphasis on virtue, refinement and good taste, these subversive novels were pornographic disrupters, featuring characters who flouted social norms – economically, domestically and sexually. One of the most controversial was John Cleland's *Fanny Hill: The Memoirs of a Woman of Pleasure*, issued in two parts in 1748 and 1749 and considered the first piece of prose pornography ever published. Cleland wrote it while in a debtors' prison, apparently to demonstrate to diarist James Boswell that he could write about 'a woman of pleasure' without using a single rude word. And how else to pass the time?

The plot of *Fanny Hill* sees our heroine writing to an old friend and reflecting on her life: working in a brothel used by wealthy men, losing her virginity, and lesbian encounters. Things then ramp up with a public orgy, anal intercourse, and a touch of sadomasochism. But *Fanny Hill* had a demure facade to hide her true nature behind. It contained no swearing or explicit naming of body parts (though did use the phrase 'nethermouth' for a vagina) and consequently flew under the radar, meaning it was freely available for a year after first publication. But in 1749 the publishers of *Fanny Hill* were arrested for 'corrupting the king's subjects', and they renounced the novel and withdrew it from sale. But *Fanny Hill* had already built up a head of steam. The ban had little effect on her reach: pirated copies were soon for sale not only in Britain but in America and on the Continent too, and by the nineteenth century illustrated editions were also circulating. Despite this proliferation of copies, however, *Fanny Hill* was not legally available to buy in England until 1970 – a decade after *Lady Chatterley's Lover* was freed from censorship. That delay was nothing, though: readers in Singapore had to wait until 2015.*

As we'll see later in this chapter, one of the most censorious states in the US was Massachusetts. *Fanny Hill* was banned there in 1821, and then by the Supreme Court, apparently without the judge even reading it. The publisher was castigated for trying to 'debauch and corrupt' the good people of Massachusetts, and she was once again available only in illegal, pirated editions. *Fanny*'s next appearance in court was in 1963, in England, where Mayflower Books had published an uncensored version. The prosecution under the Obscene Publications Act was upheld, based on one scene of flagellation, but it was widely accepted that all the court case did was highlight the growing gulf between the UK's obscenity laws and the social changes of the twentieth century. In the same year an edition had been published in the US, and in 1964 *Fanny* was in the dock again, once more in Massachusetts. The defence outlined that a recent case against Henry Miller's *Tropic of Cancer* had made it clear that if a book had 'redeeming social importance', or 'literary attributes', that would be enough to save it. A Boston professor called in defence of the book was cross-examined by the state:

---

* In that year Singapore cut its list of banned books (and magazines) from 257 to seventeen. Another almost-victory for the words.

'But does it contain the type of language you would use over the breakfast table?'

'There's not a single dirty word in the book.'

'That's not what I asked. Would you use this kind of language over the breakfast table?'

'Yes, definitely.'

Despite this unusual breakfast-table defence, it was banned again in Massachusetts. But this time, the publisher took the decision to the Supreme Court, and in 1966 *Fanny* was finally victorious. Well, sort of. The book was ruled 'patently offensive' and appealing to 'prurient interest', but the court could not prove she had no redeeming social value, so free she was.

But *Fanny* continued to do what she did best: generate headlines. In 2017 the *Mail on Sunday* ran with 'Erotic novel first banned 270 years ago for describing a young girl's sexual exploits is censored AGAIN – in case it upsets students' – claiming that Cleland's book had been removed from a reading list for a course on eighteenth-century literature at a London university. In fact, *Fanny Hill* was never on the reading list and so couldn't have been removed from it: the story was, said the academic at the centre of the row, 'a chain of news-as-gossip – recognisable both from our internet age and the 18th-century coffee houses beloved of *Fanny Hill*'s readers – a comment I had made on the radio had been twisted into headlines.' Nearly 300 years on from her first appearance, *Fanny* still retains her capacity as a troublemaker. She probably wouldn't have it any other way.

I'm with the banned

> 'Our Civilization cannot afford to let the censor-moron loose. The censor-moron does not really hate anything but the living and growing human consciousness. It is our developing and extending consciousness that he threatens – and our consciousness in its newest, most sensitive activity, its vital growth. To arrest or circumscribe the vital consciousness is to produce morons, and nothing but a moron would wish to do it.'
>
> D. H. Lawrence

Fanny was banned for her controversial eroticism in the eighteenth century, and nearly three centuries later she was still causing upset. But while we might assume that progressive change would mean that by the twentieth century censorship of novels would be in decline and that audiences could be trusted to make their own decisions about what they read, D. H. Lawrence wrote his howl of anguish against the 'censor-moron' in 1928, the same year that *The Well of Loneliness* by Radclyffe Hall – a story about two women falling in love – was published. Hall's book cost about double that of most books of the time – an attempt by its publisher, Jonathan Cape, to make it less attractive to readers who were interested only in the novelty of it; keeping casual sensation-seekers far away from titillation. Restricted words are allowed to be read by some: the well-off, and readers who have ostensibly the 'right' reasons for perusing them.

When *The Well of Loneliness* was published, the editor of the *Sunday Express*, James Douglas, declared that 'I would rather give a healthy boy or a healthy girl a phial of prussic acid than this novel', and although almost all reviewers (and many readers, who wrote to the author in support) felt that the book was not offensive (one reviewer wrote that 'the poignant situations are set forth with a complete absence of offence'), Douglas's campaign against *The Well of Loneliness* was successful. One line in the novel ('and that night they were not divided') was enough for a magistrate to have copies of it destroyed, claiming that it would 'glorify the horrible tendency of lesbianism'. In the judgement, the judge noted that the well-written nature of the book meant that it was even more harmful than a poorly written one – in this case, the power of the words was used against them.*

But the weight of the state to interfere with words was beginning to wane. *The Well of Loneliness* garnered support from E. M. Forster, T. S. Eliot, Vera Brittain and Virginia Woolf. That so many well-known authors were moved to challenge a ruling under the Obscenity Act showed that things were slowly changing.

In 1915, copies of D. H. Lawrence's novel *The Rainbow* had been seized and burned (for its frank exploration of sexuality), and in 1928 his collection of verse, *Pansies*, had thirteen poems removed before it was considered suitable to be published in the UK. *Lady Chatterley's Lover* was also published in 1928 (albeit in a limited private edition), with Lawrence writing to his literary agent: 'I stand by her: and am perfectly content she should do me harm with such people as take offence at her. I am out against such people.' From the beginning, Lawrence knew that *Lady* C would sail in rough seas; the book was an extension of his work to 'make the sex relations valid and precious, instead of shameful',

* The judge's view of *The Well of Loneliness* as being well written is not shared by Jeanette Winterson, who has called it 'one of the worst books yet written'.

and in this, he said, it was 'the furthest I have gone'. Lawrence's story of upper-class, married Lady Chatterley's affair with her working-class gamekeeper contained thirteen sex scenes, fourteen mentions of the 'c' word, and numerous instances of 'fuck' or 'fucking', but, as Lawrence explained: 'If I use taboo words, there is a reason.'

Lawrence died in 1930, two years before *Lady Chatterley's Lover* became available in several expurgated editions, i.e. with all the bits that were considered unsuitable for the public removed. If you wanted the uncut cut, you'd have to smuggle a copy in from the Continent. But as people began to travel further and ideas circulated faster and with increasing freedom across borders and populations, it became difficult to restrict words in one jurisdiction when they were available in another.

Alongside travel freedoms, the mid-twentieth century saw a more equitable society. But the battle for literary meritocracy was a hard-fought one. The arrival of Penguin Books in 1935, followed by other paperback publishers all promoting cheap, mass-market paperbacks that were affordable to the average man and woman on the street, demonstrated that words were no longer the preserve of a literary and cultural elite. Paperback books allowed words and ideas to circulate further and faster, and publishers could be much more responsive to fast-changing tastes.

By the 1950s, it had been legally established that 'literary merit' could overrule censorship, but despite this, prosecutions for obscenity reached a high point in the middle of that decade. After all, who, or what, decided the literary merit of a particular book? *Madame Bovary* was legally available to buy in the UK in the 1950s, yet at the same time featured on a secret government blacklist, and chief constables were commanded to seize and destroy any copies they discovered.

The famously vague laws on obscenity at that time (material that 'tends to deprave or corrupt') were neatly summed up by E. M. Forster: 'I have never been able to follow the legal definition of obscenity. The law tells me that obscenity may deprave and corrupt, but as far as I know, it offers no definition of depravity or corruption.'* The law considered that nothing could be published that wouldn't be acceptable for a fourteen-year-old girl to read, regardless of whether a teenage girl would want, or was able, to read the controversial books it was concerned with.

The Obscene Publications Act, passed in 1959, revolutionised how books that might fall foul of the act were viewed. They now had to be considered as a whole, rather than with a focus just on the controversial bits, and a defence of the public good (backed up by expert witnesses) was permitted. But the act had only been used to prosecute out-and-out pornography, not serious literature like *Lady Chatterley*. Sensing that the state's power and appetite for restricting words was waning, Allen Lane, Penguin's founder, decided that 'there's a time in a publishing firm, especially when things are going well, when to chuck a jemmy in the works is a very good thing because it gives everyone a lift', and, encouraged by an unexpurgated edition appearing in the US in 1959 (the court there found that *Lady Chatterley* had 'a power and tenderness which was compelling'), decided to go ahead in early 1960 with an uncensored UK publication.

Allen Lane was as resolved to publish as the authorities were

* Forster's own 1914 novel *Maurice* was not published until 1971, a year after his death. The novel dealt with homosexual love, and the author believed it to be unpublishable due to the public and legal attitudes towards same-sex relationships present during his lifetime.

determined to prosecute. His view was that Penguin was 'a University Press in paperback' that could provide a form of education for 'people like myself who left school at sixteen', and while he had said that *Lady C* was 'no great novel', he felt that it provided an excellent test of the Obscene Publications Act. Famously, when asked how he decided whether to prosecute or not, the prosecuting counsel explained that 'I put my feet up on the desk and start reading. If I get an erection, we prosecute.'

Penguin assembled thirty-five witnesses to speak out on behalf of the novel and actively invited the prosecution, knowing that they had 200,000 subscription orders for the book ready to go.* The defence struggled to find anyone of literary distinction to support a ban of the novel, ultimately relying on only two witnesses.

As ever, not all readers were considered equal or trusted – one of the key objections to publication was that it would allow a relatively cheap edition to be published, which meant a bigger circulation and far wider audience – one that might have included women and the working class.

The practicalities of prosecuting threw up complexities. How could copies of the book be given to the jury, when 'the copying process would have to be undertaken by a staff composed mainly of young girls'? And where would the jury read their copies, given that the book was censored at the start of the trial? What would happen if copies were given out to the press, but the prosecution succeeded?

* One of the authors they approached was Enid Blyton, who replied 'I'd love to help Penguin Books Ltd – they are doing a fine job with their publications – but I don't see how I can. For one thing I haven't read the book – and for another thing my husband said NO at once. The thought of me standing up in Court solemnly advocating a book "like that" (his words, not mine – I feel he must have read the book!) made his hair stand on end.'

Ultimately, the defence of *Lady Chatterley* was successful, partly due to the out-of-touch feel of the prosecution, which infamously asked: 'Is it a book you would have lying around in your own house? Is it a book you would even wish your wife or your servants to read?', while the defence argued persuasively that *Lady Chatterley* explored 'the relationship between a man and a woman in love, in which there was no shame and nothing wrong, nothing unclean, nothing which anybody was not entitled to discuss.'*

Over the next few months, Penguin sold 3 million copies of the book. Their first choice of printer had turned down the commission after a compositor, whose job it was to lay out the text, complained. After a change of heart, they took on some of the print orders. The second edition of the book, published in 1961, included this dedication:

> For having published this book, Penguin Books was prosecuted under the Obscene Publications Act, 1959 at the Old Bailey in London from 20 October to 2 November 1960. This edition is therefore dedicated to the twelve jurors, three women and nine men, who returned a verdict of 'not guilty' and thus made D. H. Lawrence's last novel available for the first time to the public in the United Kingdom.

---

* Ironically, six decades after attempting to ban *Lady Chatterley*, the British government intervened to prevent the sale of the trial judge's copy of the book to a private individual. The book, and the damask bag the judge's wife had sewn for him to make sure it couldn't be seen on his commute, had originally been purchased at auction by an American buyer. After an 'export deferral' and a crowdfunding campaign launched by English PEN, the auction price was matched and the bag and book were secured for the Penguin archives at Bristol University. The book was 'an enticing and important object' tweeted Stephen Fry, who backed the campaign.

Lawrence's stepdaughter commented that 'I feel as if a window has been opened and a fresh air has blown right through England.' The trial had demonstrated that no work of 'literary merit' could now be censored on grounds of obscenity. Over the next few years, Henry Miller's *Tropic of Cancer* and William Burroughs' *Naked Lunch* both became freely available for readers to buy in the UK, and in 1968 the role of the Lord Chamberlain was abolished (from 1737 until 1968 this member of the Royal Household had the power to grant – or not – a licence for plays to be performed). In an article to commemorate the fiftieth anniversary of the trial, Geoffrey Robertson KC wrote that 'The verdict was a crucial step towards the freedom of the written word . . . the *Chatterley* trial marked the first symbolic moral battle between the humanitarian force of English liberalism and the dead hand of those described by George Orwell as "the striped-trousered ones who rule".'

Striped-trousered, censor-morons and grey-haired ones no longer had power over the words.

Literature under lockdown

'My moral defense of the book is the book itself . . . On the ethical plane, it is of supreme indifference to me what opinion French, British or any other courts, magistrates, or philistine readers in general, may have of my book. However, I appreciate your difficulties,' wrote Vladimir Nabokov to his French publisher Maurice Girodias in 1957. Nabokov was responding to the legal problems that Girodias was faced with when he published the first edition of *Lolita* in 1955. 'I appreciate your difficulties' was a typically Nabokovian way of playing down the consequences; in fact Girodias faced repeated arrest and years of legal tangles for publishing *Lolita*. Ultimately, for that and other reasons, he left France in 1964.

In the UK, the response to publication of *Lolita* had been complete indifference, until Graham Greene called it one of the 'three best books' of the year in the *Sunday Times*. The *Sunday Express* decided a gauntlet had been thrown down, and in turn described *Lolita* as 'sheer unrestrained pornography'. This led to panic at the Home Office, which instructed all copies of *Lolita* entering the country to be seized by customs.

These experiences in France and the UK left Nabokov determined that publication of the book in the US should go much more smoothly, and he planned a careful campaign beforehand, which he referred to as 'Lolitigation'. This involved complex strategising on Nabokov's part to find the right publisher: one he believed '[would] have to agree to defend it, at his own expense, and to carry this defense through the courts as far as the Supreme Court, if necessary'. The Supreme Court in the US was no idle threat, as Nabokov outlined in another letter to Girodias:

> As you probably know, the Supreme Court has just handed down some very disappointing decisions. Although the cases judged were far removed from LOLITA's case, the important thing is that the Court did not bother with the definition of the term 'obscenity', and did not take any measures against local censorship. This means that any small-town postmaster can set in motion the machine of censorship, starting the case on its way from Court to Court, until it reached the Supreme Court, which probably (though by no means certainly) would exonerate my book.

Nabokov's letter highlights how book bans in the US were very different from those in Europe. The Supreme Court could restrict a book, but so could individual states. Indeed, the first recorded banning of a book in colonial America was *New English Canaan* in 1647, written by Thomas Morton. Most of the book was an unexceptional look at the flora and fauna of New England, but it finished with an attack on the treatment meted out to the indigenous population by the Puritan settlers, and a critique of the society they were building. The Puritans were ever on the lookout for threats to their newly established colonies and shored up their own freedoms by cracking down on any dissent. *New English Canaan* was a potential existential threat, hence the Puritans took a, well, puritanical line.

The Puritans were the first significant wave of migrants to New England, following the Pilgrims who had established the first colony in 1620. In the mid-nineteenth century Irish Catholics began to immigrate to the region to work in the rapidly expanding textile industry. Between 1860 and 1890 the number of Catholics in the United States tripled. Both Puritans and Catholics were socially conservative, and by the late nineteenth century so many books in Massachusetts had been banned that the phrase 'banned in Boston' had been coined. Books (along with other forms of entertainment) in the state were policed by the New England Watch and Ward Society,* which was hugely powerful locally. The Watch and Ward had no official legislation to back up its bans and was run by private citizens – an example of localised censorship, still prevalent in the United States today. While the Supreme Court and other judicial bodies had (and have) a narrow and specific definition of pornography, states could be far more

* Nabokov was alert to the power of such local groups, writing that 'we have here all sorts of Watch and Ward Societies, Catholic Legions of Decency, etc., and that, moreover, every postmaster in the country can start censorship trouble'.

wide-ranging in considering what words to take issue with.

For years, if you had sent a copy of Geoffrey Chaucer's fourteenth-century *Canterbury Tales* in the United States post, you could have been prosecuted. Chaucer's bawdy tale (swearing! sex! blasphemy!) was too much for US censors, and was restricted under the 1873 anti-obscenity Comstock Laws, which made it an offence to use the mail to distribute books deemed offensive. While previous attempts to censor books might have meant refusing to print or distribute them, or destroying existing copies, the Comstock Laws were a way in a more connected age to achieve the same ends. In the United States, what might be tolerated in one state might not be in another, but with the postal service covering the entire country, the Comstock Laws were an effective way of censoring words across the nation.

Much of the outrage of the citizens of Boston was directed particularly towards young readers checking out popular fiction titles from the library. Books by writers like Horatio Alger and Oliver Optic – full of rollicking adventures and dashing exploits – were phenomenally popular in the nineteenth century. 'Think of the condition of these children's minds at the end of such a carnival of sensations!' wrote the *New Hampshire Sentinel*, perhaps missing the obvious – that access to 'a carnival of sensations' was exactly what young readers craved.

As happens over and over in the history of censorship, those who held power over nineteenth-century libraries did not consider all readers equal.* They weren't necessarily interested in preventing

* The British Library has a 'Private Case' – a home for books that aren't available in the public catalogue, or, indeed, to the public (mostly erotica and pornography). It has grown and shrunk over the years, depending on donations and declassifications. No new entries have been made since 1990.

'pen-poison'* books from existing – but they did want to make sure that they couldn't be read by those whose minds they thought needed protecting: the young, the working class, and 'fallen women, and, in general, the denizens of the midnight world, night-owls, prowlers, and those who live upon sin and its wages'.

The battle over who could read what in Boston raged. The *Boston Daily Advertiser* commented that the library was

> justified in providing the kind of reading which is sought for by a large class; gives them pleasure; does them at least no harm; and, being suited to them, brings them a certain amount of intellectual profit and a kind of moral instruction; and, finally, attracts them to the library, where there is a chance that something better may get hold of them.

But this more liberal view of what a library was for was undermined by a cataloguer at the Boston Public Library called James M. Hubbard, who in 1881 began a campaign to persuade the library to stop lending 'series fiction' to children. 'I do not believe it is the proper business for the city to furnish amusing literature to the people free of expense,' he wrote. He believed the library should practise this censorship to preserve the minds of its citizens – and to influence other libraries around the country. Hubbard drew up a list of 100 titles he considered offensive (labelling them as 'vulgar', 'immoral', and 'reeking with sin'), and sent it to the trustees of the library, urging them to return to the principles of the library's founders, and petitioning the

* This description was given in 1882 by a reporter for the *Californian and Overland Monthly*, to describe true crime stories often found for sale in bars and barbershops.

Boston Common Council to close those parts of the library that circulated such material. The library trustees initially refused on the grounds that there were millions of people who wanted to read these books. In 1881 Hubbard moved from a petition to a pamphlet, listing the titles that offended him (including several written, in his words, by a 'base herd of female novelists'), and the trustees gave in to his demands.

Seeking a compromise, the library found a way to get round the controversy. By the late nineteenth century and well into the twentieth, Hubbard's banned books could be read – but only in a locked room of the library, known as the 'Inferno'. Readers had to fill out a piece of paper with their name, age and occupation, along with a reason for wanting to read the book, and a character reference. Once again, books were available for Bostonian citizens to read: but only if they could prove they were of the 'right' character.

The Inferno persisted. A 1952 article in the *Harvard Crimson* explains that the books within it were there for a variety of reasons: some were editions that were too valuable to display, some were erotica (the library had a surprisingly extensive collection of books on sadomasochism, kept in the Inferno in order to 'limit circulation to serious scholars', according to Keyes D. Metcalf, librarian of Harvard College at the time; once again, this was a judgement not so much on the words, but on the types of minds that might need protection), and some were books that had been banned in the state.

Alongside books that you might expect – the unexpurgated *Lady Chatterley's Lover* and Henry Miller's *Tropic of Capricorn*, both banned – was a collection of 'drug-store novels' – the descendants of the literature that had so vexed James M. Hubbard in the nineteenth century. They were there, the *Crimson* reported, because 'several years ago, when these cheaply bound, cheaply written books dotted the

Library's modern literature sections, officials discovered that the strong attraction of the novels detracted from the efficiency of some librarians'. As the history of the Boston Public Library shows over and over again, what people *want* to read is not necessarily what others think they *should* read.

The debates over what should be allowed on the shelves of the Boston Public Library were just one front in the city's attempts to censor literature. The Watch and Ward Society, active from the late nineteenth century (it continued until the 1950s, although with less intensity for the final twenty years of its existence), was busy censoring plays and films alongside books, which remained a central preoccupation.

The Watch and Ward list of banned titles included *The Sun Also Rises* (Hemingway), *Leaves of Grass* (Whitman) and *The Decameron* (Boccaccio). But eventually, as so often when attempts at censorship are made, the laws of unintended consequences began to assert themselves. By the 1920s, writers were beginning to deliberately print their books in Boston in the hope of having them banned – and thereby driving up sales in other parts of the country. In 1927 Upton Sinclair (who described himself as a 'prize prude') published *Oil!*, banned in Boston for a motel sex scene. The publisher printed 150 copies of a 'fig-leaf' edition, with the offending pages blacked out, which Sinclair sold on the streets of Boston. He hoped to have the book the subject of an obscenity trial, to drive up its sales.

By the 1950s, the expansion of civil liberties via court cases that curtailed the reach of municipalities meant that it was far easier for bans like those practised in Boston to be overturned. Massachusetts played a part in attempting to ban William Burroughs' novel *Naked Lunch* in the 1960s – the last major attempt to censor a controversial text in the US. While the book was found obscene in Massachusetts, the state Supreme Court overturned the decision, establishing that it had literary value. Given that *Naked Lunch* features a talking anus and extensive descriptions of opioid use, it's unlikely the Puritans who founded Boston would have agreed.

Silencing the story: *samizdat*

The Boston Public Library continued to find itself embroiled in questions about censorship throughout the twentieth century. In the 1950s, at the height of McCarthyism, it was attacked by the *Boston Post* for having a copy of *The Communist Manifesto* on display, with the *Post* opining that the library should 'label its poison', as many other libraries across the country had done, and place a stamp in every book with communist leanings. Not only that, the *Post* believed that all socialist works should be locked away from casual readers.

This kind of controversy, stemming from the political anxieties of mid-century America, reflects a specific type of censorship battle. Yet the struggle against censorship has taken different and more ingrained forms elsewhere. In Russia, the expectation of censorship was so pervasive that it shaped the act of creation. Alexander Pushkin burned most of the tenth chapter of his novel in verse *Eugene Onegin*, fearful of being prosecuted as it included criticism of the Russian emperor. 'In Russia,' wrote Vladimir Nabokov in *The Gift*, 'the censorship department arose before literature; its fateful seniority has always been in evidence.'

The earliest list of banned books in Russia was drawn up in 1073, and the first official censorship document in 1551. The state was always a powerful and active censor – initially via the Russian emperor, then delegated through various synods, academies and ministries. By the reign of Peter I in the eighteenth century, printing was a monopoly in the gift of the ruler, with penalties for materials produced by anyone other than the state-appointed printer and all books having to be published 'for the glory of the great sovereign'. The state (via the Orthodox Church) retained control of all publishing until 1783, and even then, although some private publishing was allowed, it could censor at will.

The Russian Revolution may have changed much, but it did not overthrow the Russian tradition of censorship. In 1922, the fledgling Soviet Union established Glavlit, an agency tasked with ensuring that top-secret information couldn't fall into the hands of enemies, but which mostly spent its time censoring material that the authorities did not like. And there was a lot of it. Over 1938 and 1939, more than 24 million copies of books were destroyed in the Soviet Union, and a 1940 report noted that there were 5,000 censors at work – a greater number than there were professional writers.

But censorship in Russia left readers and writers in a pre-industrial literary stasis. The poet Anna Akhmatova used the phrase 'pre-Gutenberg' to describe how she lived as a writer. After she wrote a poem about the horrors of the gulag called 'Requiem' in the 1930s, she destroyed her written copies and instead learned it by heart: she knew that leaving *any* physical trace of it was too risky. She then taught her closest friends the poem, too, so that if something happened to her, it would live on. Soviet writers who wished to write critically had to exist in an oral culture – as if the printing press had simply never been invented. And neither could Russian writers reach an international audience: after 1929, not a single Russian-language book was published abroad without approval from the Kremlin (except if it had been smuggled out). Despite the 'Khrushchev thaw', which became possible after the death of Joseph Stalin in 1953, with a relaxation of censorship taking place during the mid-1950s and 1960s, the Soviet leadership was always alarmed by the power of writing. Vladimir Lenin had been radicalised by a book – Nikolai Chernyshevsky's 1863 novel *What Is to Be Done?* – and it simultaneously feted, protected and indulged the *right* writers, while persecuting mercilessly those who they felt wrote to undermine the Soviet cause. Books are 'the most important and most powerful weapons in socialist culture', said Maxim Gorky at the First Congress of Soviet Writers in 1934.

The effect of this draconian and long-established state interference in the world of writing and publication led to the Russian practice of *samizdat*: self-publishing. 'I write it myself, edit it myself, censor it myself, publish it myself, distribute it myself, and spend jail time for it myself,' noted Russian writer Vladimir Bukovsky. Even the simplest literary freedoms in the Soviet Union were restricted: all typewriters (and later, photocopiers) had to be registered (initially with the NKVD, then the KGB). This meant that for Russian writers, the only way to reach their readers was clandestinely: often through handwritten copies of stories passed from reader to reader. Eventually, these self-published books were produced as carbon copies, on cheap, thin paper, with nondescript covers. The underground nature of *samizdat* and the difficulties in producing physical copies of texts meant that their circulation was small, but significant. They tended to be read by two groups with no common ground: the cultural intelligentsia who circulated them among trusted contacts, and government officials charged with knowing what out there needed to be censored.

Samizdat texts are a literary world of their own: they exist as outsiders, in a liminal space of unstable and unofficial versions of a text (they were often annotated by hand by readers as they circulated) – produced in numbers that were both small-scale by necessity, but large enough to disseminate with sufficient effect to draw the attention of the authorities. And sometimes, that effect could be out of all proportion to the number of copies that existed.

Doctor Zhivago

The first full-length *samizdat* novel was Boris Pasternak's *Doctor Zhivago*: no mean feat on a practical level when you consider the length of it (most editions are over 500 pages long). Refused publication in Russia in 1955 for being anti-Soviet (the censors found it critical of a clean sweep of Stalinism, the gulag system and collectivisation), *Doctor Zhivago* was only available unofficially in *samizdat*. It could, however, be read in Italy – the manuscript had been smuggled out of Russia by an Italian literary agent in 1956, before making its way to the publisher Giangiacomo Feltrinelli. 'You are hereby invited to watch me face the firing squad,' said Pasternak, according to the agent, on Pasternak's handing over of the manuscript.

It was at this point that *Doctor Zhivago* found itself on the literary front line of the Cold War. Pasternak had sent the manuscript to Glavlit for approval but heard nothing back. He knew he was unlikely to find a Russian publisher, but still he was determined it should be published. 'I wrote the novel to be published and read, and that remains my only wish,' he wrote in 1957. 'Ideas are not born to be hidden or smothered at birth, but to be communicated to others'.

In the US, meanwhile, the CIA had identified that the anti-Soviet themes of the book and Pasternak's reputation presented it with a moment to seize. In 2014, a series of declassified CIA documents outlined how the CIA felt about *Doctor Zhivago*: 'We have the opportunity to make Soviet citizens wonder what is wrong with their government, when a fine literary work by the man acknowledged to be the greatest living Russian writer is not even available in his own country in his own language for his own people to read.'

Having identified it as possessing 'great propaganda value', the CIA set about getting a copy of the manuscript of *Doctor Zhivago*, which it managed with the help of British intelligence. 'Books were weapons,' write Peter Finn and Petra Couvée in *The Zhivago Affair: The Kremlin, The CIA, and the Battle Over a Forbidden Book*, and *Doctor Zhivago* was about to be sent into battle. In 1958 the CIA worked with the Dutch security services to find a European printer for a Russian-language edition, and 3,000 hardback copies were printed. Of these, 365 were sent to Brussels, to be distributed to Soviet citizens visiting the 1958 Brussels Exposition (the Exposition was unusual in that a relatively large number of Soviet citizens – about 16,000 – were issued visas for it).

Their hope, of course, was that these copies of the book, and their primed readers, would absorb Pasternak's message of freedom, return to the Soviet Union and, according to a CIA memo, promote 'cultural and intellectual freedom, and dissatisfaction with its absence'. 'Books', wrote a CIA chief, 'differ from all other propaganda media, primarily because one single book can significantly change the reader's attitude and action to an extent unmatched by the impact of any other single medium.' The CIA, of course, could not be seen to be involved in the project; copies could hardly be distributed by the American stand at the Exposition, so instead they were handed out via a hidden library in the Vatican pavilion – often by priests.

By the end of the first month of the exhibition, a Russian émigré magazine noted that 'The greatest contemporary work of Russian literature – Boris Pasternak's novel *Doctor Zhivago*, which is banned there – is able to find its way into the country.' The news also reached Pasternak – and the American press. *The New York Times* wrote that 'during the closing days of the Brussels Fair, unknown parties stood before the Soviet Pavillion* giving copies of "Doctor Zhivago" – in Russian – to those interested . . . Origin of these copies? Classified.'

All these efforts, however, could not come in time for Pasternak to accept the Nobel Prize in Literature, which he was awarded in the same year, 1958. Pressured by the Soviet regime, Pasternak turned it down, and he died just two years later of lung cancer at the age of seventy. *Doctor Zhivago* continued to circulate in *samizdat* in Russia for another thirty years, until 1988, when it was finally legally published in the Russian literary journal *Novy Mir.*

'Some might say it's too late for me to express regret that the book wasn't published,' Khrushchev, who once described Pasternak as 'worse than a pig', later wrote in his memoirs. 'Yes, maybe it is too late. But better late than never.'

From shelves to shadows

Samizdat was a logical response to an overbearing state that stopped writers from reaching readers inside and outside of their country. *Doctor Zhivago* was only able to evade censorship because of the Russian tradition of keeping controversial texts alive and in the hands of readers,

* *The New York Times* presumably meant the Vatican pavilion, not the Soviet.

as well as the bravery of Pasternak's Italian publisher. But publishers can also be the first line of censorship: a writer can write whatever they want, but to find a wide readership, they need a publisher, and a publisher's interests and those of an author are not necessarily the same. That gap (and recent technological advances) has driven the rise of self-publishing, a way for writers to connect with a readership without having to negotiate with the caution of established publishers or other gatekeepers.

While the twentieth century saw the chipping away of laws controlling who could read what, there are now new restrictions that all writers and publishers must consider. Libel and privacy laws have evolved not to shield readers from words, but to protect the subjects of books. Defamation cases can be brought against writers and publishers for saying something that is either untrue about a person, or that damages their reputation. The risk of being sued is a constant. Sometimes they win – as in the case of David Irving versus Penguin Books and Deborah Lipstadt, author of a book which described Irving as a Holocaust denier. After a high-profile trial, Irving lost the case and had to pay costs. Sometimes they lose, as in a case brought by Mineko Iwasaki versus publisher Random House. Iwasaki was the inspiration for the protagonist of *Memoirs of a Geisha* and argued that parts of her biography were misrepresented in the book, and the case was settled out of court for an undisclosed sum.

In 2015 the Supreme Court in Britain overturned a ban on a book that had prevented the classical pianist James Rhodes from publishing an autobiography detailing the sexual abuse he had suffered as a child at school. Rhodes's ex-wife sought to suppress the book, arguing it would be detrimental to the mental health of their son. However, the judge delivering the judgement stated that 'Freedom to report the truth is a basic right to which the law gives a very high level of protection and the author's right to his story includes the right to tell it as he wishes.' The ruling underlines that a writer's right to be able to tell a truthful story can override the potential harmful effects on one person.

As books are now often published simultaneously across the globe, discrepancies in jurisdictions throw up challenges and anomalies that authors and publishers must grapple with. In the US, the person who believes they have been libelled or defamed must prove that what was said about them was false. In the UK this is reversed, and the person who made the alleged defamatory statement must prove it is true. This means that a book published in one jurisdiction may need to have changes made – or for text to be redacted – to make it safe for publication in another.

In the introduction to *Redacted: Writing in the Negative Space of the State*, a collection of essays, poems, artworks and memes, the editors describe 'text-based censorship that conspicuously masks parts of printed discourse, conveying a sense of the secret, the impossible, the inaccessible, and the indefinitely unknowable'. In 2016 Jarett Kobek's book *I Hate the Internet* was published in the United States, and when an edition in the UK followed, he was required to make changes to the text to ensure it did not break UK law. In a prefatory note to the British edition, Kobek explains how defamation law in the UK puts the burden of proof on the defendant: 'Instituted to keep people from killing each other over insults about small penises and big noses, it's evolved into the primary method by which the ultra-rich prevent disparaging information about themselves from appearing in the press.' Kobek chose a novel way of indicating to his British readers where his text had been changed in response to England's libel laws. 'Sir Jimmy Savile,' he writes, 'a living depravity who preyed on the young, the disabled and the dead . . . through the persistent threat of defamation suits . . . managed to stop any third-party reporting on his status as a living depravity.' Hence, says Kobek to his readers: 'When this book says [JIM'LL FIX IT], then you, the reader, will know that something from this book's original US edition has been changed on advice of counsel for fear of provoking litigation under English defamation law.'

While publishers may rightly be wary of falling foul of defamation and libel laws, these risks are part and parcel of their trade – to be managed and mitigated through in-house legal counsel and internal assessment. Sometimes that goes wrong, and a publisher ends up in court. But while that might draw some coverage and headlines and certainly be of interest to the parties involved, it is rarely of interest to anyone outside the world of publishing.

The far bigger threat, and one which publishers are increasingly wary of, is the court of public opinion. In 2020 a novel called *American Dirt* was published to great fanfare. The author, Jeanine Cummins, had been paid a seven-figure advance for the book, and it was selected by Oprah Winfrey for her book club. It's the story of a Mexican family who are forced to flee to the US, and it became one of the best-selling books of the year. But Cummins soon found herself in the centre of a media storm; despite initial positive reviews, *American Dirt* was attacked for its inauthenticity, with some readers accusing its author (who is of Irish and Puerto Rican heritage) of peddling stereotypes. Author Celeste Ng tweeted a review that called Cummins' depictions of Mexico 'laughably inaccurate', while other critics claim the book exploits the suffering of Mexican immigrants as 'pity porn'.

And in a meta-narrative, the controversy around sensitivity reads was a key part of the plot of the novel *Yellowface* by R. F. Kuang, published to acclaim in 2023, which examines themes of tokenism, plagiarism and cultural appropriation in publishing. *Yellowface* uses satire to explore these real-life controversies through a fictional story.

In 2015 American poet Michael Derrick Hudson submitted a poem to a literary periodical that was then selected for an anthology series called *Best American Poetry*. Hudson claimed that the poem had been submitted – and rejected – forty times under his own name, before he had decided to submit it using a female Chinese pseudonym. After ten attempts using this name, he was successful. His decision ignited a heated online debate about literary censorship: was Hudson's adoption of a different name an attempt to game the literary system, or did it shine a spotlight on the anomalies of affirmative action? Sherman Alexie, who selected the poem for the *Best American Poetry* 2015 anthology, explained in his introduction how: 'I did exactly what that pseudonym-user feared other editors had done to him in the past: I paid more initial attention to his poem because of my perception and misperception of the poet's identity. Bluntly stated, I was more amenable to the poem because I thought the author was Chinese American.'

Publishers have lately had to find ways to safeguard themselves and their authors from criticisms of cultural appropriation and inauthenticity. The instant court of social media has led to increased focus on the sensitivity reader, whose job is to scrutinise a text before publication and advise the author on any parts of their writing that might be offensive, to pre-empt any criticism that a writer is being inauthentic or insensitive. Of course, 'sensitivity' readers have been around for a long time, just under different names: one of the responsibilities of a book's editor has always been to read a text with a critical eye as to how it might be perceived by a variety of audiences.

If an author is writing characters that aren't part of their own lived experience, perhaps it makes sense to have someone with that background checking the text for any potential offence. But even that is not necessarily enough. 'All sensitivity readers can do is raise awareness of potential bias, but an author doesn't have to listen,' I was told by someone who worked in children's publishing for many years (children's and Young Adult publishing have been at the forefront of the use of sensitivity readers). And sometimes, authors listen but choose not to act. In 2021 author Kate Clanchy was accused of racism in some of the descriptions in her memoir *Some Kids I Taught and What They Taught Me*, published in 2019. Clanchy's book had won the prestigious Orwell Prize, with the judges praising a 'brilliantly honest writer'. But after Clanchy responded to criticism on review site Goodreads, such as that of a teacher who expressed their view that *Some Kids* was 'centred on this white middle-class woman's harmful, judgmental and bigoted views on race, class and body image', the controversy snowballed, drawing in other writers on social media both in her defence and against her. Eventually, Clanchy's publisher Picador, an imprint of Pan Macmillan, decided to give the book a retrospective and belated sensitivity read. Clanchy, however, felt that this would 'help create a book that would play better on Twitter, not one that is better written'. Although Clanchy did rewrite some parts of the book in light of the controversy, saying 'I was glad to re-engage with the text – it is a privilege for any writer' – she also publicly took issue with the sensitivity readers that Picador had commissioned, saying that her memoir had been 'sullied to suit their agenda'. Eventually Clanchy and her publisher agreed to part ways by mutual agreement. In a *Guardian* article titled 'The Book That Tore Publishing Apart', about the book and its effect on the wider publishing industry, one editor was quoted as saying that 'There are certain authors or subjects people just won't touch, because you know what the reaction will be on social media.' And it is not just online reactions that worry publishers – it's that of their staff, too. 'The fear is not just of inadvertently publishing something problematic but of being accused of "micro-aggressions" against junior staff. "You might think we have a lot of power, but they have a lot of power on social media to destroy someone. Everyone's saying half-jokingly: Am I going to get cancelled?"'

Publishers are usually accused of having a left-leaning bias, which makes them ripe targets for criticism in the culture wars. Milo Yiannopoulos, a British far-right political commentator, self-published his memoir *Dangerous* after his original publisher Simon & Schuster, who had reportedly paid him a $255,000 advance, withdrew from the contract. Court documents from 2017 (Yiannopoulos had sued for $10 million for breach of contract) show that Simon & Schuster had problems with the manuscript from the start. 'Throughout the book, your best points seem to be lost in a sea of self-aggrandizement and scattershot thinking,' read one comment; another, 'The use of phrases like "two-faced backstabbing bitches" diminishes your overall point'; with another piece of feedback: 'Unclear, unfunny, delete' perhaps serving as a shortcut to describe the whole mess. Eventually, after trying to represent himself in the lawsuit, Yiannopoulos withdrew it.

Likewise in the US, publisher Hachette reversed its decision to publish Woody Allen's memoir after protests and walkouts by its staff. Allen's daughter Dylan Farrow has alleged that he abused her in the 1990s, although he has never been charged. While the CEO of Hachette claimed that 'each book has its own mission. Our job as a publisher is to help the author achieve what they have set out to do in the creation of their book', staff at the company said that they 'stand in solidarity with Ronan Farrow, Dylan Farrow and survivors of sexual assault'. The freedom to choose to publish or not publish a book is fundamental to all publishers and editors, but in a world of increasingly polarised viewpoints, fuelled by social media, these decisions now receive far more scrutiny and cause much more controversy than they used to.

In today's culture wars, public libraries and librarians have become flashpoints in the battle over who gets to tell stories, and who gets to read them. Conservative groups have dominated recent headlines for pushing book bans in schools and libraries, often targeting works on race, gender identity and sexuality, but some of the arguments they use, especially around the need to protect children, echo earlier efforts by progressives to remove books deemed offensive or psychologically damaging.

This overlap isn't about political alignment so much as shared rhetorical strategies. Both right- and left-leaning activists have, at different times, appealed to the emotional safety of young readers as a justification for censorship. For example, conservatives in the US have recently succeeded in removing books like *Gender Queer* by Maia Kobabe and *The Hate U Give* by Angie Thomas from school libraries, citing sexually explicit content or anti-police themes. Meanwhile, progressive voices have criticised classics like *To Kill a Mockingbird* or *Of Mice and Men* for their use of racial slurs or outdated portrayals of marginalised groups – calling not necessarily for bans, but for removal from required reading lists or library shelves in certain school contexts.

Where these campaigns have common ground is in a desire to shield young readers from discomfort. The result is that the terrain of censorship is much more complex than a simple liberal/reactionary binary. While it's true that publishing is often *perceived* as liberal, the industry remains disproportionately white, male and elite – a reality that complicates any narrative of progressive dominance. And once books are published, access to them in schools and libraries is increasingly dictated not by publishers but by local politics, school boards, and activist parents on both sides of the aisle.

In this contested space, librarians have found themselves not just curators of collections, but defenders of intellectual freedom. At the entrance to the New York Public Library's Main Reading Room, John Milton's words are etched in stone: 'A good Booke is the precious life-blood of a master spirit, imbalm'd and treasur'd up on purpose to a life beyond life.' Yet this reverence for literature is under increasingly sustained threat. According to PEN America, more than 3,000 book bans were recorded in the US between 2021 and 2023 – an unprecedented spike.

Libraries, once passive targets, have become active battlegrounds. In 2023, the Boston Public Library joined a national initiative allowing young readers (aged thirteen to twenty-six) across the country to apply for digital library cards, giving them access to e-books and audiobooks often banned in their own states. 'Every young person in the nation should have free and open access to books from all points of view,' explained the library's president. It's a far cry from the nineteenth-century practice of locking controversial books in special collections like the Boston Inferno, accessible only to the vetted few.

As Kurt Vonnegut wrote in 1973, responding to the attempted censorship of his novel *Slaughterhouse-Five*: 'I want to congratulate librarians . . . who . . . have staunchly resisted anti-democratic bullies who have tried to remove certain books from their shelves, and have refused to reveal to thought police the names of persons who have checked out those titles.'

Today's librarians inherit that resistance. And while we may imagine we live in an era of open information, they know better: the freedom to read remains a right constantly under siege – from many directions at once.

The struggle over who controls stories and who gets to read them persists. Banned Books Week was first launched in 1982 as a response to rising attempts to remove books from schools and libraries. Where early censorship often targeted religious dissent or critiques of authority, contemporary bans have evolved to focus on materials labelled problematic by some – a definition that continues to shift. Today, it's not sex itself that provokes controversy, but sexuality.

Most recent challenges target books by LGBTQIA+ authors or writers of colour. In 2023, the most frequently challenged titles included the aforementioned *Gender Queer*, *This Book Is Gay* by Juno Dawson and *All Boys Aren't Blue* by George M. Johnson – all flagged for their LGBTQIA+ themes and sexual content. By contrast, in 2001, the most challenged books were *Harry Potter and the Sorcerer's Stone* (for promoting satanism and the occult), *Of Mice and Men* (for racial slurs, violence and profanity) and *The Catcher in the Rye* (offensive language and suitability for age group, and because it seems to be a reflexive habit in the United States for each generation to ban it).

Banning books used to be so much simpler. If 'unclear, unfunny, delete' is where we've ended up, 'redact, rewrite, ban' is where we began. Writing, like every creative process, has always demanded the right to offend, even if others have tried with varying degrees of success to neuter it. Creativity is often about upending the existing order and charging up and over established boundaries in a flurry of ink and glue.

The seesaw of freedom and restriction for words will last for as long as readers and their opinions do. The threat of censorship continues to hover not just over books and words, but real people, too. In China, books are banned, bookshops closed down, publishers kidnapped and party officials fired for the simple act of reading. In 2024 a Chinese municipal official was expelled from the Chinese Communist Party for privately reading 'an illegal publication containing contents that undermined the unity and solidarity of the Party'. Banned titles in China unsurprisingly include books scrutinising the Chinese political system, but also *The Prince* by Machiavelli; Hillary Clinton's memoir, and Hannah Arendt's *The Origins of Totalitarianism*. As with the Index of Forbidden Books, this list tells us much about how China perceives the outside world, and the real-life consequences for booksellers and writers highlight the very real power that words still have.

While Boston has been flinging open its electronic shelves, in Iowa, in a move more worthy of the State of Gilead, Margaret Atwood's novel *The Handmaid's Tale* was recently moved from the shelves of a library and into storage. School texts there must be 'age appropriate', and without any 'descriptions or visual depictions of a sex act', according to a law passed in April 2023, and since then school districts in the state have removed nearly 1,000 unique titles by over 300 different authors. But Iowa's law-makers have found dealing with the volume of titles that had to be assessed a challenge. New tools are being used in the role of censor – ones that can work tirelessly and without breaks – and without being corrupted as they read. The assistant superintendent of curriculum and instruction for the state said that it was 'simply not feasible to read every book and filter for these new requirements'. Instead, Iowa's books were assessed by ChatGPT, with administrators asking it, 'Does [book] contain a description or depiction of a sex act?' At least when *Ulysses* was described as a 'filthy book' by the censor in the UK in 1922, before it was banned the legal officer responsible bothered to read forty-two of its 732 pages.

Allowing ChatGPT to suggest what should and shouldn't be banned takes us right back to the time when a single passage deemed offensive was enough to stop a book in its tracks; after all, ChatGPT can't consider broader contexts, or assess literary merit. If only we could ask it to keep in mind Atwood's paraphrasing of Geoffrey Chaucer: 'If you don't like this tale, turn over the page and read something else', and keep *The Handmaid's Tale*, and others, on the shelves. Ultimately, censoring books is a bad plot twist: it *always* ruins the story for someone.

4.

Bad Apples: Plagiarism, Plunder, Pretence and Pranks

'Books have led some to learning and others to madness.'

Petrarch

Words are a mirror to the soul, both fragile and formidable in their power. We approach books with reverence – these repositories of thought, these universes bound between covers – and trust implicitly that the name on the spine truly represents the mind behind the words. Yet this trust, this unspoken contract between writer and reader, rests upon a foundation more precarious than we might care to admit. For centuries, a shadowy undercurrent has rippled beneath literature's grand edifice: a world of borrowed phrases, purloined pages, fabricated identities and calculated deceptions. In the realm of books, that most civil of territories, lurks a surprisingly lawless history of kidnapped words, stolen volumes, pretenders to greatness, and literary tricksters – all merrily exploiting the gaps between what we write, what we read, and what we believe to be true.

'Your word is truth,' said Jesus – and we are our words. Writing is initially a private act. It's just you, the writer, with your words. You don't need to second-guess trusting or believing them – they are solid and dependable – and you know their provenance exactly. Because a writer must believe wholeheartedly in the truth of their own words (otherwise they fail to believe in themselves), it follows that they might expect readers to approach their writing with the same level of absolute trust.

But readers come with different (and varied) agendas. They engage with a writer's words because they are curious about that person, their experiences and what they have to say: by reading their thoughts and fantasies, they are privileged to get a glimpse into who the author is and what makes them tick. Whether it's the stylistic choice of a novelist, or the bold claim of a polemicist, words are read as revealing something about the person who stands by them. It's crucial that readers believe that what they are reading *really* came from the mind of the author – that the person whose name is on the cover of the book is showing their authentic self – and that they haven't stolen someone else's words or are pretending to be someone else. There's an implicit contract of absolute trust between writer and reader: the writer vouches that what is written under their name reflects their honest thoughts, and the reader accepts that reassurance at face value.

For hundreds of years (until the novel developed them in a different direction), books were *fact*. Oral histories were mutable, but books fixed a story forever. That's why people studied, collected, debated and desired them. And it's why, despite the current dominance of social media, it remains true that the book is *still* the format in which people want to tell their story. The authenticity of the book is an unearned, baked-in positive for any author. While social media is a series of surface jabs, the book is the knock-out blow that can cement reputations. The truth is, while it's far easier to bash out 280 characters every hour to your social-media followers, there's status in a book that simply can't be earned any other way. Whether you're a Dick or a Dickens, publishing a book showers you in gravitas, even if you, the author, might personally lack it. You get to perch on the shoulders of giants and bask in the reflected glory of all the authors that came before you, no matter what your message might be.

Readers and writers are all human: protean, mercurial, and seeking connection. But while we look to books as bearers of fact, authoritative and trustworthy, their history demonstrates that things are not always as they seem. We assume we're being told the truth: that the name on the cover is the author's, and the writer's claims about being an expert on the topic are real. But since a writer isn't present to explain or prove their authenticity when we curl up with a book, texts are open to interpretation, and dependent on trust. And sometimes these gaps can be exploited – by another author, or, these days, a large language model.*

Because readers must take writers on trust, the literary world has a long tradition of fraudulent behaviour – more, perhaps, than any other creative endeavour. This history is an indication that the invisible contract doesn't always hold: inevitably, people being people, other

* Someone recently sent me a link to LibGen, which is a database made up of pirated books used by Meta to train AI. I searched it, and my first book was in there. My thoughts have been consumed by a voracious, faceless large language model without me knowing. I don't know how I feel about this ripple effect, but my words are taking an exhilarating journey all of their own.

motivations can get in the way. Plagiarism, literary hoaxes and forgeries mean we can never be quite sure that what we are reading *is* the truth – or that a writer is who they claim to be. As readers we come to words with preconceptions and expectations, but the space available for deception might be exploited by a writer for numerous reasons: infamy, money, plain old dupers' delight. It's hardly surprising: we are all familiar with unreliable narrators, those creations of the page whose perspective allows us differing levels of insight into their world. We might think, with varying levels of fondness, of Holden Caulfield in *The Catcher in the Rye*, Nick Carraway in *The Great Gatsby*, or Amy Dunne in *Gone Girl*. But while an unreliable narrator might add a frisson of welcome pleasurable tension to the reading experience, do we feel so forgiving towards an author who lies about who *they* are?

Plagiarism: the kidnap of the self

Imagine a writer sneaking about with a net, kidnapping another author's words. That's where the word plagiarism comes from – its etymological root is *plaga*, which refers to a hunting net, or a trap. A *plaga* could be used to kidnap another man's slaves, but the Roman poet Martial used *plaga* in a literary context in the first century AD to describe the theft of words – almost as valuable as slaves. So, the word for stealing someone's words (are you still with me?) had its roots in the physical theft of a person: apt, perhaps, if writers are their words, and their words are them. Plagiarism betrays honour for the reader (though they might not know it) and the writer (who certainly does know, and who is betraying themselves).

Martial wrote a number of epigrams on *plaga*. He drew distinctions between those who recited his poems as their own (plain old plagiarism); writers who tampered with his texts and inserted their own words into them (forgery, effectively); and finally, those who wrote offensively bad poems and passed them off as Martial's own (downright defamatory, and rude, to boot). 'A known book can't change its master,' he wrote, presumably in exasperated hope rather than real expectation; given that he bothered to write about word theft, he presumably understood and accepted that *all* writers are plagiarists, to a greater or lesser extent – it's part of the job description. In Martial's era, the temptation to cheat was obvious: the world felt larger, news travelled slowly, and readers were connected only by word of mouth. The chances of your deception being uncovered were minuscule – the risk–reward ratio was in your favour.

And if someone accused you of plagiarism, how could they prove it? After all, it's more akin to poaching than outright theft: who owns a word, or an idea? You surely can't be punished if a phrase or fragment strays into your fertile mind and you later act on it, consciously or unconsciously. Speaking of poaching, author Carson McCullers once complained that fellow Southern Gothic writer Harper Lee had been 'poaching on my literary preserves' when Lee wrote *To Kill a Mockingbird*, suggesting that one of the difficulties with defining and detecting plagiarism is that it isn't an out-and-out land grab, more a crossing of friable and invisible boundaries.

Ovid, Cicero, Shakespeare, Dryden, Sterne – all used, adapted and stole stories from others and made them their own. The list stretches back, and will no doubt reach forward into the future, too, in an endless process of literary recycling. 'The ugly fact', acknowledges author Cormac McCarthy, 'is books are made out of books.' Words are endlessly kidnapped from one text and put to work in another, and the only word we have for it is plagiarism – but is this even the right word for a process that seems inherent to the very fabric of literature?

McCarthy's accusation doesn't seem so ugly when we read lines in *The Waste Land* like: 'The Chair she sat in, like a burnished throne,/ Glowed on the marble . . .', and hear the echo of Shakespeare's lines from *Antony and Cleopatra*: 'The barge she sat in, like a burnished throne,/ Burned on the water.' And Shakespeare himself stole this scene from a translation of Plutarch: 'She disdained to set forward otherwise but to take her barge in the river of Cydnus, the poop whereof was of gold, the sails of purple, and the oars of silver.' What we might call 'plagiarism' can, in fact, be a series of signposts, alerting the attentive reader to a wider web of meaning and significance. Rather than the violence of a kidnapping or the violation of stealing another's thoughts, it suggests a more careful process of sieving, grafting and knitting.

T. S. Eliot wrote that 'The good poet welds his theft into a whole of feeling which is unique, utterly different from that from which it was torn; the bad poet throws it into something which has no cohesion.' This then seems the key: thieving writers are forgiven if they can merge the stolen words, images or stories with their own vision, and turn it into something new. But who is doing the forgiving, and who decides when something is unique *enough*? And while a reader might not mind (or even notice), the original author may have stronger feelings about it – when you've slaved over your words for months or years, having someone else reuse them without acknowledgement feels like the deepest of insults.

Martial's frustrations about his words being stolen weren't just about his reputation. Vexed after hearing that a rival poet, Fidentius, had stolen his words and claimed them as his own, Martial countered that 'Fame has it that you, Fidentius, recite my books to the crowd as if none other than your own. If you're willing that they be called mine, I'll send you the poems for free. If you want them to be called yours, buy this one, so that they won't be mine' – a nod that literary theft is not just about ownership, but also about financial reward.

While the act of borrowing from and imitating other writers has always existed, and plenty of writers have complained about it, there was no legal framework to define what plagiarism was until the primacy of the author as an individual was established post-Enlightenment. The first mention of plagiarism to describe literary theft in English came 1,500 years after Martial, by playwright Ben Jonson, and the word appeared in Samuel Johnson's *Dictionary* in 1755 ('Theft; literary adoption of the thoughts or works of another'). In between these two events, as we've seen, in 1710 the first copyright act was passed in England, which established that an author could have copyright over their own work, rather than their printer. Until this point, the author was an afterthought: the printer took on the financial and legal risk (which could be significant) of publication, and in return, the money made by a book went directly to them, as did the right to print it. The copyright act was one of the most consequential legal acts in publishing history: it meant that 'theft' of words as defined by Johnson's dictionary had become quite literally true.

In *What Is an Author?* the philosopher Michel Foucault wrote that the 'possibility of transgression attached to the act of writing' was only in reach once 'a system of ownership for texts came into being'. When stories were told, retold, added to and reframed, whether in the oral traditions of the ancient Romans or the intertextual hothouses of Renaissance London theatres, it was hard to know for sure who owned them. But once copyright over texts was established, words became an author's property – and the argument over what is inspiration, imitation or outright word-kidnapping has raged ever since.

Ownership of words is now spiritual and legal: to quote extensively from another writer's words, you must pay for them, either to the author, or their estate (unless, that is, the work is out of copyright).* They are literal property, and while you might be able to rent them out for a specific job, you can never own them outright. Readers and writers might disagree that words can be owned, but as soon as a writer publishes a run of linked phrases, they can, and do. Copyright is the legal mechanism that *allows* ownership and disallows anyone but the author from profiting. Copyright means that a particular phrase now belongs to a particular writer – and if someone else wants to use the same words in the same order, then they need to either acknowledge where they originated, or pay to use them – usually both.

T. S. Eliot wrote in his essay collection *The Sacred Wood* that 'Immature poets imitate; mature poets steal; bad poets deface what they take, and good poets make it into something better, or at least something different,' and we've seen in this chapter that Eliot's *The Waste Land* is a perfect example of a mature poet borrowing words from other writers, and weaving them into something different – a way of writing he clearly felt comfortable with. And sometimes other writers have used the spirit of Eliot to defend themselves against accusations of plagiarism. In 2022 the Australian author John Hughes had his novel *The Dogs* withdrawn from the longlist of a literary prize after he was accused of multiple acts of plagiarism by using unacknowledged passages from *Anna Karenina* and *The Great Gatsby*, along with

* In the United Kingdom, copyright for literary works lasts for seventy years from the end of the calendar year of an author's death.

more than fifty similarities found between *The Dogs* and Svetlana Alexievich's 2017 non-fiction book *The Unwomanly Face of War.*

Hughes apologised, explaining that

> I don't think I am a plagiarist more than any other writer who has been influenced by the greats who have come before them . . . I've always used the work of other writers in my own. It's a rare writer who doesn't . . . It's a question of degree . . . That great centrepiece of modernism, The Wasteland, is itself a kind of anthology of the great words of others. Does this make Eliot a plagiarist? Not at all, it seems. You take, that is, and make something else out of it; you make it your own.

Being accused of plagiarism is one of the worst things that can happen to an author: it's reputationally very difficult to recover from. And it's hard not to feel sympathy for Hughes, who described how: 'there is nothing more disturbing than discovering your creative process is not what you had assumed'. This explanation gets straight to the heart of the matter (to borrow from Graham Greene) – it's a rare writer who sets out to deceive, and far more likely that instead they have unconsciously weaved another's writing into their work. After all, writers are the biggest readers out there, and none of us are starting with a spotless mind, more's the pity. And unlike for earlier authors, the risk–reward ratio has now flipped: algorithms and AI mean it's easier than ever for plagiarism to be uncovered, and for the news to subsequently reach every corner of the world in the time it takes to send an email.

But, as one academic pointed out, Hughes's defence of *The Dogs* didn't make much sense. On the one hand, he was claiming that he had plagiarised by mistake, due to an untidy creative process (he said of Alexievich's stories and his own work that 'I could no longer unpick them, even if I had wanted to'), but on the other, he seemed to want readers to believe that it was intentional and meaningful, like Eliot's. But, as the academic also pointed out, Eliot used copious footnotes in *The Waste Land*, which carefully acknowledged his debts to other authors. Hughes did not.

Hughes might have been better to refer critics to the arguments of Roland Barthes, like Foucault a French literary critic who believed that there was no such thing as *a* writer, because all writing involves collaboration – unconscious or otherwise. How can an author possibly create without using their experiences and those of the people and places they encounter? When we write, we use as unacknowledged scaffolding every phrase, sentence and argument we have read or heard – on the page, in conversation. It's impossible to avoid – at least, without wiping your mind clean. And it is not just on the level of the sentence, or phrase, that a writer can plagiarise. Graham Greene spoke of the 'ice chip in the heart' that all writers must have to allow them to 'plagiarise' the lives of their family and friends in their work. And that brings us right back round to Martial, who argued that plagiarists kidnap the 'inner life' of their victims.

Purloining: tome raiders

It's not just words that get purloined. It's books, too. 'Books are not absolutely dead things, but do contain a potency of life in them,' wrote Milton. Perhaps that's why readers have coveted them so fervently – is there any other portable project out there that can say the same? We sense, like journalist Susan Orlean, that 'once words and thoughts are poured into them, books are no longer just paper and ink and glue'. There is *life* between the pages. While we can't (yet) download the contents of someone's mind to peruse, by reading their words we can enter into their mind, another world, using words that are portals to new ways of thinking and seeing. We get a sense of who they are, what they think, and how they want to present themselves to the world; more than that, as readers, a book is a jumping-off point for examining ourselves and learning something about our own inner life.

To start this journey of self-knowledge, we need to crack the spine. The book itself is simply a physical object, a vessel, that contains something magical and ephemeral: it's what's inside that counts. Right? Wrong. Ask any publisher about the demise of physical books in the wake of e-books and they will laugh in your face; ask anyone with shelf-loads of books if they have read them all and they will blush. For the most voracious readers the vessel itself still *matters*; we want to possess the book, own it – words, thoughts and all. It's a blurry line between owning the medium and consuming the message. We want it all. And the materiality of books, the 'paper, ink and glue', means we can have it. But this materiality also means that books can be taken by those they don't belong to. There's something about gathering up sheets of paper, covering them in ink, slapping a cover on them and calling it a book that leads to some truly unhinged behaviour.

The desire to possess books is one encountered from the earliest days of their production. Medieval books were hand-scribed, personalised and mostly irreplaceable. A book was as unique and precious as the mind (and hands) that made it. Early printed books were expensive and in short supply. They were stringently controlled by the elite – monasteries and universities – who were ferocious gatekeepers to the circulation of ideas and what was acceptable knowledge. The first libraries were formidable and protective institutions: you couldn't just walk in, select a book to read, and take it home with you. Each volume had enormous value and had to be preserved, and even the few readers allowed access couldn't be trusted – which is why books were kept on the shelves in chains, a practice that began in the Middle Ages and lasted until the eighteenth century. You can still see chained books in Hereford Cathedral and Wimborne Minster, although I won't be visiting – the idea of 'chaining' a book so it can never feel the sun on its spine, have its margins annotated or coffee spilt on it is too sad to contemplate for long.

By the nineteenth and twentieth centuries, libraries had pivoted from book jails to public institutions whose utopian vision was to give access to all – sharing books and their words with as many readers as possible. But, alas, with no chains to deter them, and despite the proliferation of cheap plastic-wrapped paperbacks, library theft has continued over the centuries. There's no absolute consensus on which library books are the most stolen of all time (indeed, there's no consensus on when a library book moves from being a 'late return' to 'stolen'), but some of the most-plundered titles from a 1996 survey in the United States were the Bible, the prophecies of Nostradamus, the *Guinness Book of Records* and *The Joy of Sex*. Self-help and how-to guides in general seem the most popular. The average library thief, it transpires, is practically minded (and has an eye on the future): they lift books that might help them solve a problem, or help them anticipate one. That's not too far removed from a library's noble aim of educating the masses. But not all library thieves are searching for a car repair manual or divine insight.

*

In 2017, the Carnegie Library* of Pittsburgh began an appraisal of its rare book room. On the first day (in fact, in the first hour), the assessors immediately noted that several titles were missing or had been gutted. Of an eighteen-volume set of rare etchings from the eighteenth century, they reported that

> The only part of this asset located during on-site inspection was its bindings. The contents have evidently been removed from the bindings and the appraiser is taking the extraordinary assumption that they have been removed from the premises.

Extraordinary indeed. By the end of the appraisal, the assessors had discovered that approximately $8 million worth of rare materials had been stolen, from the oldest book in the collection to first editions of Boccaccio and George Eliot to irreplaceable lithographs and maps. The eighteenth-century etchings alone were worth $600,000; many items were priceless. But how had they been stolen? Greg Priore, the manager of the rare book room, had designed it to make it impregnable to thieves. There was only one entrance, limited opening hours, constant surveillance. Since 1992, he himself had sat guard at its entrance. But therein lay the catch: the one person he had failed to guard against was himself. Over twenty-five years, Priore had snuck out precious material and sold it on via a local bookseller: it turns out that you *can* put a price on the priceless. Priore's defence was that he needed the money to pay

---

* A 'Carnegie library' is one built with money donated by the philanthropist Andrew Carnegie; he was so dedicated to libraries (and so rich) that he funded 2,509 of them between 1881 and 1929 (he died in 1919, but his Foundation continued his work).

for the schooling of his four children – stretching the boundaries of a library as a place to find an education by just a little.

But this was not the first, and is unlikely to be the last, time a library was plundered by the very people put in charge of protecting it. In Naples, the sixteenth-century Girolamini library had been closed to the public for years before a curious academic managed to gain access in 2012. He found shelves emptied and drink cans littering the floor alongside discarded books, even a dog roaming around with a bone in its mouth, perhaps searching for a copy of Kafka's *Investigations of a Dog*. The art historian who alerted the police to the decay and decline of the library wrote in a story for a newspaper that leaving the light-fingered director in charge was like having an arsonist in charge of a forest. Marino Massimo de Caro, the director, would wait until the evening, disable the CCTV, and then with a group of associates proceed to take the most valuable titles from the shelves. The looting was systematic, with the books having their library seals and stamps cut out or defaced (some even had their bindings stripped) before being sold on the international book market. In a belt-and-braces measure, the thieves had also stolen the library catalogue, to make sure investigators couldn't even be certain what books the shelves didn't hold. De Caro was arrested and charged, and eventually sentenced to seven years in jail. Because he cooperated with the authorities, this was commuted to house arrest. Plenty of time to catch up on his reading.

The Carnegie and Girolamini library heists show that the biggest threat to valuable books is not the casual thief, but the organised inside job. The people most trusted with rare and precious books are often those who are stealing, defacing and destroying them. These supposed book lovers have the means and the opportunity, and once motive is supplied, then they don't seem to be able to stop themselves. But perhaps for some librarians, a career spent taking care of books and building relationships with them can blur important boundaries. In the end, these individuals seem to lose sight of the fact that the books they serve as custodians for don't belong to them.

In 2017, the same year that Priore's theft was being discovered across the Atlantic, 240 rare books were stolen from a warehouse in West London. They included copies of Dante's *Divine Comedy*, and *On the Revolutions of the Heavenly Spheres* by Copernicus. Heady stuff for bibliophiles. The missing books were estimated to have been worth $3.4 million, less than half Priore's haul, but many, which contained handwritten notes by previous owners that spanned centuries, were irreplaceable. The raiders had pulled off an incredible heist: they climbed up the side of the warehouse, scaled the roof, cut open a skylight and descended through it, all while avoiding cameras, alarms and motion sensors.

But that effort wasn't matched by the end product. Having expended their energy in the planning and execution of the raid, the thieves had failed to think through what might happen if they were successful. Rare books are difficult to store and to get rid of: pesky antiquarian booksellers want proof of provenance before they'll buy them off you, and it's a small and intimate profession. They ask questions and talk to each other. Unless you know exactly what you're stealing and have good contacts, stolen books quickly become a liability. And that's what seems to have happened in this case: after a long investigation, nearly all the volumes were recovered, buried under a house in Romania. Too hot to handle, and not suitable beach reads.

Book lovers don't like to think of precious old books being buried, or ripped apart, or treated as commodities. Old books have lived long lives, collecting along the way fingerprints, tears, dust, stains, the scribblings of previous readers. It's difficult to quantify their value – in the same way that we can't quantify the value of a life. But we acknowledge that venerable old age itself is something to be protected and shielded. The Carnegie Library of Pittsburgh should probably have invested in some stout chains to keep its charges safe. But there are also books in danger at the opposite end of a lifespan – young books, just starting out in the world. While their bindings might be workaday and nothing special, the power of the book means that they are still coveted for what's inside the covers.

Steal this book

In 1971 the political and social activist Abbie Hoffman wrote *Steal This Book*, intended as a guide to overthrowing governments and organisations. While *Steal This Book* went on to sell enough copies for its author to note that 'It's embarrassing when you try to overthrow the government and you wind up on the Best Seller's List',* it doesn't seem to have influenced the generations of book thieves that followed. Apparently, shoplifters who steal from bookshops are definitely interested in capitalism, but not in overthrowing it: just like publishers, they focus their efforts on what they know there is an appetite for. A couple of *Guardian* investigations on the problem of 'shrinkage', as booksellers coyly refer to book theft, highlighted the differences in book markets across the globe. In Canada, that means they steal literary superstars like Haruki Murakami, whereas in the UK recognisable brands – like Harry Potter and Peppa Pig – are more at risk. Beatrix Potter is a

* It is not known how many copies of *Steal This Book* itself were stolen.

particular problem for booksellers, as her books are small enough to be easily concealed in a pocket.

One bookshop in a town south-east of London lamented that 'We can no longer stock any of the lovely small hardback editions of *The Tale of Peter Rabbit*, or any of the other small Beatrix Potter books, as they are continually pinched. And in Beckenham, too. Shocking.' Shocking it might be, but it's increasingly difficult to detect book theft after the fact. Most professional lifters now sell their wares anonymously online, avoiding the scrutiny that might come from walking into a second-hand bookshop to dispose of them.

Booksellers tend to be sanguine about a certain level of liftage: 'a certain percentage of books will wander off, and over time you know what they'll be,' says James Daunt, the chief executive of Waterstones. Booksellers across the UK report theft of a heady mix of the *Wisden Cricketers' Almanack* (small but pricy, and what might be its downfall, updated every year); local authors (apparently at Blackwell's in Oxford there is an 'ongoing love' of stealing books by noted past resident J. R. R. Tolkien); reading-list staples ('we had a stage of keeping Cormac McCarthy's *The Road* behind the till to limit theft. One spring saw 15 taken from our shelves,') and, by more erudite light fingers, philosophers. In 2017 the London Review Bookshop reported its most-stolen authors (in order) as 'Baudrillard, Freud, Nietzsche, Graham Greene, Lacan, Camus, and whoever puts together the *Wisden Almanack*.' Those cricketers at it again. If this sounds impressive, however, many booksellers feel that book thieves have dumbed down in recent years. One Hove bookseller reported that 'In the 1980s, Albert Camus, Jean-Paul Sartre, Sylvia Plath and Jack Kerouac were the most likely to go missing, *The Bell Jar* and *On the Road* competing for being the least profitable books in the shop. We are now forced to keep Asterix, Tintin, Beatrix Potter and Dr Seuss behind the counter.' From philosophers to picture books.

And the demographic of book thieves is surprisingly broad. Cricketers, students, fantasy fans to be sure; but in Forum Books in Northumberland it's 'the under-fives who, once they've found a book, hug it and won't let go or try to march straight out'. A former manager of a London book store reported a woman who stole 'the Andrew Morton Princess Diana biography and then burst into tears as soon as she was stopped, only able to say "she was the people's princess" over and over'.

Anecdotally, booksellers note that some thieves steal to order for a market, but others seem to do it just for the thrill of it – or for 'a radical reappropriation of knowledge', as one shoplifter justified when he was caught with £400 worth of books about his person.

Abbie Hoffman's injunction to 'steal this book' was a straight-up invitation, but *How to Shoplift Books* by artist David Horvitz 'details 80 ways in which one can steal a book, from the very practical, to the witty, imaginative and romantic'. Methods include hiding a book inside a fake rock, cooking some garlic in-store and exiting with your chosen books as everyone else is 'caught in the ecstasy of the aroma', or 'Smash a hole in the store's window. Throw the book through the hole.'

As Horvitz notes, 'we rarely come across a message encouraging us to steal – especially not one with the authority that print still carries'. Book theft is a juxtaposition: no one could seriously argue that a book is necessary for life, and stealing books – books! – seems so wrong – anti-culture, against civilised society. Yet as all dedicated readers know, the desire to possess one can be almost overwhelming. There's even a word for book thieves: biblioklepts. But is there a word for a person who steals words before they've made it into print?

The spine collector

'Book Thief Who Stole More Than 1,000 Manuscripts "Wanted to Cherish Them Before Anyone Else"' read a 2023 headline. In the years prior, publishing insiders across the globe had been subject to a strange series of events, beginning with innocuous-sounding emails asking that the recipient kindly supply a manuscript to the sender. This type of request happens all the time: agents, publishers and authors are forever sending submissions and manuscripts to each other; why would these politely worded requests in the standard language of publishing be any different from hundreds of others? A relatively small and sociable industry, publishing runs on high levels of trust, white wine and book-launch-fuelled gossip. So mostly, the recipients did as asked. But gradually, it became clear these requests weren't genuine. Someone, somewhere, was making a lot of effort to intercept words that they had no official business with. But who? And why?

The 'who' part was answered in 2021 when Filippo Bernardini, later dubbed 'the spine collector', was arrested and charged with a spree of digital thefts spanning more than five years. Bernardini had spent that time impersonating editors, translators and literary scouts to try and steal unpublished manuscripts. His approach was scattergun and baffling: he targeted (although didn't necessarily manage to obtain) manuscripts by big-name authors like Margaret Atwood and Sally Rooney, but he also requested manuscripts by unknown or less well-established authors. And what he did with the manuscripts he convinced people to send him was equally strange: he read them, but after that – nothing. The manuscripts weren't leaked online; there was no blackmail attempt. The words simply disappeared into the digital ether – a crime that appeared to hurt no one.

That's not true, of course. Author Peter Baker wrote of his experience of being persuaded by Bernardini to hand his manuscript over to him (Bernardini had emailed him via a spoof email address, posing as his agent and requesting a version of his manuscript in a format different to that originally supplied): 'It was the first book I'd ever tried writing, and, during the previous near-decade, it had become an overburdened locus of my ambitions, hopes, doubts, and fears. Many times, I'd looked at the manuscript and wondered if I was fooling myself. Getting fooled into handing it over made me feel sick.' The feelings a writer has about their manuscript are intense, meaningful, profound. A manuscript is your initial attempt at your book – it's not for a wide audience. This is *your* work, and showing it to someone else takes an enormous amount of courage and confidence. You choose your earliest readers extremely carefully, so to be duped into sending it to someone who it turns out is not who they say they are must be incredibly destabilising. During the court case in 2023, Bernardini said

> One day, I created a spoof email address for someone I knew of in the publishing industry, and I sent an email to someone else that I knew of asking for a pre-publication manuscript . . . I wrote in the style and using the language that my former colleagues had used. When that request was successful, from that moment on, this behaviour became an obsession, a compulsive behaviour.

Publishers are increasingly vulnerable to cyber-attacks and ransom attempts online. Atwood's 2019 sequel to *The Handmaid's Tale, The Testaments*, was the target of repeated attempts to steal the manuscript.

'People were trying to steal it. Really, they were trying to steal it and we had to use a lot of code words and passwords,' she told the BBC. Big-name authors and their publishers must now deal with shielding an author's words all the way from manuscript to finished copies – carefully controlling who can see what, and when, in well-choreographed releases.

When Bernardini initially appeared in court in New York, even the judge appeared confused about what he intended to do with all these manuscripts. 'So he wanted to read books before they were published?' she asked. 'Interesting. Very interesting.' Perhaps the judge would have been less confused if she had realised Bernardini's CV stated he had written his dissertation on a translation of *Pinocchio*.

The why did eventually become a little clearer. 'There is a relationship between tormentors and victims, something close to a real friendship, or even love. A person cannot live without others, just as the tormentor cannot live without his victim.' Bernardini wrote these words in a novel published in 2008 (it was called *Bulli*, Italian for bullies). He had worked in the publishing world for several years: as an intern, a rights assistant, a translator, and at a literary agency. His relationships with people in the industry seemed to be part of the psychology of his crimes: during the years he was active, some victims would challenge him via email when they realised that he was a fraud. His responses became personal, and unpleasant.

Court papers report Bernardini explaining that when reading the manuscripts, he had a 'special and unique connection with the author, almost like I was the editor of that book'. Perhaps it was a way of creating his own highly exclusive book club of one – 'cosplaying what people in publishing were doing as editors or literary agents'. In publishing, status can be indicated by how early a copy of a book you can procure. An advance copy of a finished book (sent out to reviewers and journalists) puts you ahead of the reading pack; an advance proof or unedited manuscript even more so. Reading a manuscript that doesn't yet have a publisher might, in your mind, give you the ultimate publishing edge. Assuming he read the manuscripts he was sent, Bernardini would have been one of the very first to do so for each – perhaps creating an intimacy in his mind between himself and the author. 'I wanted to keep them closely to my chest and be one of the fewest to cherish them before anyone else, before they ended up in bookshops,' he said. He seemed to want to create an exclusive relationship with the author, with him as the original, and best, reader. Once a manuscript is published as a book, it becomes open to anyone to read, but not all readers, Bernardini seems to be suggesting, would cherish or even deserve an author's words in the way he would. 'I had a burning desire to feel like I was still one of these publishing professionals and read these new books . . . My name will always be associated with this crime. It is my scarlet letter and I will carry it for the rest of my life.'

Even in his attempt at explanation Bernardini's literary obsession shines through.

Possessing: 'men who become books'

Marie Kondo, doyenne of tidying, once described books as a 'praying mantis lurking in the grass'. According to her, we should 'ideally keep fewer than 30 books' in our home, and she experimented with ripping out certain pages of books so that she only kept the words that 'sparked joy'. As if that wasn't nightmarish enough, she kept her mutilated mantes hidden away in a *cupboard*. It's advice that will make most book lovers shudder, then stop listening. The compulsive collection of anything is generally viewed as a negative – but not so much when it comes to books. Instead, an extensive book collection is usually something to be celebrated, or at least tolerated, in a way that collecting other objects isn't. After all, books are education, entertainment and home decor, all in one neat package.

The number of books that we *should* keep in our homes has been contested for a long time; recognition that, for most readers, there will always be more books than places to put them. And mechanised printing on an industrial scale means there now really is no limit to the number of books an individual can possess, other than the resources necessary to buy and to house them. While we might think that e-books would help solve the latter problem, they may simply push it in a new, and potentially more overwhelming, direction. Yes, on Reddit there is a subreddit called r/DataHoarder, for those who just can't press delete. The Japanese phrase *tsundoku* refers to the phenomenon of piling up books (in flagrant disregard of the rules of Kondoing), never to read them; now, of course, the only limits are your data storage arrangements.

Ever since Gutenberg cranked up his press, and long before, the question of how many books is enough has been tormenting readers and frustrating the people who live with them. In the tenth century the Islamist scholar Sahib ibn Abbad apparently had a collection of 117,000 books. Impressive, but even more so when you consider that he also had a herd of 400 camels which he used to transport them – trained to walk in alphabetical order. And spare a thought for the family of the comedian Barry Humphries, who had 25,000 books in his house when he died in 2023, and who had described himself (presumably proudly) as a 'compulsive bibliomaniac'.

In a time when printed books were difficult to come by, before mass printing, having a large collection of books told you a lot about someone. In ancient Rome, every family of good standing had a *bibliothēca* in their home. This was an outward symbol of your education, taste and social position. Then, as now, some book lovers would buy books (or scrolls) for their library with absolutely no intention of reading them – the act of possession was enough satisfaction. But the printing press unleashed a torrent of books that could eventually be bought by the masses, an avalanche that continues to this day.

Each individual bibliomaniac has their own personal definition of how and what books they seek to possess. Some collect first editions or signed copies, while others want to possess a particular series or specific collection. Poet Alfred Tennyson was filled with horror at the idea of collecting first editions (which he considered to be the worst, as they contained more errors), while Samuel Johnson wanted 'the original, and all the translations, and all the editions which had any variations in the text'. The lunatic.

Nowadays, Bookstagram and BookTok are full of freshly hatched bibliophiles, lusting after exquisite new editions of old titles. Publishers are wise to this, hence their continued focus on producing covetable, collectable series of books, from clothbound hardbacks to beautiful box-sets. Along with booksellers, they are busy creating virgin markets and new justifications to persuade us to consume titles both new *and* old. In 2025 Puffin Books reissued six of Jane Austen's novels for the TikTok generation. With cartoon illustrations and bold colours on the covers, the new blurbs for plain ol' Jane promised stories that were 'full of meet-cutes, missed connections and drama', according to the marketing. Of course, what hasn't changed is the stories inside the day-glo covers, which makes you wonder how the average TikToker will feel when they realise that *Sense and Sensibility* is not *Bridgerton*, no matter how much neon is splashed on the cover. But since the point of these books is perhaps not to be read but to have them be seen in carefully curated bedroom reels, maybe it doesn't matter.

'If fortune turns her face once more in kindness upon me before I go, I may chance, some quiet day, to lay my overheating temples on a book, and so have the death I most envy,' wrote Romantic poet Leigh Hunt (and author of *The Romance of Book-Collecting*), who you just *know* would have been on BookTok making endless reels to show off his collection.

We might like to tell ourselves that we keep books because we're going to read them one day, but even the most ardent book lover would have to eventually concede to Kondo that they have a slight problem. And what happens when the romance of book collecting spirals into something very different? Sir Thomas Phillipps was a nineteenth-century collector who referred to himself as a 'vellomaniac' – his real obsession was manuscripts, of which he owned 60,000 – but he also had a significant side hustle as a bibliomaniac, owning 40,000 books. He had twenty rooms in his house, and sixteen of them were given over to books. The keeper of manuscripts of the British Museum described visiting:

> The state of things is really inconceivable. Lady P is absent, and were I in her place, I would never return to so wretched an abode . . . Every room is filled with heaps of papers, MSS, books, charters, packages & other things, lying in heaps under your feet, piled upon tables, beds, chairs, ladders &c.&c. and in every room, piles of huge boxes, up to the ceiling, containing the more valuable volumes! It is quite sickening . . . The windows of

> the house are never opened, and the close confined air & smell of the paper & MSS is almost unbearable.

There is nothing romantic here about book collecting. Untidy, stench-filled rooms crammed with towers of mouldering books and boxes. No wonder 'Lady P' was absent. As well as attempting to live in this state, Phillipps confronted the perennial problem faced (although not often enough faced up to) by all bibliomaniacs: what to do with his collection when he died. His wife had clearly tapped out, and by the end of his life he was estranged from his only daughter. The cause of this estrangement was intimately tied to his obsession with books. In 1841, the writer and charlatan James Orchard Halliwell had dedicated a book he had written to Phillipps, and the older gentleman, flattered, had then invited him to stay at his house. It was a foolhardy decision. Halliwell had a lifelong habit of cutting up books and pasting the pages into scrapbooks; he had also, as a student, been accused by Trinity College of stealing manuscripts. Phillipps quickly came to regret inviting the light-fingered scissor-happy Halliwell into his home: he claimed that Halliwell had stolen a 1603 copy of *Hamlet* from him and sold it to the British Museum. Meanwhile, Halliwell was busy stealing Phillipps' daughter's heart. When in 1842 Halliwell eloped with Harriet Phillipps, his new father-in-law was enraged and cut off all contact with the pair. In his will, Phillipps stipulated that no bookseller, stranger or Roman Catholic (not coincidentally, Halliwell was one) should be allowed to even *view* his book collection. We may hope that it was a happy ending for Harriet Phillipps, who had escaped the squalor of her father's obsession, but since she had simply swapped one bibliomaniac for another, we can't be sure that history didn't repeat itself, with her ending up just like her long-suffering mother, Lady P.

If bibliophiles love books, where does that leave bibliomaniacs like Phillipps? Bibliomaniacs are readers who have passed beyond love and headfirst into obsession. The first use of the word came in 1802, when a French librarian, Étienne-Gabriel Peignot, described bibliomania as 'the overwhelming compulsion to own books, not so much as to inform oneself as to possess them and feast one's eyes on them'. In 1809 the Reverend Thomas Frognall Dibdin published a 782-page book called *Bibliomania* – an exhaustive, and presumably exhausting, treatise on the topic. 'What renders it particularly formidable is that it rages in all seasons of the year, and at all periods of human existence,' explained Dibdin. It did not, however, rage equally across all peoples: bibliomaniacs, said Dibdin, were mostly men, and 'the artificer, labourer and peasant have escaped wholly uninjured'. The affliction of bibliomania was at least one less thing to worry about if you were scraping a living.

Unsurprisingly, a common side effect of bibliomania saw avid readers transform into writers and produce long and detailed books on the topic. Dibdin led the way, and was followed in 1930 by Holbrook Jackson, who wrote *The Anatomy of Bibliomania* – another extremely long and densely footnoted history of the disorder. In it, Jackson explored all the many facets of book obsession. According to him, for a bibliomaniac (as opposed to a more casual reader or amateur collector), 'the difference lies in the intensity of the desire'. For Jackson, book collectors don't just *dabble*, they are slaves to their book collections, which take over every aspect of life. 'They can as little bear the thought of better collections than their own as they can that of profane hands touching their books.' Jackson might have found BookTok equal parts inspiring and confronting; what if someone else had a better shelf display than him?

But bibliomaniacs are small fry compared to bibliotaphs, who are essentially book misers. For them, it's not enough to just possess a book – they often bury them. You know, to keep their precious safe from wandering eyes. Biblioclasts go even further: they collect, then destroy, books. Better to destroy them than let anyone else have a peek.

Jackson's conclusion was that in the end, bibliomaniacs can't even find pleasure in their books: some would refuse to read them in case the book got spoiled. It is not the book *itself* that is the prize, but the idea of owning it, the covetousness, the finding the next win: 'in their frenzy for particular books they are tormented by delusions of conspiracies to deprive them of the ecstasy of possession.' Books eventually become a source of torment, and, says Jackson, the bibliomaniac 'can never be said to enjoy his books; and I would doubt if he enjoys even the pursuit of them: he is too anxious, too passionately inclined to hunt'.

It's hard to know how seriously to take *The Anatomy of Bibliomania*. You would need to be a bibliophile at least to read it; perhaps a bibliomaniac to source a copy. Its title is a nod to Robert Burton's *The Anatomy of Melancholy*, and as well as being the last word on the peculiarities of the bibliomaniac, it includes chapters on 'How Bookmen Conquer Time and Place', 'They Are God-like and Immortal' (books, that is), 'They Are the Best Company' (ditto), 'A Diet of Books Considered', 'Books as Furniture', and 'Reading at the Toilet': 'Reading during the ritual of the toilet . . . has a long but mostly unrecorded history . . . Every bookman . . . knows how fruitful in meditation are the solitary moments of the toilet when we are faced only by our own soapy visages.' Ultimately, it feels as if Jackson could have gone on writing forever about his book obsession, proving that he was both the right and the wrong man for the job.

As well as discussing the physical properties of books alongside more ephemeral ones, Jackson covers readers, libraries, those who merely dabble, and those completely obsessed. Some bibliomaniacs never read their books; others read obsessively. Eventually, Jackson reaches the final cliffhanger of bibliomania: 'Men Who Become Books'. These are collectors who have absorbed enough words that they have become a library themselves, 'A walking university, a library of flesh'. In the end, cautions Jackson, 'The sum of it all is: read what you like, because you like it, seeking no other reason and no other profit than the experience of reading.' Don't hoard your books – enjoy them.

In recent years, enforced time at home has led many readers (including myself) to reflect on the books we share our homes with. During the Covid-19 pandemic books were a mighty solace, but they were also there, in our space, 24/7. With nothing else to do, many bibliophiles decided to sort out their shelves at last. Ultimately, book lovers must face the hardbacked truth: that each volume we collect, store or hoard has specific meaning and value only to us. That's what is so difficult to face up to: that when we are gone, those tasked with clearing out our books just won't appreciate them in the way we do. In fact, they might not appreciate them at all. After Thomas Phillipps died in 1872, it took 100 years for his collection to be dispersed. *One hundred years*. His grandson spent fifty years of his life supervising the sale of his collection. What a legacy to leave. Far from being a universe unto themselves, Phillipps' books had become a Herculean time-consuming waste disposal issue. Marie Kondo might have had the right idea.

Novel deceptions

Writers have been playing with questions of authorship and authenticity since at least the fourth century BC. Dionysius the Renegade (his name might have been a clue) was the earliest hoaxer in recorded history. He was a Stoic who manufactured a fake play allegedly written by Sophocles. Dionysius wrote his play to entrap another philosopher, Heraclides Ponticus. The fake play contained a clue to its author – which makes it an early example of a particular type of literary hoax: one designed to target a specific person, or group of people. The aim of this hoax is not for the writer to get away with their deception, but rather for the target to be fooled – and for the author to then reveal the truth. Being unmasked is the point of this type of hoax – it is only then that it can be appreciated for what it is.

But most hoaxes are not deliberate in this way. Instead, they are genuine literary creations whose provenance is never meant to be uncovered. They are self-serving on the part of the originator: done for some kind of gain, be it financial or emotional. But why do they happen? In his 2018 book *Impostors: Literary Hoaxes and Cultural Authenticity*, Christopher Miller writes that 'Demand exceeds supply, creating a market for fakes.' That demand is driven by readers, as explained by critic and essayist Louis Menand in a *New Yorker* article: 'We are complicit in the attempt to get us to believe because we already want to believe. Writing is a weak medium. It has to rely on readers bringing a lot of preconceptions to the encounter, which is why it is so easily exploited.'

And hoaxing follows the market. James Macpherson and Thomas Chatterton hoaxed readers with poems in the eighteenth century – partly because, at the time, poets had high profiles. Macpherson claimed to have discovered the 'Ossian' poems – an early Gaelic epic cycle, which despite being invented, counted Napoleon and Thomas Jefferson as fans. Chatterton, meanwhile, dealt in manufacturing poems purportedly from the fifteenth century. This brought both opprobrium in his lifetime and celebration after his death (the Romantic poets in particular praised his genius).

These days a hoax is more likely to arrive in the form of a misery memoir or other first-hand story – the Holocaust, for example, has generated several high-profile cases of fraudulent storytelling. And the stakes are higher, and occasionally very high: American author James Frey made at least $4.3 million in royalties for his memoir *A Million Little Pieces*, and then $1.5 million more even after he admitted that parts of it were fabricated. One fake book about the Holocaust, *Misha: A Mémoire of the Holocaust Years*, published in 1997 by Monique De Wael under the name Misha Defonseca, sold more than 30,000 copies in France, and was made into a film in Belgium and an opera in Italy. It told the story of a young Jewish Belgian girl who during the Second World War hid in woods and was raised by wolves. This far-fetched story was initially accepted as true, but the book eventually became mired in legal controversy and challenges to its authenticity in the United States, and in 2008 De Wael confessed that none of it was true. She blamed her US publisher – 'She made me believe, and I believed it' – for encouraging her to continue the deception she had started ten years earlier.

There are numerous psychological reasons why some writers are drawn to hoaxing, but hoaxers are often people who have had some exposure to the world of literature, perhaps been rejected by it, and left wanting more of it. They may have had early literary promise that never quite led to anything, and feel that if they can just get their name out there, they will finally be recognised and be able to sustain a career. Hoaxing can have consequences that last for many years, far beyond what the original writer might have planned or anticipated. Pseudo-Dionysius the Areopagite was a Greek mystical writer who falsely wrote under the name of Dionysius, a convert of the Apostle Paul. It took more than a thousand years for the fraud to be uncovered; during this time his works had a profound influence, even though the author of the works was not who he claimed to be. And from the earliest times, hoaxers realised that it wasn't enough to simply present work written under someone else's name: a plausible origin story was required, too, for cover. One of the earliest examples of this type of literary fraud was *Dictys Cretensis Ephemeris belli Trojani* ('Dictys of Crete, Chronicle of the Trojan War'); this fake manuscript was given an elaborate backstory to explain its provenance: 'There it remained undisturbed for ages, when in the thirteenth year of Nero's reign, the sepulchre was burst open by a terrible earthquake . . .' – and the manuscript was discovered. Yes, it's a bit of a *deus ex machina*, but it did the job.

The emergence of the novel saw writers smudging the lines between truth and fiction, and encouraging readers to play along. Many early novels included the word 'histories' in their titles or were written in a way that parodied popular historical titles. 'The Editor believes the thing to be a just History of Fact; neither is there any Appearance of Fiction in it,' wrote Daniel Defoe in the Preface of *Robinson Crusoe* – encouraging readers to suspend their disbelief and come along for the ride. The claim that a story was true, not made up, became one that readers were happy to be complicit in – because it added to the pleasure and intrigue of the storytelling.

It wasn't just the subject matter that was duplicitous. Female writers often wrote under male names, since historically women were marginalised from the literary world. Mary Ann Evans wrote her novels as George Eliot, although Charles Dickens was one of the first people to guess that the author of *Scenes of Clerical Life* was a woman. 'I should have been strongly disposed, if I had been left to my own devices, to address the said writer as a woman,' Dickens wrote to Eliot, obviously fishing for clues.

> I have observed what seem to me to be such womanly touches, in those moving fictions, that the assurance on the title-page is insufficient to satisfy me, even now. If they originated with no woman, I believe that no man ever before had the art of making himself, mentally, so like a woman, since the world began.

The name on the cover did not satisfy Dickens as to the author's true persona. But Eliot's reasons for writing as a man were purely practical, and genuine: she did not set out to hoax or fool people, but merely to be able to have her work published.

The Narrative of Arthur Gordon Pym, the only novel that Edgar Allan Poe wrote, gave on its title page a precis of the story intended to make readers believe it was a true story, including a precise location for the setting: ('eighty-fourth parallel of southern latitude'). Poe built on the deception of *Gordon Pym* with his 1845 short story 'The Facts in the Case of M. Valdemar', which when published was believed by many readers to be a true story. This deliberate confusion wouldn't have mattered quite so much were it not for the plot, which described a man at the point of death being mesmerised, and then maintained in a state between life and death for seven months. While some readers thought the story was a real scientific report, others offered up their own 'true' (and disturbing) experiences of similarly rousing people from the dead. So, it's clear that authors were happy to knowingly deceive their readers about the origins of their work. Historical fiction was serious and learned, whereas novels could be construed as frivolous. By adding a little pretend 'fact' to their fiction, writers could muddy the waters and hope to be taken more seriously.

Pranks: 'the black swan of trespass'

In 1943, two Australians, James McAuley and Harold Stewart, set out to hoax a magazine called *Angry Penguins*. It had been founded in 1940 by a young surrealist poet called Max Harris, and championed modernist writers. McAuley and Stewart believed that the magazine was pretentious (well, it *was* called *Angry Penguins**), and that modernist poetry was nonsense. So strong were their feelings that one slow afternoon at their day jobs (they were working for the army) they dreamt up an entire collection of poems to illustrate their point. Together, they wrote sixteen poems and created an entire fictional backstory and life for their poet–author, whom they named Ern Malley (using 'Ernest' as the first name of their fictional author suggested that the creators were . . . not). The deliberately artificial poems were influenced by McAuley and Stewart's previous attempts at writing their own poetry, and the books that happened to be on their desks: a dictionary of quotations, a Shakespeare dictionary, the *Concise Oxford Dictionary*, and less conventionally, a report on the drainage of mosquito breeding grounds.

The poems were written in one day: 'a poem every half an hour, a rate slightly less than a line a minute,' says Michael Heyward, who has

* The phrase 'angry penguins' came from a line in a poem of Max Harris's: 'as drunks, the angry penguins of the night' – he decided the phrase was suitable to represent the magazine's rebellious stance about the prevailing conservative literary order.

written a book called *The Ern Malley Affair* on the hoax. McAuley and Stewart improvised their poems: 'We'd think of a line or two each, or we'd play with this bit and put a bit in here and take a bit out there,' explained Stewart many years later in a 1989 interview. Using improvisation and free association, 'it was a hard day's work creating the poems,' said McAuley.

The hoaxers made a statement in a magazine called *Fact* in June 1943 that explained both their motive: 'For some years now we have observed with distaste the gradual decay of meaning and craftsmanship in poetry . . . what we wished to find out was: Can those who write, and those who praise so lavishly, this kind of writing tell the real product from consciously and deliberately concocted nonsense?' – and their method: 'We opened books at random, choosing a word or phrase haphazardly. We made lists of those and wove them into nonsensical sentences. We misquoted and made false allusions. We deliberately perpetrated bad verse, and selected awkward rhymes.'

The poems set out to imitate the modernist literary fashion of the day, containing echoes of Shakespeare, Keats, T. S. Eliot and Oscar Wilde. The random source material, coupled with subversive intent, led to McAuley and Stewart writing sixteen surrealist poems that somehow . . . worked. Okay, 'Culture as Exhibit' may have leant a little *too* heavily on the mosquito drainage report for its opening:

Swamps, marshes, borrow-pits and other
Areas of stagnant water serve
As breeding-grounds . . . Now
Have I found you, my Anopheles!

But if you didn't know the truth, it would be easy to believe that the poems were what they seemed: real. To a casual reader unaware of how they had been put together, they seemed on the surface just like many other modernist poems of the time, even if they were purposely written to showcase what the writers believed were the worst excesses of that literary movement.

Once they were written, the poems were 'carefully mistyped and erased', wrote Stewart, 'we rolled the paper in the dust, we put our wet cups of tea on it to make ringed stains, we "aged" the ink in the sun.' And the authors were at pains to give their efforts a plausible origin story. To make their hoax really fly, McAuley and Stewart also created an elaborate history to explain who Ern Malley was, and where he had come from. He had been born in Liverpool, moved to Australia with his mother and sister, become a car mechanic and insurance salesman, suffered from Graves' disease (causing him to live with his sister, Ethel), refused treatment, and died at the very precise age of 25 years and 4 months – the exact same age as John Keats at his death. If you knew what you were looking for, the clues were all there in a poem called 'Colloquy with John Keats', which included the line: 'Yet we are as the double almond concealed in one shell.'

Ern Malley was an ordinary suburban Australian, living an unremarkable and undistinguished life (well, bar his uncanny connection with John Keats), until the emergence of his poems after his early death. After he died, the fictional Ethel 'discovered' his collection of poems among his belongings. She then wrote a letter, beginning 'Dear Sir, When I was going through my brother's things after his death I found some poetry he had written.' According to the legend created for Ethel, she then called at her local library and spoke with the librarian, who advised her to send the poems to a magazine called *Angry Penguins*.

This was the fictional story behind how the poems came to be published – in reality, they had been sent directly to the magazine by their creators. Stewart later commented that 'the letters required much more literary skill and much more time and trouble . . . not only did we have to create the character of Ethel Malley, the middle-aged, middle-brow, middle-class young lady of no great education . . . also we had to create his [Ern's] character through her letters.' Composing fake poems is one thing, but inventing credible people is another entirely.

McAuley and Stewart's Ethel letter, and the poems, were then sent to Max Harris at *Angry Penguins*. He was astounded. He showed the poems to his colleagues at the magazine, and his fellow writers in the Australian modernist movement. Harris and his colleagues felt they had discovered a significant new poetic voice in Australia. It's not that surprising: lines from some of the poems – 'Do not speak of secret matters in a field full of little hills', 'I assert my original glory in the dark eclipse' and 'the black swan of trespass on alien waters' – were truly memorable.

Harris published the poems in *Angry Penguins* in June 1944. Their reception was out of all proportion to anything that he might have expected. The question of exactly who was behind the poems took hold immediately. One lecturer in English at Adelaide University who knew Max Harris became convinced that Harris had written them in a bizarre hoax against himself. Other readers fervently believed that a new modernist poetic genius had been found, while others concluded that the poems were a fabrication from beginning to end. In short, like all good hoaxes, the poems reinforced each reader's existing preconceptions about literature. For a week, booksellers hungrily capitalised on the story of who this mysterious young poet Ern Malley was, selling copy after copy of *Angry Penguins*. McAuley and Stewart took all this interest as proof 'that a literary fashion can become so hypnotically powerful that it can suspend the operation of critical intelligence in quite a large number of people'.

The ripples of the Ern Malley affair were far-reaching. *Angry Penguins* was prosecuted for obscenity, fined, and eventually folded. Max Harris was prosecuted in Adelaide for obscenity as a result of publishing the poems. The prosecution had just one witness, a policeman who stated that: 'I don't know what "incestuous" means, but I think there is a suggestion of indecency about it,' and that he found it 'unusual for the sexual parts to be referred to in poetry' (the words 'genitals' and 'incestuous' appeared in the poems). While Harris countered that 'some people could place an indecent interpretation on anything', he was found guilty and fined £5. Harris's reputation as a literary talent-spotter was destroyed, alongside the modernist poetry movement in Australia. By the 1960s, 'experimental' and 'avant-garde' writing in Australia had ceased to exist; no writer wanted to risk being associated with Malley's literary style. But the poems took on a vigorous life of their own. The *Angry Penguins* editors were so enraged by the hoax that they decided attack was the best form of defence, and published the poems in book form, quickly selling out the first print run. *The Darkening Ecliptic* has been through many reprints, and the affair inspired Booker Prize-winning author Peter Carey's 2003 novel *My Life as a Fake*.

Ern Malley's poems are in fact completely believable as real, intentional works. They are sad, touching, emotion-driven, and seem to speak from the heart. Readers responded to them then – and now. That's one of the reasons why eventually Malley became far better known than his creators. McAuley and Stewart may have set out to make a literary point, but Malley's afterlife eclipsed theirs. The final poem in the collection, called 'Petit Testament', ends with the lines: 'I have split the infinitive. Beyond is anything.' The first edition of *The Darkening Ecliptic* contained a misprint in this line (if indeed something entirely artificially created can be said to have a misprint) so that it read 'I have split the infinite', rather than infinitive. But both versions work beautifully. We might judge the hoax and how the poems came to be, but the writing has its own power – as much as any authentic examples. It's no wonder that Harris was taken in. I would have been, too. Who could resist: 'It was a night when the planets/ Were wreathed in dying garlands', or 'I have avoided your wide English eyes:/ But now I am whirled in their vortex'?

Our tour of literary malfeasance has taken us from Martial's frustrated epigrams on word theft to modern algorithm-based plagiarism detectors, chained medieval manuscripts to imagined poets and poems. But the essential tensions between creation and appropriation, possession and sharing, authenticity and artifice remain unchanged over centuries.* Only the methods evolve. In our digital age, when a large

* As I was writing this book, one of the most high-profile literary scandals in recent years broke. Best-selling 2018 memoir *The Salt Path* by Raynor Winn was heavily criticised for an apparent lack of authenticity and honesty, with questions being asked about the author's claims about the events that led her and her husband to embark on the walking adventure that became the basis for the book, which has sold 2 million copies and been made into a film. Among other issues, the scandal raised questions about who is responsible for fact-checking in publishing, and how far publishers should go to confirm what their authors say is true. As a *Guardian* article on the furore highlighted, part of the difficulty with these types of memoirs is that readers (and publicity and marketing teams) like a neat and tidy narrative arc – which potentially encourages writers to bend the truth to satisfy our desire for a compelling plot.

language model can craft a passable sonnet in seconds (McAuley and Stewart claimed that it took them an afternoon to compose their sixteen poems), the boundaries between genuine and artificial expression grow ever more porous. AI may soon become both the ultimate literary hoaxer and the perfect tool for unmasking such deceptions, an endless cycle of words creating and consuming one another on shifting sands of authenticity. And no matter how careful a reader is, they will eventually be taken in. The bibliomaniacs, plagiarists and pranksters of tomorrow will wield new tools, but their motivations – ambition, obsession, mischief – remain timeless. We're told you shouldn't judge a book by its cover, but as this history of literary subterfuge demonstrates, perhaps you shouldn't trust one by it, either. The space between words and truth has always been perilously wide – and in that chasm, the bad apples of the literary world will continue to flourish. Happily, they make for great stories.

5.

Bad Blood: Veins to Pick

> 'Don't like to write, but like having written. Hate the effort of driving pen from line to line, work only three hours a day, but work every day.'
>
> Frank Norris

'I hate writing; I love having written,' said Dorothy Parker. Have you ever stared at a blank page, convinced the words have packed their bags and left for good? Or perhaps you've poured heart and soul into a manuscript, only to have it returned with a rejection slip so sharp it could double up as a weapon? Welcome to the writing life, a journey often less about being anointed with poetic inspiration and more about wrestling with writer's block, navigating a sea of 'thanks, but NO WAY', and enduring critiques that sometimes feel like they've confused the inkstand with a vial of poison. This chapter delves into the less glamorous, often maddening, but undeniably universal experiences that forge – or break – a writer: the dreaded block, the soul-crushing knocks, the occupational hazard of literary rivalry, and the brutal public dissection hiding under the benign name of 'the review'. Forget the romantic ideal; let's talk about the bad blood and spilt ink.

Blocked: when even a bad word would be a relief

'I feel confident that in amount no writer contributed so much during that time to English literature,' humble-bragged overachieving Victorian novelist Anthony Trollope. Up at 5.30 with his watch in front of him, he aimed to write 250 words every quarter of an hour. Few writers measure their success based solely on output, but Trollope kept a close eye on his, and it worked: he published forty-seven novels in his lifetime. He was also the granddaddy of data: despite writing long before the era of the automated word count, every week he set himself the challenge of filling a particular number of pages. 'As words, if not watched, will have a tendency to straggle, I have had every word counted as I went,' he wrote, fuelled by the early-morning coffee he paid to be brought to him before he headed to his day job at the Post Office.

Trollope reflected that he allowed 'no mercy' when it came to writing. He did not 'sit nibbling his pen, and gazing at the wall before him, till he shall have found the words with which he wants to express his ideas'. Somehow, through sheer force of will, he imposed himself on his pages. He never entertained the idea that one morning he might have got up and found himself *unable* to write. Writer's block (such an apt phrase, bringing to mind a slab of concrete standing between you and your paper or screen), the 'noonday devil'* of writers from the dawn of time, was a scourge of the Romantics, and would afflict generations of writers to come, but for Trollope it was simply not an option.

Perhaps this was because, in an era of manic industry, Trollope was surrounded by fellow nineteenth-century novelists also known for their productivity. Charles Dickens wrote roughly 2,000 words a day between 9 a.m. and 2 p.m., leading to a total output of about 4.6 million words over his career. That's maybe why he called himself 'the Inimitable'. Victor Hugo published more than fifty works over his lifetime – although his method of ensuring that he got words on the page was even more punishing than Trollope's early starts. Hugo's wife described how he wrote in 'a huge grey knitted shawl, which swathed him from head to foot, locked his formal clothes away so that he would not be tempted to go out and entered his novel as if it were a prison'. Whatever works: American short story writer John Cheever got up every morning, dressed in a suit, then removed it to write in his underwear, while D. H. Lawrence climbed mulberry trees naked to 'stimulate his thoughts'.

Whether it's outlandish (or no) garb, punishingly early starts or tree-climbing, it's true that many writers have gone to extreme lengths to ensure they fulfil the job description and *write*. But these pens are outliers: a study of creative impasses shows that the most effective antidote to an imagination drought is also the most mundane: 'applying the

* The 'noonday devil' was a demonic presence from early Christian writings onwards and was mentioned in the Bible. It described the mysterious force that encouraged monks to lose motivation and neglect their duties as midday approached.

seat of the pants to the seat of the chair'.* In other words, consistently sitting at a desk and putting words to paper, with no mercy. Just like Trollope.

You might not think there would be anything in common between the writing processes of Anthony Trollope, Graham Greene and Barbara Cartland, but their literary success was built on the same simple ingredient: consistency. Greene described how, over twenty years, he averaged roughly 500 words every weekday morning. 'I have always been very methodical, and when my quota of work is done I break off, even in the middle of a scene . . . When I was young not even a love affair would alter my schedule. A love affair had to begin after lunch.'

Speaking of love affairs, undisputed Queen of Romance Barbara Cartland followed the same driving principle. Still writing well into her nineties, during her life she published over 700 books, which she would dictate to her secretary (well, presumably several long-suffering secretaries). Whatever was happening outside her four walls – her life spanned almost the entire twentieth century, from 1901 to 2000 – or in her personal life, she made progress every day. Cartland's prescription against writer's block was 'yoga, clairvoyance, fruit sugar, ginseng, garlic and honey', but whichever brought the magic (my money is on clairvoyance), by the time she died over a billion copies of her books had been sold. No wonder – she wrote a cool 8,000 words a day. Cartland once explained how: 'I say a prayer. I really do. I say, "Please God, get me a plot." It's absolutely extraordinary: then the

* These are the words of a writer called Mary Heaton Vorse. It was advice she gave to Sinclair Lewis in 1911, and by 1930 he had won the Nobel Prize in Literature.

plot comes.' Turns out that the big man enjoys a slushy romance as much as the next deity.

But whether it's 8,000 or 500 words a day, or 1,000 words an hour, most writers struggle to work in such a metronomic fashion. There are peaks and troughs – times when they can't stop writing, and times of despair when they can't find a way to even start. But while writers have probably always struggled to put paint to cave wall or pen to paper, 'writer's block' as an official diagnosis has only been around since the twentieth century, and we've got the Romantic poets (and the emergence of an interest in the inner workings of the mind) to blame – or thank – for that.

Unlike the metronomic Trollope, Percy Bysshe Shelley, in common with most of the Romantics, treated the act of writing as a mysterious and mercurial undertaking. He described the process of creation as coming from 'some invisible influence, like an inconstant wind', while beyond his twenties, Samuel Taylor Coleridge felt 'an indefinite indescribable Terror' (the capital 'T' was his own) whenever asked to embark on a writing project (same here). So tormented was Coleridge by his failure to sustain his poetry career after his youthful success that he increasingly relied on the opium he had become addicted to in his late twenties. Not a solution that I would recommend. The Romantics became known for *not* writing as much as they were for writing, and this is where the idea of the tortured poet, waiting in vain for inspiration, comes from.

Much like Coleridge's reliance on opium to encourage his muse and deal with her failure to appear, F. Scott Fitzgerald increasingly turned to alcohol as his writing career disintegrated. The pattern of early success for a young writer that quickly burns out is a recurring one in literature: early praise can lead to heightened expectations and such pressure that the words just stop coming. In a 1937 essay called 'Early Success', which explored the issue head-on, Fitzgerald wrote that 'premature success gives one an almost mystical conception of destiny as opposed to will-power . . . The man who arrives young believes that he exercises his will because his star is shining.' The 'difficult second album syndrome' is as true for writers as it is for musicians. This is my second book, so I know what I'm writing about.

Waiting for an 'inconstant wind' is a romantic, writerly way of saying that you're currently not writing – a phrase that suggests that although you can't put pen to paper right now, surely it's just a matter of time before the wind changes direction. Novelist Ann Patchett described how sometimes her creative muse had 'gone out back for a smoke' (in writing, either you, or the words, are inhaling something). Patchett tried to overcome writerly procrastination by attaching a sign-in sheet to her office door, to make herself accountable; she also had forthright views on writer's block: 'I've never understood why other professions don't get to claim blocks . . . they have to call a failure a failure.' Writers, it seems, have found a more palatable way to describe the universal struggle of not being able to knuckle down and do one's job.

Originally, writers wrote in constrained forms that they, and their audiences, knew well: sonnet or ode, play or elegy. These structures might have helped keep them on the rails, but modernist writing – free-form, lacking structure or boundaries by virtue – paradoxically made writing much more difficult. If it was possible to write *anything*, where to even start?

While the mantle of writer's block had skipped a generation with the industrious novelists of Trollope's era it could never be entirely vanquished. Gradually, twentieth-century writers began to reframe writer's block as the price to be paid for, well, being a writer. Creative inhibition was formalised as 'writer's block' in 1947 by an Austrian psychoanalyst, Edmund Bergler. 'I have never seen a "normal" writer,' he proclaimed, which explained, presumably, why men and women of letters were such metaphorically constipated basket cases. But at least there was now an official diagnosis, and a diagnosis, could, perhaps, lead to a cure.

Bergler was dedicated to understanding the analysis paralysis his patients faced, and over twenty years he made a study of blocked writers and their 'neurotic inhibitions of productivity'. He was able to ascertain that existing popular theories were untrue: writers didn't run out of inspiration like a car running out of fuel, and neither were they much affected by external factors – the idea that a writer becomes blocked once they have enough money in the bank to comfortably pay their rent, or retire on. It wasn't laziness (the writers he studied put the hours in at their desks, trying and failing to produce) or a lack of talent (many of his clients were already successful). Instead, Bergler came to believe that writers are like psychoanalysts: they unconsciously try to solve their internal problems 'via the sublimatory medium of writing'. To unblock a writer, they simply needed therapy to resolve their specific psychological issues, and then the words would flow.

So, the rise of psychotherapy and increasing knowledge about how humans functioned meant that a failure to write was no longer part and parcel of the creative process, something an author had to accept and endure, but instead something that could (and should) be fixed, just like any other psychological issue. Instead of the 'indescribable Terror' of Coleridge, Bergler saw writer's block as a medical problem, with medical solutions – he claimed to have a 100 per cent success rate in treating it. And once successfully treated and the block lifted, 'the megalomaniac pleasure of creation produces a type of elation which cannot be compared with that experienced by other mortals,' Bergler wrote. Of course, while a cure for writer's block might seem something for an author to hang their writerly dreams on, the stories of blocked writers suggest that it's just not that simple – because writers aren't simple, either.

If you can't write, you can at least write about that experience. So one good thing about investigating writer's block is that, unsurprisingly, it's something that sufferers tend to explore through words on a page, which gives us some insight into what the patients enduring it really think about it. After the commercial and critical success of *To Kill a Mockingbird*, Harper Lee struggled for years to publish anything else. Lee's second novel, *Go Set a Watchman*, appeared in 2015, fifty-five years after her first, but was written before *To Kill a Mockingbird* – she had been unable to overcome her writer's block. 'To be a serious writer requires discipline that is iron fisted,' she explained. 'It's sitting down and doing it whether you think you have it in you or not. Every day. Alone. Without interruption. Contrary to what most people think, there is no glamour in writing. In fact, it's heartbreak most of the time.' Ralph Ellison described his writer's block being 'as big as the Ritz and as stubborn as a grease stain on a gabardine suit', which might seem like hyperbole, but not when you consider that after the success of *The Invisible Man* in 1952 his writer's block lasted for forty years.

More recently, George R. R. Martin, author of the *Song of Ice and Fire* series, has been suffering from one of the most prominent and commented-upon cases of writer's block in history. He's been writing *The Winds of Winter*, the penultimate volume in the series, since 2010. Martin describes himself as a 'gardener' rather than an 'architect' when it comes to writing – he relies on his words coming to him organically, rather than through intricate advance plotting. More 'inconstant wind' than 'metronomic pen-pusher'. When asked what he would change about his books he replied: 'If I could change one thing about one of my books, I'd have them finished.' And the public, interactive, impatient online world that authors now face doesn't help, as Martin explains: 'I will make no predictions on when I will finish. Every time I do, assholes on the Internet take that as a "promise", and then wait eagerly to crucify me when I miss the deadline. All I will say is that I am hopeful.'

Some writers stop writing because life gets in the way, or they are battling with addiction (which may emerge as a way of dealing with not being able to write) or other mental health issues. And a writer's career is a vocation – a lifelong one – which means sustaining it over decades (it's a rare writer who officially retires); sometimes an author begins to feel that they are falling out of step with the times, and that the world or audience they *were* writing for is no longer there.

Ultimately, the most obvious reason that so many writers start out promisingly but can't sustain their success is that they eventually get ground down by the mental struggle involved in writing. Anthony Burgess summed it up: 'The anxiety involved is intolerable. And . . . the financial rewards just don't make up for the expenditure of energy, the damage to health caused by stimulants and narcotics, the fear that one's work isn't good enough. I think, if I had enough money, I'd give up writing tomorrow.' It's no wonder that many writers have turned to therapists as ways to help them cope with the stress of the job; there are few other areas of employment where your psyche is so intimately bound up with your output.

In 1966 Truman Capote signed a contract to write a book that was 'going to do to America what Proust did to France' – a contemporary American version of Marcel Proust's *In Search of Lost Time*. By 1981, the contract had been renegotiated several times (as had the advance), but the book still hadn't been delivered. 'Capote spent the last 10 years of his life pretending to write a novel that was never there,' observed Martin Amis. But you can see why: it must be difficult to acknowledge final defeat and give up the ghost. 'Either I'm going to kill it, or it's going to kill me,' Capote said of the book, *Answered Prayers*. In the end the manuscript won. Capote died in 1984 with it still unfinished, stating the morning before his death that '[the chapters] will be found when they want to be found'.

Capote is not the only writer whose struggle with their text has ended in defeat (as the millions of unpublished, half-finished, barely started manuscripts in the world attest to). Anyone who has attempted to write something understands. And many writers struggle to even begin to write, because to do so means you can no longer linger in the comforting fantasy land of potential perfection. As William Faulkner said, 'The work never matches the dream of perfection the artist has to start with.' To write is to force a future reckoning with yourself: that's a psychologically punishing way of earning a living.

So, what *is* the cure to writer's block? Willa Cather read aloud from the Bible to warm up her creative juices, while Hemingway would sharpen pencils. He would also trick himself by ending a writing day in mid-sentence, so that he had something to return to and start from the next day. John Steinbeck advised that 'The simplest way to overcome this is to write it to someone, like me. Write it as a letter aimed at one person. This removes the vague terror of addressing the large and faceless audience and it also, you will find, will give a sense of freedom and a lack of self-consciousness.' Joan Didion's editor noted that 'If she's feeling stuck on something, she'll put it in the freezer . . . The manuscript, in the freezer, in a bag.'

Perhaps it's finding the right conditions – the perfect desk, the right tree to climb, the . . . but no. 'A writer who waits for ideal conditions under which to work will die without putting a word on paper,' warned E. B. White, author of *Charlotte's Web*. Fair enough. Is it refusing to countenance the idea of writer's block entirely, treating it as you would a potentially contagious and deadly condition? The fear of bringing on a block by contemplating it was summed up by the prolific and bestselling Judy Blume: 'I don't believe in writer's block. For me there's no such thing as writer's block – don't even *say* writer's block.' Touchy.

One option, not available to all, is to try another language if the words aren't flowing in your own. T. S. Eliot told *The Paris Review* how:

> I thought I'd dried up completely. I hadn't written anything for some time and was rather desperate. I started writing a few things in French and found I could . . . Then I suddenly began writing in English again and lost all desire to go on with French. I think it was just something that helped me get started again.

At the start of this chapter, we learned that Graham Greene was one of those writers who set themselves a schedule each day to make sure they kept writing. But this productivity wasn't a given. Greene suffered from writer's block in his fifties, by which point he was a well-established novelist. His way through was to use a dream journal, where he could scribble down his nocturnal thoughts – a way of getting *something* down on paper that no one else would see, or judge, but that might also stimulate his imagination. Who wouldn't be inspired by a dream like this one, which Greene assiduously recorded: 'I was working one day for a poetry competition and had written one line – "Beauty makes crime noble" – when I was interrupted by a criticism flung at me from behind by T. S. Eliot. "What does that mean? How can crime be noble?" He had, I noticed, grown a moustache.' Sounds like the start of a brilliant short story.

While Bergler and his fellow psychoanalysts treated writer's block as a medical, or at least psychiatric, condition that could be overcome by therapy, that is not, of course, an option for all writers. Therapy takes time and money (both often in short supply in the literary life) and can be frustratingly unspecific and impractical. Dream diaries and writing in a different language might nudge things along, but can't be relied upon. Ultimately, the simplest approach is probably the best, as summed up by Sylvia Plath in a letter considering how she planned to overcome her creative log-jam: 'I have no idea how to begin. I shall, perhaps, just begin.'* We have returned to a gentler version of Trollope's 'no mercy'. Probably the best way through is to get up early, take a blank page, and consider this advice from Terry Pratchett: 'There's no such thing as writer's block. That was invented by people in California who couldn't write.' The only way through is to get out of bed, get dressed, get undressed, and 'just begin'.

* Plath acknowledged that when she couldn't write, the positive was that 'I wait and live harder, eyes, ears, and heart open, and when the productive time comes, it is that much richer.'

Shelf awareness: rejection

Once a writer has found a way through the bottleneck of writer's block to the wide sunlit vistas on the other side, they could be forgiven for thinking things might become a little easier. After all, they have something material to show for their efforts: a manuscript, something that, with a little help and attention from the right people, could become a book. But having reached the motorway, what comes next is often a tedious series of roadblocks that see you driving in circles: this time in the form of rejection. Stephen Marche writes in his 2023 book *On Writing and Failure* that 'Failure is the body of a writer's life. Success is only ever an attire,' and that there's an entire book on the topic suggests it's a rich seam for study. There are also many diverse ways to fail as a writer. There's not writing, or writing but not being published, or being published and being met with criticism and no financial success. Truly, it's a set of Russian dolls, each failure tucked inside another.

Your reward for all that effort, which you must face head on, is, almost certainly, rejection. That's it. For most writers, the sweet sweat of creation is followed by the abject terror of sending your book to agents and publishers, to receive in return a resounding 'thanks, but no thanks!' The publishing industry is *predicated* on rejection – it would be impossible to say 'yes' to every submission – and there are far more writers out there than the world of readers can possibly handle. Supply outstrips demand, so we should spare a thought for the people doing the rejecting – those who have to wade through endless speculative submissions and then find a kind-yet-firm way of turning the majority of them down. It's no coincidence that a tower of unrequested manuscripts is referred to as a slush pile – and no one likes spending hours with damp feet and indifferent reading material.

But the good news about rejection is that a writer needs just one person to say 'yes', and all other knock-backs fade away into the shadows. Chinua Achebe's *Things Fall Apart* was rejected by every publisher bar one and then went on to be the biggest-selling book in modern African literature. Kathryn Stockett's *The Help* racked up sixty rejections before it was taken on by an agent, and then a publisher, and sold 15 million copies. Robert M. Pirsig's *Zen and the Art of Motorcycle Maintenance* made a virtue out of rejection: it found itself in the *Guinness Book of Records* for having been rejected 121 times – eventually selling a cool 5 million copies. You must admire any author who doesn't just keep going, but maintains a careful rejection tally, too.

While a writer might eventually come to terms with being rejected, it surely helps if those doing the rejecting are at least polite about it – unlike the person who told Louisa May Alcott 'You can't write.' There's nowhere to go with that. Robert Louis Stevenson said that 'Our business in life is not to succeed, but to continue to fail in good spirits' – something Ernest Hemingway excelled at. He received numerous rejections early on in his career, and the upside to this was that he became extremely good both at writing, and at finding ways to cope with being told 'No'. Hemingway was up for punting back the rejection, clapping back:

> When you get a printed form attached to a story you wrote and worked on very hard and believed in, that printed rejection slip is hard to take on an empty stomach. 'Dear sir: We regret to tell you that your submission does not meet our editorial needs.' Well, fuck it. I regret to tell you that your rejection slip does not meet MY editorial needs.

Hemingway was the kind of guy who would accelerate round the roadblock, and he had learned the hard way to keep his foot on the pedal. In 1926, his first long work, *The Torrents of Spring*, was rejected almost immediately by his publishers, who responded that 'It would be extremely rotten taste, to say nothing of being horribly cruel, should we want to publish it.'

That rejection was tame compared to the one Hemingway received for *The Sun Also Rises*. A publisher called Peacock & Peacock began their letter with the bad news:

> If I may be frank – you certainly are in your prose – I found your efforts to be both tedious and offensive. You really are a man's man, aren't you? I wouldn't be surprised to hear that you had penned this entire story locked up at the club, ink in one hand, brandy in the other. Your bombastic, dipsomaniac, where-to-now characters had me reaching for my own glass of brandy . . . what is not needed are treatises about bullfights and underemployed men who drink too much.

In among this were two paragraphs more of the same. But like all rejections, this one is just the opinion of a solitary reader (it was signed by someone with the improbable name of Mrs Moberley Luger), and one publication. If Hemingway had internalised Peacock & Peacock's refusal as a judgement of all his work, and as the opinion of all readers, he'd have given up. Luckily, he wasn't one to be derailed by this (or any) rebuff. He promptly sent *The Torrents of Spring* to a different publisher, who agreed to take it on, along with his future work, which included *The Sun Also Rises*, which has never been out of print since 1926. Writers need thick skin and a full tank.

Like Hemingway, Marcel Proust was not a writer to back down. In 1912, he sent a copy of *Swann's Way*, the first part of his epic *In Search of Lost Time*, to an editor called Marc Humblot, who replied: 'My dear fellow, I may perhaps be dead from the neck up, but rack my brains as I may I can't see why a chap should need thirty pages to describe how he turns over in bed. I clutched my head.' I mean, he's not wrong – Humblot was trying to politely say that Proust's prose did his head in, a sentiment that many readers of *In Search of Lost Time* will share.

Proust responded to M. Humblot that

> I find Monsieur Humblot's letter (which I return herewith) completely idiotic . . . The significance, as should be obvious, is not that I want to describe how I twist and turn in bed – which I could certainly do in much fewer pages – but that the twisting and turning provides me with a means of analysis.

Proust was evidently onboard with Edmund Bergler's idea – not yet expressed – that writing was therapy. But clearly disgusted by the literary establishment's failure to recognise his genius, and perhaps unwilling to subject himself to further rounds of rejection, Proust decided that the best way through this particular roadblock was to dismantle it himself: he knuckled down, finished writing the book and went ahead and published. *Swann's Way* was a vanity publication in that Proust paid a publisher to produce it for him.

Not all editors are dullards or fools and incapable of understanding what is staring them in the face; some are even quite talented writers themselves. T. S. Eliot, whose day job was as a director at Faber & Faber, had the unenviable job of rejecting *Animal Farm* in a letter to George Orwell, writing that 'it is a distinguished piece of writing; that the fable is very skilfully handled . . . I am very sorry, because whoever publishes this, will naturally have the opportunity of publishing your future work: and I have a regard for your work, because it is good writing of fundamental integrity.' This #sorrynotsorry rejection was based on Eliot's belief that Orwell's positive point of view about Trotskyism wasn't convincing, but perhaps because he was a writer himself, Eliot was at least able to reject *Animal Farm* with sensitivity and thoughtfulness. Unlike an editor at Dial Press in the US who wrote to Orwell to refuse the novel by saying that it was 'impossible to sell animal stories in the USA' – somewhat missing the point of the book.

But though they might be cruel, or idiotic, one must admire the creativity that some editors put into writing rejection letters. Occasionally, it's even possible to feel sympathy for the person doing the rejecting, like this harsh but heartfelt rejection letter to Gertrude Stein, who was renowned for being repetitious in her writing:

> Dear Madam,
>
> I am only one, only one, only one. Only one being, one at the same time. Not two, not three, only one. Only one life to live, only sixty minutes in one hour. Only one pair of eyes. Only one brain. Only one being. Being only one, having only one pair of eyes, having only one time, having only one life, I cannot read your M.S. three or four times. Not even one time. Only one look, only one look is enough. Hardly one copy would sell here. Hardly one. Hardly one.
>
> Many thanks. I am returning the M.S. by registered post. Only one M.S. by one post.
>
> Sincerely yours,
>
> A. C. Fifield

Ultimately, however, our sympathies should probably remain on the side of the writers. Rudyard Kipling kept a rejection letter that read: 'I'm sorry, Mr Kipling, but you just don't know how to use the English language' – while there's an apocryphal story that Joseph Heller settled on *Catch-22* as a title after receiving twenty-two rejection letters. That both Heller and Kipling, like numberless others out there, didn't let cruelty, rudeness or indifference put them off is something to be admired.

If knock-backs can be reframed as just another experience along the way to ultimate success, they would be far easier to deal with. 'Rejection' is just another word for feedback, and that's always helpful. Or it should be. I'm not sure how useful it is receiving the news that 'The author of this book is beyond psychiatric help', which happened to J. G. Ballard. Vladimir Nabokov was told that *Lolita* 'should be buried under a stone for a thousand years', while H. G. Wells had to absorb this assessment of *The War of the Worlds*: 'An endless nightmare. I think the verdict would be, "Oh don't read that horrid book."'

Edgar Rice Burroughs received this very specific feedback as part of a rejection letter: 'It is not at all probable, we think, that we can make use of the story of a Virginian soldier of fortune miraculously transported to Mars.' A shame, but Burroughs was sanguine: 'If you write one story, it may be bad; if you write a hundred, you have the odds in your favor.' Eventually the odds worked for him, and Burroughs wrote *Tarzan of the Apes*, one of the biggest sellers of all time.

Managing rejection is all about endurance, and if you can stay the course, the hope remains that it will pay off. There's irony in rejection when you're on the receiving end of it one year, and proved right in your persistence the next. The schadenfreude must be delicious. Imagine how the recipient of this rejection felt: 'We are not interested in science fiction which deals with negative utopias. They do not sell.' Actually, they do. The negative utopia mentioned here is *Carrie*, by Stephen King, which went on to sell over 3 million copies. King had dedicated himself not just to the craft of writing at a young age, but also to the craft of mentally managing the inevitable. He described how: 'By the time I was fourteen the nail in my wall would no longer support the weight of the rejection slips impaled upon it. I replaced the nail with a spike and went on writing.'

While rejection is a fundamental part of the writing life, there's a conspiracy of silence round it. The literary world likes to hide it away and pretend it doesn't happen; writers often only want to talk about it in retrospect, once they've broken through, and moved on to acceptance and success. Writing is all about the long, slow, messy slog, but that's not a story we want to hear. Instead, we'd much rather focus on the stories that give us hope; the unlikely zero-to-hero stories of publishing success; those who seemingly become overnight sensations. But even a cursory study of these will show you that overnight success in writing just doesn't happen. What we see is the highlight reel – the book tours, the rave reviews – but not the years of sweat, ink and rejection. We should look to those writers who didn't let rejection deter them, who kept going, and kept going. 'I love my rejection slips. They show me I try,' said Sylvia Plath. She persevered and overcame being told that 'There certainly isn't enough genuine talent for us to take notice.' Authors who can rise above rejection and can see it for what it is – a step on the road towards success – are those who might eventually be able to describe, like Ray Bradbury, how:

> I have several walls in several rooms of my house covered with the snowstorm of rejections, but they didn't realize what a strong person I was; I persevered and wrote a thousand more dreadful short stories, which were rejected in turn . . . The blizzard doesn't last forever; it just seems so.

But not every rejection story ends happily with the loose ends neatly tied into an overcoming-the-odds bow. John Kennedy Toole took his own life in 1969, when he was only in his early thirties, after his publisher lost interest in the progress of his manuscript of *A Confederacy of Dunces*. 'With all its wonderfulness,' said his publisher, the book 'does not have a reason . . . it isn't *really* about anything. And that's something no one can do anything about.' Granted, Toole didn't make the decision to end his life entirely because of his troubles with writing – like all of us, he contained multitudes, and the reasons behind his decision were doubtless complex. But his correspondence with his publisher demonstrates the toll that writing took. 'I have to come out of this though, or I'll never do anything,' he despaired. His editor's advice, 'Cheer up. Work', wasn't enough to save him.

But the rejection that Toole experienced was a spur to his mother, who was determined to see his manuscript published after his death. She began submitting it to other publishers, and eventually saw it become a book. It won a Pulitzer Prize and was translated into twenty-two languages. The sadness at the heart of Toole's response to rejection is balanced by the beauty of his mother's perseverance on his behalf. It's a tragedy, of course, that he never lived to see his writing have success, for the greatest rejection for a writer is to reject yourself without giving your words a chance to live. Writers can be their own worst enemy, sabotaging their prospects at every turn.

Perhaps better to keep in mind Saul Bellow, who said 'I discovered that rejections are not altogether a bad thing. They teach a writer to rely on his own judgment and to say in his heart of hearts, "To hell with you."'

'You must keep sending work out; you must never let a manuscript do nothing but eat its head off in a drawer. You send that work out again and again, while you're working on another one. If you have talent, you will receive some measure of success – but only if you persist,' wrote Isaac Asimov. Even if it's someone else persisting on your behalf, these are words for all writers to live by.

'Snuffed out by an article': reviews

One blessing about rejections is that they can be kept private until a writer decides to share them with the world – something that they are usually only comfortable doing once they have overcome all those roadblocks and diversions and completed the perilous journey to their final destination of becoming a published author. That's when you can laugh at the absurdity of all those who failed to notice your talent. It's a moment that should be one of absolute triumph – blocks vanquished, knock-backs firmly in the rear-view mirror.

Alas, the moment of publication is also the moment that criticism moves from something you can keep between yourself and the closed circle of the publishing industry, to a free-for-all bloodbath where anyone, anywhere, anytime can have their say. Just when you imagine yourself gliding serenely into the literary sunset – manuscript under arm, modest book deal gently twinkling on the horizon – you encounter a fresh antagonist: the review. The reader who reads not in hope or haste, but in judgement. The professional (or not) who, with a stroke of their pen – or worse, a star rating – can tip you from soaring with the eagles to literary roadkill. The Greek chorus of critics is vast, contradictory, and rarely silent, and once a book leaves your desk, there's no unhearing what they say.

Take this cautionary tale. In 1821, Percy Bysshe Shelley wrote a poem about his friend John Keats, who had died three months earlier:

> Oh gentle child, beautiful as thou wert,
> Why didst thou leave the trodden paths of men
> Too soon, and with weak hands though mighty heart
> Dare the unpastured dragon in his den?

The 'dragon' in these lines was Scottish writer and critic John Gibson Lockhart, who had written a mocking review of Keats' 1818 poem *Endymion*, telling the young writer that 'It is a better and a wiser thing to be a starved apothecary than a starved poet.' Okay, the stiletto to the heart here is somewhat subtle: is being a starved apothecary any better than being a starved writer? Bearing in mind that Keats was apprenticed to a doctor as a teenager and then trained as a surgeon, Lockhart is perhaps suggesting that there is more honour, and potentially more money, in wielding a knife over a pen.

Whatever delicate allusion Lockhart was drawing in his review, Lord Byron saw Shelley's effort and decided to wade in boots first, writing in *Don Juan* that Keats 'was kill'd off by one critique . . . 'Tis strange the mind, that very fiery particle,/ Should let itself be snuff'd out by an article'. The mocking tone is unlikely to be an accident; the two poets had no love for each other. Keats had been jealous of Byron's success and privilege, commenting tartly after reading a positive review of his work: 'You see what it is to be six foot tall and a lord!', while Byron described Keats as a 'little dirty blackguard'.

Keats wasn't *directly* snuffed out by a bad review, of course. He died of tuberculosis. But in the last few months of his life, as he battled his failing health, he was more and more preoccupied with his critics. Although he tried to rise above all the chatter by commenting that 'Praise or blame has but a momentary effect on the man whose love of beauty in the abstract makes him a severe critic on his own Works,' the criticism of *Endymion* certainly added to a spiral of stress and ill-health that ended in his death.

Criticism, feedback and personal responses to books have been around forever, along with gossip, literary salons and chat. And while writers might think they believe in the merits of free speech, this philosophy might find itself under severe strain once you are on the end of a public hatchet job.* A ninth-century leader in Byzantium called Photius wrote a book called *Bibliotheca*, which was his review of 279 books (he'd have loved Goodreads). Like a lot of online reviewers today, Photius was unimpressed by most of what he read, criticising one book as 'without urbanity or elegance, and soon palls, or positively disgusts . . . a tasteless effusion'. He was even disappointed by Herodotus' *Histories*, which was generally considered one of the greatest works of ancient Greece, commenting that 'He is fond of old wives' tales and digressions, pervaded by charming sentiments, which, however, sometimes

* The original 'hatchet' job referred to clearing the way ahead of troops, then in the nineteenth century it came to mean a Chinese assassin, hired to, ahem, clear the way of whomever you wanted out the way. Quite how such a brutal term came to be applied to the gentle art of the book review is unclear, but from the 1920s onwards it has been used in such a way.

obscure the due appreciation of history and its correct and proper character.' Historians note that we're lucky to have *Bibliotheca* to study as many of the books it considers are now lost to us – our only way to know anything about them is through Photius' book reviews.

The earliest book reviews were for the elites, and written by them, too – they tended to be academic and specialist, targeting a narrow group of readers. It wasn't until the rise of newspapers in the eighteenth century that reviews became more approachable and written for the generalist reader. But the 'book review' as an official way of letting people know something about a book – or, indeed, letting them know a book existed at all – wasn't a big thing until the nineteenth century. Before then, advertisements and notices might let you know a book was coming, but they wouldn't tell you what to make of it, or if it was any good – the reader paid their money and took their chances.

Edgar Allan Poe's critiques for *Graham's Magazine* in the 1840s were the first sustained collection of reviews, and Poe kicked off with a gripe that would be voiced again and again as the process of reviewing books became entrenched: that publishing was nepotistic, and a sham: 'We place on paper without hesitation a tissue of flatteries, to which in society we could not give utterance, for our lives, without either blushing or laughing outright.' Sparing his own blushes and hysterics, a 'tissue of flatteries' was not the approach that Poe himself took, with one writer complaining that his harsh reviews sometimes confused 'his phial of prussic acid for his inkstand'. Poe described one novel called *Norman Leslie* as being 'unworthy of a school-boy', and of the author's follow-up book, *Paul Ulric,* he wrote: 'When we called *Norman Leslie* the silliest book in the world we had certainly never seen *Paul Ulric.*' I enjoy how Poe hides behind the 'we' here, as if it's not him writing these words, but some committee of critics. And on title alone, neither *Norman* nor *Paul* really set the imagination on fire.

For lovers of literature, reviews provide an excellent time machine. It's hard to get a real sense of what the earliest readers of now-famous books really thought about them, before an author was famous, or before critical opinion coalesced, and they were entrenched in the literary canon. Imagine how F. Scott Fitzgerald might have felt on reading one of the first reviews of *The Great Gatsby* in 1925, whose headline was: 'F. Scott Fitzgerald's Latest a Dud'. That's both cutting to the chase and cutting. We don't need to imagine how Marcel Proust felt about a review of his first novel, *Pleasures and Days*, in 1897. The critic Jean Lorrain called the book 'pretentious in style' and a work of 'elegiac spinelessness'. He then moved away from criticism of the book, and on to Proust's private life, hinting that Proust was having an affair with fellow writer Lucien Daudet. Incensed, Proust challenged Lorrain to a duel, with *Le Figaro* covering the event: 'Two bullets were exchanged without result, and the witnesses, by agreement, have decided that this meeting ended the dispute.' While the duel might have ended as a non-event, it goes to show how a book review can lead to the settling of decidedly unliterary scores.

By 1891 Henry James was already bemoaning both the number of reviews being published, and the lack of critical thinking shown in them, sentiments echoed by Edmund Wilson in 1928 in an essay called 'The Critic Who Does Not Exist', kicking off with a gripe that 'What we lack . . . in the United States, is not writers or even literary parties, but simply serious literary criticism.' Wilson believed reviews should put a book in the context of literary history, and help reveal to readers the inner secrets of how writers worked; but he let his profession down by writing an infamous review of *The Lord of the Rings* (it was titled

'Oo, Those Awful Orcs') and an essay called 'Who Cares Who Killed Roger Ackroyd?' – a denunciation of, well, all of crime fiction. At least with that one you could just read the title, and move on.

So the book review has come in for serious criticism itself – either too elite, too mediocre, too negative, too positive, or badly written, unfair and uninteresting. For a review to be useful, it needs to hold in mind the potential reader, who will possibly be coming at both topic and author cold. But of course, not all readers are created equal, so it's not easy to assume what level of knowledge they will already have. A book review should be written by someone who has a decent chance of being able to understand the book they are reviewing, explain it to the average man or woman in the street, and then get off the fence and make a clear recommendation.

In a 1985 interview, the novelist and critic Elizabeth Hardwick explained that literary criticism is 'a natural response to the existence in the world of works of art. It is an honorable and even an exalted endeavor. Without it, works of art would appear in a vacuum, as if they had no relation to the minds experiencing them.'*

A helpful review needs to be objective, give context, and be consistent in its opinions; in a world where we're all short of headspace, we need a sage guide to untangle where a book sits in time and space, and let us know whether it is worth our investment. But this 'honorable' and 'exalted endeavor' has the potential to be dangerously divisive. While a reviewer might feel they are serving the interests of *their* audiences, an

* Hardwick wrote an essay for *Harper's Magazine* in 1959 called 'The Decline of Book Reviewing', in which she complained about the state of the American review experience. 'A genius may indeed go to his grave unread, but he will hardly have gone to it unpraised. Sweet, bland commendations fall everywhere upon the scene; a universal, if somewhat lobotomized, accommodation reigns.'

author might well disagree with a review's view of what their words are worth.

Who's wielding the hatchet?

On the one hand, we might consider it best that the reviewers of books are authors themselves. We hope that they can review sensitively, with the struggles of a writer in mind, and perhaps try to offer a balance of praise, criticism and encouragement. On the other, it's hard to be judged by a fellow professional: someone who you might, or might not, admire; equally, we have to account for human nature, which, when it comes down to it, can be petty, competitive, biased and jealous. And is it ethical for a writer to review a fellow writer – someone who they might be friends with? The reader of a review must presume the reviewer is coming to a book with an open mind, unswayed by reputation – but just how likely is that?

The politics of reviewing in public are very different from those of reviewing anonymously. Novelist John Updike was also a public (and prolific) reviewer, who set out his own rules for reviews after what he called 'youthful trauma' from having his own books critiqued – an experience that perhaps was behind his description of reviewers as 'pigs at the pastry cart' in one of his novels. Maybe his guidelines allowed him to think of himself as an even-handed critic: after all, if there are rules to follow, criticism becomes more like cricket, even if there's no umpire to appeal to. At least this way both reviewer and reviewee could have had a chance of understanding the parameters of the exchange. Updike's first rule was probably the most important – 'Try to understand what the author wished to do, and do not blame him for not achieving what he did not attempt' – while others reminded a reviewer that their job was not to reveal too much of the plot, and, if they came to the conclusion that the book was not much good, to try and find other examples from the writer's oeuvre, to make sure that the failure of the book truly was with the writer, not the reviewer.

Updike also had what he called a 'vague' rule, which addressed the spirit in which a review should be undertaken. 'Review the book, not the reputation. Submit to whatever spell, weak or strong, is being cast. Better to praise and share than blame and ban. The communion between reviewer and his public is based upon the presumption of certain possible joys in reading, and all our discriminations should curve toward that end', a reminder that a good review, one which helps potential readers decide what to read, and which gives useful feedback to an author – should be the main aim. Updike strove to respect and uphold the sacred bond between writer and reader – those 'certain possible joys'. Alas, Updike's gentleman's code of reviewerly conduct wasn't enough to save him from a posthumous mauling by the poet and novelist Patricia Lockwood in 2019. Her critique began: 'I was hired as an assassin. You don't bring in a 37-year-old woman . . . to review John Updike unless you're hoping to see blood on the ceiling.' That was just the opening line.

Perhaps Updike would have been okay with Lockwood's review, what with it coming from a fellow writer. But for most authors now, it's not the professional reviewers that cause the most controversy, but the hordes of reviewers online, sharing opinions worldwide and amplified at the touch of a button, and with no bona fides to present. Whereas in the past a writer might expect to be reviewed by a 'professional' – a fellow author, a literary critic, an academic in a shared field – all authors must now run the gamut of the World

Wide Web – or the worldwide whinge. We're all critics now. Before the digital revolution, we would discuss what we'd read only with the people we could reach – face to face, or by letter. There was an inbuilt trust (and a broader personal context to place an opinion in) implicit in these reviews – you had some sort of prior relationship with the reviewer, and could be confident that their views were authentic, even if you didn't agree with them. And reviews took time and effort to write – unlike now, where a knee-jerk opinion can be posted online the moment it is thought of.

The volume of faceless online reviews means they have become increasingly devalued. In recent years Goodreads has seen fake accounts used by authors to 'review bomb' rivals, while other authors have been drawn into responding directly and immediately to reviewers they feel have been unfair. The lack of oversight on Goodreads and other websites means that anything goes, with no opinion more or less valid than another. Simultaneously, Goodreads holds increasing sway among the publishing establishment, who can use it as a form of direct market research or to try and pick out the next literary trend. In this way it can feel like an unending nightmare for authors – a place where unfair criticism can make or break a career, with no way to answer back. And the criticism is often targeted disproportionately towards minority authors or those writing on culturally sensitive topics, with pile-ons and attempts to cancel writers.

In 2024 author Cait Corrain had her novel *Crown of Starlight* dropped by Penguin Random House after she admitted she had 'boosted the rating of my book, bombed the ratings of several fellow debut authors, and left reviews that ranged from kind of mean to downright abusive' on Goodreads. Notably, Corrain had mainly left one-star reviews for books by people of colour, explaining on X that while she felt 'no ill will' towards the writers she targeted, 'fear about how my book would be received running out of control' was how she justified her actions. Lack of moderation on Goodreads means that writers – and invariably this will apply particularly to those of colour, or those who deal with sensitive subjects – can find themselves victims of sustained and targeted campaigns against them. As one author described Goodreads: 'It's like an Armageddon energy there that is destructive and devoid of value.' What writer wants all that creative sweat to be reduced to a star rating?

It's not all end-of-the-world energy, though. Online reviewers sometimes have a habit of being able to get right to the heart of a book for us in a way that a thousand-word op-ed just can't. 'I've read more interesting cereal boxes,' wrote one reviewer on Amazon about William Faulkner's *As I Lay Dying*. Another approached D. H. Lawrence's *Sons and Lovers* with this doom-laden line: 'I have not read this book yet; but am not looking forward to it.' 'Too many words so far,' was the plaintive response to reading some David Foster Wallace, while another succinctly summarised *Frankenstein*: 'an annoying scientist and an ugly tall man fight over who is more depressed.' My favourite, however, might be this review of John Steinbeck's *The Grapes of Wrath*: 'This is a great book. Very well written and important. I hated it.' Well, we can't all like everything.

All this criticism, and criticism of criticism, can make the strongest of writers feel like they never want to hear another opinion on their work, or anyone else's. We'll leave the final words of this section with American author Philip Roth, who has been enjoying none of it.

> Shut down all literature departments, close the book reviews, ban the critics. The readers should be alone with the books, and if

> anyone dared to say anything about them, they would be shot or imprisoned right on the spot. Yes, shot. A 100-year moratorium on insufferable literary talk. You should let people fight with the books on their own and rediscover what they are and what they are not. Anything other than this talk.

I don't like to think what Roth would have made of this book.

Hot type: rivals

If reviews can be the rocket fuel on the bonfire of literary rivalry, a writer's ego supplies the initial spark. The reviews that a writer is likely to take most notice of are, we've seen, from those of fellow writers. But feedback from a fellow professional can also be the most difficult to swallow, cutting to the heart in a way that an anonymous online review could never. Sometimes, these public opinions culminate in a book-related feud. Like most things literary, rivalry between writers is complex and multi-layered. Professional jealousy, ideological disagreements, media manipulation and plain old personal loathing can all drive it. And they have existed since writers first picked up their pens – indeed, a feud was a sign that you had arrived as a serious man of letters. Defining yourself in opposition to another writer has always been a useful form of self-publicity.

Vladimir Nabokov took feuding to new and sustained heights: there was a long list of well-known writers whom he hated. T. S. Eliot was 'not quite first rate'. He had no time for William Faulkner ('ridiculous'), D. H. Lawrence ('execrable'), Ezra Pound ('total fake') or Albert Camus ('awful'). 'Many accepted authors simply do not exist for me,' he declared. Not for nothing was a collection of essays of his called *Strong Opinions*. This collection contained a 1965 interview with Australian critic Robert Hughes in which Nabokov described the 'great books' that journalists wrote about as 'an absurd delusion, as when a hypnotized person makes love to a chair'. You what now?

Nabokov's most vitriolic literary loathing was reserved for an ex-friend, the writer and critic Edmund Wilson, whom we met a few pages back. Although Wilson isn't as well known to us today as Nabokov, in his time he was a big shot – one of the most respected literary critics of the twentieth century. The list of topics Nabokov and Wilson fell out over included the Russian Revolution, the pronunciation of 'nihilism', and whether it was possible to make love in the back of a cab. Truly, Nabokov was seriously invested in that particular question. The feud even entrapped Nabokov's wife Vera in its orbit – she managed to fall out with Wilson over the meaning of the French adjective *fastidieux*. These guys were fastidious, all right.

Perhaps because they had once been good friends, this particular feud was Nabokov's most sustained. Although Nabokov and Wilson's friendship managed to survive the many arguments listed above, it was eventually torpedoed by a long, complex and exhausting fallout over Alexander Pushkin's novel in verse *Eugene Onegin* – specifically, a falling-out over Wilson's review of Nabokov's translation of it. A classic example of something where the stakes are so low as to be invisible to anyone not intimately involved. The Nabokov–Wilson feud has been compared to the balletic rituals of a duel, playing out over years, not days, with a steady response–reply–response pattern. Nabokov was even primed for it to go beyond the grave. 'I would like to see my edition printed before confronting an irate Pushkin and a grinning E. Wilson beyond the cypress curtain,' he wrote, and after his death in 1977 his son Dmitri stepped up as a proxy and continued the disagreement on his behalf.

The duel – whether real or implied – is a favourite way for writers to settle their differences. In 1598, Ben Jonson killed the actor Gabriel Spenser in a sword fight,* and in 1772 Richard Brinsley Sheridan (author of the play *The Rivals*, funnily enough) challenged Captain Thomas Mathews to a duel in which he was nearly killed by him. In 1931 American writers Theodore Dreiser and Sinclair Lewis got into a physical fight at a dinner (Lewis accused Dreiser of plagiarising from a book his wife had written), with Dreiser hitting Lewis. The next day, a canny boxing promoter offered to arrange a fight between both, with them sharing the takings.

The most intense and profound feuds are of course between those who have been friends, and who operate in the same small world. Look at Ernest Hemingway and F. Scott Fitzgerald. Fitzgerald complained that Hemingway was 'always willing to lend a helping hand to the one above him' (I think he meant that Hemingway was not averse to a bit of obsequiousness), while Hemingway compared Fitzgerald variously to a dying butterfly, a glass-jawed boxer and a missile crashing to earth on a 'very steep trajectory'.

In a 1929 letter, Fitzgerald made a long list of suggested changes for Hemingway's *A Farewell to Arms*. There were so many that the letter was ten pages long. Fitzgerald concluded with the heartening line, 'a beautiful book it is!', while Hemingway responded by scribbling

* We don't know why they were fighting, but we do know that Spenser's sword was ten inches longer than Jonson's. Jonson pleaded guilty to manslaughter and should have been hanged, but because he was able to read Psalm 51 out in court in Latin he was able to claim 'benefit of clergy' (a loophole dating back to the medieval tussle between Church and state) and walk away with just a branded 'M' on his thumb.

underneath: 'kiss my ass'. Hemingway followed up by writing a long letter to Fitzgerald in 1934 about *Tender Is the Night*: 'a long time ago you stopped listening except to the answers to your own questions . . . You see well enough. But you stop listening. It's a lot better than I say. But it's not as good as you can do.'

At least Hemingway and Fitzgerald's feud was about the actual nuts and bolts of writing, not the marginal stuff – but despite their niggles, the two did care about and help to advance the career of the other. 'Our poor old friendship probably won't survive this but there you are – better me than some nobody in the Literary Review that doesn't care about you & your future,' wrote Fitzgerald to Hemingway – and they managed to remain the best of frenemies. Theirs was a seesaw friendship, with Hemingway's star rising as Fitzgerald's was lost in drink, with Fitzgerald writing poignantly to Hemingway on the success of *For Whom the Bell Tolls*: 'Congratulations too on your new book's great success. I envy you like hell and there is no irony in this.'

Author Hua Hsu writes that 'It stands to reason that artists who possess a sensitivity to human nature would themselves be hypersensitive people. And it makes sense that those with gifts for storytelling and narration are capable of shaping petty jealousy into something noble and epic.' Perhaps this sentiment helps explain just why the literary world lends itself to feuds: no matter how trivial one might seem (or be), it can always be dressed up as a noble, and indeed necessary, intervention. The world of ancient Greek literature was shaped round the writerly rumpus: poets and playwrights competed at festivals, which actively encouraged them into conflict.

Having a literary target to define yourself against was an integral part of being a Greek writer – and a modern one. Ruth Rendell said that 'to say that Agatha Christie's characters are cardboard cut-outs is an insult to cardboard cut-outs', while Truman Capote commented of Jack Kerouac's books: 'that's not writing, that's typing' – with both Rendell and Capote presumably finding having a literary nemesis a spur to their own writing. Writing (especially fiction) is such a hard-to-pin-down and ephemeral process that you can see how having a concrete 'other' to set against might be useful, indeed necessary, motivation.

Sharing an opinion about your rivals is easy. Drawing a response is harder. And a true literary feud requires a public forum – there's no point if it's just kept between the protagonists. Poetry historically leant itself to feuding – the word *flyting* describes two parties exchanging insults with each other, usually through verse. In Norse literature the gods would flyt with each other, but it also took place in real life. Shakespeare and Chaucer both indulged in it, but it was especially prevalent in Scotland in the fifteenth and sixteenth centuries, encouraged by the courts of James IV and V. In *The Flyting of Dunbar and Kennedy*, performed by poets William Dunbar and Walter Kennedy for James IV, Kennedy referred to Dunbar as a 'shit without wit' – the first recorded instance of a scatological insult among men of letters. Crucially, flyting was ritualistic – structured, and with mutually agreed-upon parameters. It was also advantageous for the combatants – win or lose (and the victor was merely a matter of opinion), it was a way of raising your profile and gaining attention.

The earliest literary feuds show that they could be both personal, but also calculated for gain, or publicity. In the sixteenth century in England, Ben Jonson was on one side of 'The War of the Theatres', facing off against fellow playwrights John Marston and Thomas

Dekker (and possibly William Shakespeare). In 1599 satire in prose or verse was banned by John Whitgift, the Archbishop of Canterbury, which left writers with no creative outlet for this type of humourous commentary; hence writers like Marston, Dekker and Jonson satirised each other instead. That meant that writers instead satirized each other, as a way to satisfy their urges. No one can be sure how deeply the antagonism was felt, or whether it was all, or partly, manufactured, but it was an outlet for writerly rivalries, as well as a way of thrashing out differences in artistic and literary style.

Using the criteria of public forum and public reprisals, the second half of the twentieth century is considered the 'Golden Age' of the literary feud, particularly in America, where celebrity culture meant that TV soon found itself the new medium for literary sparring. The flames of these creative disagreements were further fanned by the media's obsession with the Great American Novel – what it was, who had written one, who might go on to fulfil their promise and write the next one. If the history of British literary feuds was like a game of chess, the American literary arena of the mid-twentieth century resembled nothing so much as a heavyweight boxing match, complete with sweaty venues, baying crowds and the occasional literal literary punch-up. Gore Vidal described himself as 'a tremendous hater, a tiresome nag, complacently positive that there is no human problem that could not be solved if people would simply do as I advise', picking fights with Norman Mailer, Tom Wolfe and Truman Capote (of whom Vidal said 'He's a full-fledged housewife from Kansas with all the prejudices'). Meanwhile, Wolfe called John Updike and Norman Mailer 'two old piles of bones'; their very different writing styles and backgrounds meaning that their feud was played out on the page, and in the pages of the tabloids. Vidal and Mailer eventually managed to patch up their feud: 'such stuff as dissertations are made on and our little careers are rounded with a boredom', but not before their public disagreements had sucked the oxygen out of their writing – the reason for them in the first place.

The Gore Vidal–Norman Mailer contretemps remains perhaps the most glorious spectacle of authorial antagonism ever to grace the literary pages – or indeed, the television screens – of America. In the early 1970s, when Vidal compared Mailer's *The Prisoner of Sex* to 'three days of menstrual flow' and Mailer responded by headbutting Vidal in the green room of *The Dick Cavett Show*, literature transcended mere words on a page to become pugilistic performance art. These were feuds writ large, played out against the backdrop of a continuing cultural obsession with the Great American Novel and fuelled by the same testosterone that powered Mailer's prose.

What makes these feuds so deliciously memorable isn't merely their performative theatrics, but that behind each barb lurked genuine artistic differences and the unbearable truth that America, vast as it was, simply wasn't big enough for all these literary egos. The feuds sold papers, boosted book sales, and occasionally even advanced the craft of writing itself – though one suspects that in the cold light of the twenty-first century, the punches thrown might be remembered longer than the paragraphs penned. Ultimately, the greatest feud for any writer is with literary oblivion.

While American literary feuds once played out in smoky television studios and booze-soaked parties, their British counterparts have in recent time found a more demure – though no less vicious – home on Twitter, where 280 characters provides just enough space for a perfectly crafted literary stiletto. Rachel Cusk and Camilla Long crossed tweets after Long's scathing review of Cusk's memoir (the Twitter spat was one thing; Long's review of Cusk's *Aftermath* was crowned 'Hatchet Job of the Year' for 2013, by one website). But overall, the risk to your reputation in getting involved in an online feud makes it an unattractive proposition (some writers, like Zadie Smith, stay away from social media entirely. She explained how doing so gives her the 'right to be wrong' in her writing – not having to face head-on the public reactions to her work). The polarisation of views and the echo chamber of social media means that writers worry about losing their audience. As Will Self explains, 'Writers have become too craven to get into disagreements with each other. They're all competing for a dwindling pool of readers, and are afraid of alienating their audience.'

The British literary establishment, once confined to the genteel pages of the *London Review of Books* or whispered asides at Hay Festival drink receptions, now finds itself exposed in the unforgiving glare of social media, where a hastily composed post can do more damage to a reputation than the most meticulously crafted review. What remains constant, however, is the delicate balance of intellectual snobbery, professional jealousy and genuine artistic disagreement that has always fuelled the British literary quarrel – just now with hashtags, and the occasional passive-aggressive emoji to soften the blow.

The writing life has always been defined by its obstacles. From Trollope's relentless early-morning word counts to modern authors dodging (or inciting) online spats, blocks (be they the writer's variety, or of enemies on social media), parries, rejection slips, scathing reviews and feuds are not simply occupational hazards, but the very crucible in which literary careers are forged – or melted down beyond recognition. The successful writer is probably not one who avoids these trials, but one who instead transforms them into eternal fuel for the lifelong creative fire. Perhaps that's the true mark of literary greatness: not the ability to pen perfect prose, but the resilience to keep writing despite the noonday devil of writer's block, the crushing blow of rejection, the public dissection of one's work, and the sharp barbs of rivals. In the end, writing isn't just about having written – it's about getting out of bed the next day and still wanting to write, even after you've experienced all the blood, sweat and spilt ink that the literary life entails. The road to authorship is littered with roadblocks and diversions, but for those who have the temperament and stamina to persist, there remains the slim but tantalising possibility that their words might eventually find their way home.

6.

Bad Endings: Old Stories, New Chapters

> 'The book is like the spoon, scissors, the hammer, the wheel. Once invented, it cannot be improved.'
>
> Umberto Eco

In 2021 a Bulgarian wine producer realised that the printing press at their vineyard used to print labels for their wine spent most of its time not in use. Once the labels for each harvest were printed, that was it. The machine sat silent. But the vineyard's owner explained how 'I remember in school learning about Gutenberg and how he had invented printing with moveable type and had used an old wine press to print his wonderful Bibles. I thought that if a wine press could be used for printing, could a modern printing press be used to make wine?' Unsurprisingly, the answer is no, and this story was, as my copy-editor pointed out to me, published on April Fool's Day.

But I imagine that if you owned a vineyard, you might start to see everything through the rosé-tinted spectacles of winemaking. What's that printing press doing there, idle? Put it to use! And winemaking and the story of how it serendipitously and unexpectedly led to printing (and consequently the book) is one of organic growth. It used technology that was already there, but which could be adapted and repurposed to take it in a direction that would be unimaginable to most winemakers – except one. As author Steven Johnson writes, Gutenberg 'took a machine designed to get people drunk and turned it into an engine for mass communication'. Some plot twist.

We don't know very much at all about Johannes Gutenberg, but we do know that he was born in Mainz, in the Rhine. As the Rhine was all about winemaking, Gutenberg just had to find a spare wine press, have a tinker, and find himself lauded as the inventor of one of the most influential machines in history. 'What the world is today,' wrote Mark Twain in 1900, 'good and bad, it owes to Gutenberg. Everything can be traced to this source.' Victor Hugo proclaimed that the invention of printing was 'the greatest event in history . . . the mother of revolution', and Francis Bacon wrote that it 'changed the appearance of the whole world'. Increases in literacy, the spread of ideas that drove the Reformation and all that followed from it were only made possible by print.

So, we're mostly in agreement about the impact of the printing press on human culture. Print – books – changed everything. But how did they come to be? Converting a wine press to print books sounds challenging even before you've drunk a case of wine, but Gutenberg didn't have to reinvent the wheel. Much of the technology he adapted had already existed for centuries in Asia, in what is now Korea. It's possible that 150 years before he was even born moveable type was being used there, and the practicalities of print gradually made their way from east to west, becoming more refined as they did so, to flourish when Gutenberg, and the world, was ready for them. But it wasn't just the physical ability to produce books that was needed for print to be successful: it also required a market – one that was ready to change how it read, and embrace this astonishing new tech.

The threads of the story of the printing press are woven into the history of the book and its development over centuries. It's a story of resilience and reinvention, retreat and rebirth. Every new iteration of the book looks both backwards and forwards – adapting what has gone before, and adding a dash of new and emerging technology, often borrowed from seemingly unrelated fields. And because books are so culturally vital to readers, every upheaval that results in changes to the form brings us a kaleidoscope of emotions. Uncertainty. Fear. Delight. Intrigue. Lawsuits.

The book's hegemony has lasted for nearly 500 years – not a bad run. At times, it has seemed unassailable: it has spread worldwide, adapted and thrived. But challenges to its supremacy have multiplied, and the story of the book in the twenty-first century is one of a fight for survival that we can't be sure it will win. There's always conflict between old and new technology, and the threats the printed book now faces are existential, with the stakes higher than ever. E-books. Audiobooks. ChatGPT. Will AI usher in a golden age of enhanced partnership and productivity, liberating and force-multiplying our ineffable human creativity with the speed, vision and precision of machine learning? Or will it instead cannibalise our creativity, collapse the publishing industry and destroy our storytelling abilities, all while disenfranchising storytellers, decimating royalties and trampling over copyright? Would it be a good thing if the book disappeared? After all, our planet's resources are increasingly scarce. Digitisation of stories, for those who have access to the technology, can lead to democratisation of readership and new audiences, and all with a far smaller carbon footprint than a book.

Given how vital stories are to us, perhaps in the end none of this will matter. We tell stories to find meaning, to connect, to pass on the truth about our legends, histories and shared ideas. As William Boyd once said, stories 'seem to answer something very deep in our nature as if, for the duration of its telling, something special has been created, some essence of our experience extrapolated, some temporary sense has been made of our common, turbulent journey towards the grave and oblivion'.

So perhaps *how* we tell each other stories – the format – isn't as important as *why*. Maybe we need to chill about the future of the book and learn to live with the thought that every few hundred years, the way we convey stories will fundamentally change. But in a digital age, the next changes will unfold at a speed that would have astonished Gutenberg – over the course of our lifetimes. Gutenberg *might* have anticipated the success of the book (certainly he would have had hopes for it), but he could never have lived long enough to see it come to full fruition. As readers living in the twenty-first century we'll live through new ways of telling stories – seeing some fail, some flare briefly but brightly, and others succeed and change the world. Again.

In 'The Magic of the Book', Hermann Hesse wrote that 'formulation in words and the handing on of these formulations through writing are . . . the only means by which humanity can have a history and a continuing consciousness of itself.' Can we continue to create meaningful history and consciousness without books? Perhaps looking at the challenges this most magical of objects has faced down, and the potential confrontations ahead of it, will give us some clues.

The manuscript men

In a time before books, our thoughts were recorded on cave walls, the sides of mountains, animal skins and papyrus. So, while we're used to thinking of books as the natural home of words and writing, that hasn't always been the case. As we've seen, the book as we recognise it only debuted in the fifteenth century, once Gutenberg and those who came after him had found a mechanical way to reproduce words quickly and accurately. Gutenberg's inspiration was an immediate threat to the existing way of presenting words – on elaborately illustrated handwritten manuscripts that took many, many hours to produce – and the book was such a success that there are few parallels in history.

This wasn't gradual change over hundreds of years. In 1452 Gutenberg began printing his first Bible, and by 1500 a thousand printing presses in Europe had already produced 8 million books. The pace of production and the speed of spread relative to the pace of life were like nothing seen before. Gutenberg himself acknowledged this, stating of his invention that: 'Through it, God will spread His Word. A spring of truth shall flow from it: like a new star, it shall scatter the darkness of ignorance, and cause a light heretofore unknown to shine amongst men.'

All this rapid change was presumably quite destabilising to live through. Life was slower, so any new technology probably made those who encountered it feel like some of us do about the development of ChatGPT, DeepSeek and other forms of AI. 'The word that has been used repeatedly is scary,' said a US senator of his constituents' feelings towards AI in a Senate Judiciary Committee hearing about how to regulate the technology. And perhaps 'scary' might have been how another Johannes – Johannes Trithemius – would have felt about these new-fangled books sweeping the Continent.

Until the mechanised printing press appeared, handwritten manuscripts were how books were produced, and Trithemius was a manuscript man. The monasteries of Europe had sewn up the manuscript market by cunningly linking the thankless task of laboriously writing someone else's words out with the (some might say equally thankless) task of serving God. Handwriting, said Trithemius, 'gives virtue to words, memory to things, and liveliness to times and circumstances'. *Virtue* to words. Words themselves couldn't be virtuous. Virtue was bestowed on them by the very act of creation and scribes were, claimed Trithemius, 'the herald of God'.

Unfortunately for Trithemius, deep down, his monks were not manuscript men. Perhaps they had heard about these wondrous new books that could be produced in their hundreds without anyone having to do hard labour. Or perhaps they hadn't, but nonetheless felt that life was too short. Apparently, his monks would come up with elaborate reasons *not* to sit still in a dark cell for hours slowly and laboriously writing; in fact, they told him that they would 'gladly go to labours outside, I will not in the least refuse to dig or carry stones'. But what was the point of that? Writing things out by hand was a way – *the* way – of serving God: spiritual and meditative, it cemented God's words in a monk's mind, with the handy side effect of preventing idleness. What was not to like?

To make sure the monks got the point, in 1492 Trithemius wrote *In Praise of Scribes*. It did what it said on the tin. But it also revealed Trithemius's inner conflict about the future of books. 'Writing books by hand must not be stopped because of printing,' he said. But contrarian Trithemius was also an early-adopter, and fan, of print. 'O blessed art of printing!' he exclaimed. And we only know what he thought and said at all because of the lasting power of print. Conversely, we know hardly anything about Gutenberg – he printed nothing about himself in his lifetime, and for hundreds of years it wasn't even clear that he *was* the inventor of print. We certainly had no idea what he thought about his world-changing invention. But we know a lot about Trithemius – and all of it printed.

We also know that when the first books began to be printed, the market was intensely competitive. Competition came from manuscripts, which had been perfected over thousands of years, which is why Gutenberg chose to start his print revolution with Bibles and other religious books – he knew there was already an audience. All he had to do was change the format and production method and convince readers to buy them.

Gutenberg had to make his new product as familiar to readers, and as beautiful, as Trimethius's beloved handwritten texts. Books might now be being produced mechanically, but Gutenberg made sure they looked like illustrated manuscripts; that's why the prosaically named B42 typeface, used in the Gutenberg Bible, mimicked handwriting. Gutenberg's books used double columns and left space on the pages for hand-coloured initial capital letters and other decorative elements that mimicked the skill of the manuscript scribes. So while Gutenberg's books were mass printed, they were finished off with handmade embellishments. And that need to retain elements of the old within the new continues throughout the history of the book. Early e-readers had virtual 'bookshelves' to display a reader's books, while apps for note-making were made with faux ripped pages and indentations to suggest depth, as on the page of a book. After all, new products can only go as fast as it takes the market to embrace them; making the new look like the old using established cultural constraints is a useful shortcut. No entrepreneur can afford to startle their audience.

The invention of mechanised printing was also an accelerant to competition. New printers sprung up everywhere, while the price of books dropped more than 60 per cent between 1460 and 1500. 'The world today is abounding with volumes . . . for the art which they call printing . . . daily produces an almost countless number of texts by old and recent authors alike,' wrote Trithemius. As soon as print took off, it created a superabundance of material (still a problem today) – completely overwhelming if you had grown up in the pre-printing age.

Trithemius eventually founded a library (first in Sponheim, then in Würzburg, in Bavaria) of about 2,000 books, but initially there were just forty on the shelves. That doesn't sound like much, but for the time, forty volumes was an average collection. That the library finished up with 2,000 tomes indicates the exponential power of print. Old and new forms of storytelling (roughly 1,200 of the collection were printed, and the rest were manuscripts) sat next to each other on the shelves, rubbing spines over the centuries.

Trithemius was able to both intuit what was being lost with the arrival of print – writing 'Who doesn't know how great is the distance between a scribed and a printed book? The scripture on parchment can persist a thousand years, but on paper, how long will it last?' – and to appreciate its potential. He lived at a time and in a place when everything must have seemed uncertain – and much of that unpredictability was driven by new ideas spread by print. The precariousness of Trithemius's time is mirrored today: there are those who feel that the internet has destabilised our society (and some who feel it has completely destroyed it) – while others recognise that it has revolutionised communication and how we access information. Like Trithemius, we are curious but cautious about the future, about the opportunities and efficiencies it brings, while still feeling an emotional connection to what has gone before.

Flying high and sinking low with Doves Type

Like any product that revolutionises, the book felt like a fait accompli: an obvious and necessary progression from the manuscript, needed to educate and liberate an expanding population in a time of social and political upheaval. But it didn't have everything its own way. For hundreds of years the manuscript and the book co-existed, each with their own strengths and weaknesses. The seventeenth-century poet John Donne, described by Ben Jonson as 'the first poet in the world in some things', might have been an original writer, but Donne's work existed mostly in the old ways: handwritten form only, circulated among small groups of trusted readers. His poetry was at times both erotic and satiric – a heady and potentially dangerous combination that might have finished his career in the Anglican Church (he ended up as Dean of St Paul's Cathedral) at a time when reputation and religious affiliation were everything.

Sticking with the manuscript form of the book, rather than print, allowed Donne to have his cake and eat it: to write, to share his work, and to continue in his public profession. Key to this was the fact that he could carefully control who had access to his writing. The restricted circulation of a handwritten manuscript was its biggest advantage: his poems were his innermost thoughts and feelings, not suitable for all eyes. Incredibly, in 2018 a bound manuscript of Donne's poems was rediscovered in a house in Suffolk. But the reason it had survived for 400 years was because it was a hybrid: the handwritten manuscript pages were treasured because they were so hard to come by, while the book-like binding that preserved them allowed them to persist over the centuries.

Donne recognised that handwritten manuscripts continued to have some advantages over the printed book. Just because mass printing and circulation was *possible* didn't mean it was appealing to all writers, or readers. For both practical and aesthetic reasons, the old forms of the book retained their allure. In the late seventeenth and early eighteenth centuries, despite print being well established in Britain, the poet William Blake reinvented the manuscript. Blake described how his work was 'a method of printing which combines the painter and the poet', which gave him complete creative control over his work in a way that no other writer had. His manuscripts were also hybrids, picking and choosing from the advantages of both book and manuscript.

William Blake lived with visions and interactions with otherworldly beings for his entire life. He was fortunate that his wife took all this in her stride, remarking that 'I have very little of Mr Blake's company; he is always in Paradise.' Perhaps his ease in moving between real and unreal worlds gave him the creative flexibility to move backwards and forwards between the old and the new ways. In 1788 Blake developed a technique of etching that allowed him to combine illustrations and text on the same page – and then print them himself. This 'relief etching' apparently came to Blake in a conversation with his brother, Robert – nothing strange in that as Robert was, like William, a printer – although what was peculiar was that at the time of this chat, Robert had been dead for several months.

When not visiting Paradise or communing with the dead, Blake worked on what he called his 'illuminated printing', a nod to the illuminated medieval manuscripts that inspired him. For Blake, each manuscript he worked on was an individual, not a copy; instead of the standardisation of mechanised printing, he embraced the variations in each of his manuscripts. He wrote the verses, created the illustrations, printed the plates, coloured the pages by hand, and finally bound the books into covers. Mechanisation had taken control away from authors, but Blake had found a way to take it back.

> No man can improve an original invention . . . I have heard many people say, 'Give me the ideas; it does not matter what words you put them into,' and others say, 'Give me the design; it is no matter for the execution.' These people knew enough of artifice but little of art. Ideas cannot be given but in their minutely appropriate words. Nor can a design be made without its minutely appropriate execution.

One of Blake's students described how Blake was able to execute 'something between a thing and a thought', and his method of execution was also something in between: a bridge spanning the individualisation of the manuscript, and the opportunities of new printing methods. In medieval manuscripts, motifs and marginal decorations created an interplay between words and images. Blake did the same; text and art were equally important.

One of the limitations of ink was that illustrations were restricted to what could be carved on a woodblock, which wasn't much. Blake found a way round this to combine the beauty of illustrations with print. He described his way of working as 'more ornamental, uniform, and grand, than any before discovered, while it produces works at less than one-fourth of the expense'. He had created a third way between the uniformity of mechanisation and the laboriousness of manuscript creation – a blend of book form where the old and the new could enhance each other.

Blake died in 1827, just before (relatively speaking) another revolutionary leap in printing technology. In 1865, American inventor William Bullock perfected the rotary press – a machine that could fold and cut paper at an astonishing 12,000 sheets per hour, enabling millions of copies to be printed in a single day. But this exponential expansion in the reach of ideas came at a tragic cost to its creator: Bullock's own leg was crushed by one of his printing presses, and he died after developing gangrene following its amputation.

By the nineteenth century's end, printing had undergone perhaps its most significant transformation with the invention of the Linotype machine. This 'line o' type' system revolutionised typesetting, allowing a single compositor to produce 6,000 characters per hour – triple the output possible by hand. The pace of change in printing technology had become relentless, each innovation building upon the last to transform how words reached the world.

But relentless change has a way of triggering a backlash against its progress. Whether it's horse-drawn cart to penny farthing, bike to car, boat to jet engine or analogue to digital, early-adopters will always be accompanied by look-backers. It's not necessarily that these people don't want progress; it's that they can still see the value in how things were done in the past and want to salvage the best of it to accompany us into the future. In the late nineteenth and early twentieth centuries this backlash led to the rise of the private presses, founded by men and women who wanted to celebrate the beauty of craft, and the idea of working for pleasure, rather than profit. Manuscript illustrating and book binding, they believed, were skills, not processes, and to lose those skills would be to misplace a whole lot of knowledge.

While you might think that the private presses' feelings on Gutenberg were that he was the worst thing to happen to books since silverfish,* they revered him – or at least, the beautiful books he produced. They weren't inspired by the production efficiencies of ink and moveable type, but they were by the astonishing beauty of the books his printing press could create. While Gutenberg's Bibles looked backwards to the age of manuscripts for inspiration, and to bridge the gap for readers between the old and new forms, the private press movement looked back to Gutenberg for theirs. Gutenberg might have ushered in an age of standardisation relative to manuscript production, but paradoxically, to the private press enthusiasts, he was a beacon of individuality and beautiful book design. We see this tension often in books: they nudge us forwards while simultaneously asking us to look backwards.

'This is the supreme Book Beautiful . . . a symbol of the infinitely beautiful in which all things of beauty rest,' wrote Thomas Cobden-Sanderson about the work of the Doves Press, which he had co-founded in 1900. The private press movement believed that every decision in book design and production had profound meaning. Binding, paper, typography and ink had to be carefully chosen to maximise the overall aesthetic appeal of every book. This was the slow, detailed and monumentally uneconomic stuff of bibliophilic dreams. Naturally, it drew

---

* Silverfish, primitive wingless insects, are bad news for books. They love the cellulose in book bindings and will eat as much of it as they can.

in eccentrics, misfits and utopians: those who were willing to sacrifice profit for perfection, whatever the personal cost. The Kelmscott Press was founded in 1891 by William Morris and Emery Walker (with some titles illustrated by Edward Burne-Jones) and leant heavily on the aesthetics of fifteenth-century text design, using smaller spaces between words and margins that reflected those of medieval manuscripts. Kelmscott folded in 1898, but its legacy in book aesthetics was outsized.

But all this beauty was eventually challenged by ugly reality. Prizing aesthetics above all else, the private presses were never truly viable. Their founders might have thought themselves utopian, but they faced accusations that the books they made were returning the world to a time when the only way to own a book was to be rich. They fetishised the past. And they induced the sort of book-mania in people that Thomas Phillipps and other bibliophiles might have recognised, and probably encouraged. Spending all your time on the micros of type, paper and binding can make you lose sight of the bigger picture. Cobden-Sanderson and his co-founder Emery Walker fell out spectacularly over the ownership of the Doves Type* which they had created for their books. The Doves Type was the most valuable asset of the Doves Press, and is often described as the most beautiful typeface in the world, but Walker and Cobden-Sanderson's tussle over who should have ownership of the font when they decided to disband the press in 1906 descended into years of ugly correspondence and legal threats, with Walker eventually being banned from entering the business he had helped establish. The dispute even dragged in their friends, most notably Sir Sydney Cockerell, who attempted to broker

* If you're wondering what Doves type looks like, gaze at any page in this book.

a deal between the two, which would see Cobden-Sanderson granted use of the type until his death, at which point it would pass to Walker. Although Cobden-Sanderson had promised Walker a copy of the type 'for his own use', as time went on, he became increasingly incensed at the thought of anyone else having control over 'his' letters, and attempted to renege on the deal.

The high ideals of beauty and elegance expressed in creating the Doves typeface did not outlast its bad-tempered end. Cobden-Sanderson was clear where he stood on the matter: 'I am . . . a visionary and a fanatic, and against a visionary and a fanatic he will beat himself in vain,' he declared. Motivated by the unbearable idea that the Doves Type might be used on books that weren't actually great works of art – 'the Doves Press type shall never be subjected to the use of a machine other than the human hand' – Cobden-Sanderson decided the best and only course of action was to drop the metal type into the Thames, to stop anyone else having control of it. In 1916, that's exactly what he did. Let's hope he's blissfully unaware that almost a hundred years later some of the Doves Type was retrieved from the bottom of the Thames by a graphic designer called Robert Green, digitally recreated, and now lives on with its own X handle.

The borrowers

The book has always had to walk a fine line between the fanatics and the pragmatics. The pragmatists usually win in the end (that's the nature of them), but the visionaries and fanatics are there to make sure that we remember the beauty of the old, so that we can use the best of it to inspire the new. But for the book to reach its full potential, it had to be able to reach an audience of millions. By the end of the Second World War the era of the private presses was over, subsumed by the mass market. What might be lost in beautiful design was gained in being able to reach readers all over the world with books that were cheap and accessible. But print didn't arrive with a ready-made audience: it had to fight for it.

Books are one of the greatest time machines we have, helping us unlock the past and imagine the future. They tell us how people long dead thought, felt and acted, and why. They are precious portals into the past that enable us to imagine times before the ones we live in. So it's only through books that we are able to understand that in the early twentieth century, there was no big market for them. Despite the book colonising the world, its reach was broad but shallow: it remained a luxury item. Relative to incomes, production costs and hence book costs were still high, and there was an added barrier: literacy. Why would you buy a book if you couldn't read? The buyers of books hadn't really changed over the centuries: they remained the preserve of universities, churches and institutions – where you'd find the literate and elite.

In Britain in the second half of the nineteenth century, literacy rates climbed dramatically. The literacy rate for men rose from 69.3 per cent to 97.2 per cent between 1851 and 1900, and for women, the change was even more pronounced: from 54.8 per cent to 96.8 per cent. The Education Act of 1870 established that the state had a duty to school children, and the classrooms and teachers that followed helped drive literacy rates up. But being able to read didn't automatically translate into buying books. Most ordinary households still only owned a handful: a family Bible, perhaps, or a few children's books. When it came to books, buying habits were out of step with the ability of manufacturers to make them. Printing had become increasingly efficient, but where was the market? Unless publishers were able to create one, what was the point of printing more and more?

In the end, it was not publishers or printers who came up with the answer. The market was created for them as an unexpected by-product of the First World War. 'We knitted him a balaclava helmet to keep his head warm and omitted to provide anything to supply the inside of his brain,' read a 1915 article in *War Illustrated* magazine. Like so much else, the book was sent off to war, and changed by it. A warm head wasn't enough; a newly literate population had been sent far from home, enduring long periods of waiting and boredom in between the fighting. Books began to carve out a niche from 'nice to have' to 'absolutely essential'.

The book was the ideal companion to distract you from the trenches, to share with your comrades, to provide talking points and entertainment. The YMCA and Red Cross set up libraries in POW camps, while Arthur Conan Doyle rose to the challenge of keeping soldiers entertained by un-retiring Sherlock Holmes in *His Last Bow*, in 1917. German engineer Theodor Koch wrote that for soldiers, 'A book must not be too formidable or sombre to look at. It's like a cyclist with a long hill in front of him – the sight makes him tired.' Writers like Rudyard Kipling, John Buchan, and, perhaps surprisingly, Jane Austen, along with poetry and anthologies, were all popular. And having had a taste of reading, soldiers brought the habit home with them.

A book's strengths are also its weakness. Portable and durable, as well as heading off to the front, it's capable of setting off on its own publicity tour: you might borrow a book, love it, and buy a copy yourself – or at least, something else by that author. But converting readers one by one is a very slow process. And books were *too* robust: they didn't fall apart and need to be replaced, like other household objects. People could read, and now they had the habit of reading. But barriers remained. 'Today accumulating printed books and shelving them in one's home may seem like mundane facts of life . . . In the first decades of the twentieth century, however, those activities couldn't be assumed and needed to be learned,' according to historian Ted Striphas. Readers were still more likely to borrow books from libraries or friends than they were to buy them.

In the post-war world, publishers ran into a double-headed problem: they had the ability to produce millions of books cheaply, but without a big enough market to support the number of books they could print. You could fire out books quickly, but only grow markets slowly. Supply and demand were completely out of whack. And book lovers were undermining any attempt at creating a decent market by persisting in using libraries, book clubs and each other as suppliers, limiting the number of books that could be sold.

Fortunately for the book, if there was one thing the mid-twentieth century knew about, it was creating markets. Henry Ford had done it with the car. Cigarette manufacturers, soft drink inventors and morphine marketers (at least, in the nineteenth century – regulation of opiates was in place by the mid-twentieth century) had all created consumers out of pretty much nothing. What was urgently needed was a way to make buying books and reading them a habit, or possibly, like morphine, an addiction: something that you would return to again and again, against your better judgement, and until you had lost everything and bankrupted yourself. Okay, maybe not quite that.

In 1933 William Lyon Phelps delivered a speech on US radio. Phelps was an author, academic and critic, and his speech was called 'The Pleasure of Books'. He began with:

> The habit of reading is one of the greatest resources of mankind; and we enjoy reading books that belong to us much more than if they are borrowed. A borrowed book is like a guest in the house; it must be treated with punctiliousness, with a certain considerate formality. You must see that it sustains no damage; it must not suffer while under your roof . . . But your own books belong to you; you treat them with that affectionate intimacy that annihilates formality.

Phelps was echoing a move that was already underway in the early 1930s: to utterly shame readers who persisted in borrowing books. A conglomerate of American publishers had hired a PR man called Edward Bernays* to make readers value books (and thus pay more for them), and stop *borrowing* them from each other. As well as standing in the way of a potentially huge market, these 'wretches' were readers who 'raised hell with book sales and deprived authors of earned royalties'. Book borrowing was *cheating*: un-American, unfair, and probably communist. Bernays decided to come up with a

* Bernays, a nephew of Sigmund Freud, is considered 'the father of public relations', but was also a controversial rogue. He wholeheartedly believed that men just like himself should use propaganda to manipulate the masses, stating that 'Intelligent men must realize that propaganda is the modern instrument by which they can fight for productive ends and help to bring order out of chaos.' He convinced Americans to use disposable plastic cups by suggesting anything else was unsanitary and would give you venereal disease, worked for the American Tobacco Company to convince more women to take up smoking (employing psychoanalyst A. A. Brill's phrase 'Torches of Freedom' to encourage women to associate smoking with emancipation), and used covert means to manipulate doctors or others in positions of authority to ostensibly agree with whatever habit he was trying to persuade the masses to adopt.

'lethal epithet' for these disgraces. He launched a nationwide competition to find a name for them, and it was obvious he wasn't the only person who couldn't bear these sorts. The entries poured in. The eventual winner was 'booksneak', which doesn't have the vitriol of some of the other suggestions: 'greader', 'libracide', 'booklooter', 'bookbum', 'bookaneer', 'greeper' and 'blifter'. *No one* wants to be known as a greeper.

Bernays attacked the problem of a lack of market for books on several fronts. When he wasn't lethally labelling readers as blifters and bookbums, he was busy setting up the Book Publishers Research Institute, which sounded impressive, but was really just a way for him to talk about bookshelves. That's right. Smartly enough, Bernays decided that 'Where there are bookshelves, there will be books' – a twist on the more usual 'where there are loads of books, someone will eventually give in and put up bookshelves'. Bernays made bookshelves a desirable, and necessary, home decor essential. And all these efforts paid off. Whereas previously American publishers had been in a zero-sum game of selling books for $1 a go to try and generate sales, Bernays saw that the way to create a market was to make readers value buying, owning and displaying books in their homes.

Bernays' biggest legacy was probably in how he changed the emotional relationship between readers and books. As Janice Radway says in *A Feeling for Books* (1997), 'Every book sale could generate two forms of profit. On the one hand, it could generate cash for its publisher. On the other hand, it could also produce perceived changes in the status of the individual who bought it.' Bernays used his institute to pump out spurious research that linked book-buying with personal success. Buying and reading books would make you better off, more attractive, more likely to be hired and more financially successful – which I think all us readers know to be true.

The twentieth century saw the beginnings of the promotion of the book as a fetish: a product that not only surprised, delighted and entertained, but that also said something profound to the world about the person reading it. Readers started to view their books as extensions of themselves. Books became aspirational: they represented an idea of your true potential. The physicality of a book means it is not just practical and portable, it's an outward signifier of what we think about ourselves, and perhaps more importantly, what we want others to think about us. The aspirations we began to lend to books led to the acceleration of PR and marketing campaigns attached to authors, and a veneration of all aspects of the physical nature of the book.

William Lyon Phelps ended his speech by saying that 'Books are of the people, by the people, for the people. Literature is the immortal part of history; it is the best and most enduring part of personality.' Bernays' brilliance was in making people believe that what they were seen to read said something about them – that it truly was an 'enduring part of their personality'. Out and about in public, with striking jacket designs so everyone knew what you were reading, with marketing campaigns and blurbs to persuade people to buy, the book was on a roll. But, having carved out a new market, it faced its next problem. It had only a small window of opportunity to establish itself as ubiquitous before it was challenged by new forms of mass entertainment – which could have stopped the presses.

New readers on the block

'All the famous novels of the world, with their well-known characters and their famous scenes, only asked, it seemed, to be put on the films. What could be easier and simpler? The cinema fell upon its prey with immense rapacity,' wrote Virginia Woolf in 1926. The book wasn't the only form of entertainment hunting for a market. Consumers now had far more choice about how they spent their time and money: in the cinema, the pub, at the races or at home listening to the radio. The book was old news – could it compete with the novelty of moving pictures and the wonder of voices broadcast from around the world?

In 1934 in England, forty-eight booksellers attended a conference set up by Basil Blackwell (whose father had established the Blackwell's chain of bookshops) and the publisher Stanley Unwin headlined 'The New Reading Public', to try and address this problem – or, perhaps more positively, see what opportunities it presented. There was a recognition that a new reading public existed, looking for quality reading experiences at an affordable price, and that the market as it was did not serve them. The phrase 'The New Reading Public' had been in circulation since the 1920s, most notably used in a 1922 lecture by journalist and critic Sidney Dark to the 'Society of Bookmen'. Dark began his lecture by talking of how the lower-middle and working classes 'have discovered that the literature of their country is a priceless possession which is their very own, and which they are eager to read, as any normal man would be to explore the highways and byways of a newly acquired estate' (this analogy perhaps suggested that Dark had limited experience of these people, or 'non normal' men, as he might have put it). Dark continued: 'Now that everyone can read, and great multitudes actually do read, the responsibility, primarily, of the writer, and incidentally of all of us who are concerned in the making and distributing of books, is obviously tremendously increased.' He was concerned to highlight that the types of literature being published needed to be relevant to these new readers: 'The book that is nothing more than a series of beautifully constructed sentences has little value in the welter of our modern world.' Dark quoted Joseph Conrad, using the writer's statement on his success: 'I saw that I had managed to please a certain number of minds busy attending to their own very real affairs' – an indication that the 'Bookmen' were discovering that to satisfy these new readers, they would need to publish books that met them on their own turf, and that dealt with their day-to-day concerns.

One man 'concerned in the making and distributing of books' was publisher Allen Lane, later behind the decision to publish *Lady Chatterley's Lover*. He recognised that this new 'reading' public might not, in fact, choose to read. Relatively speaking, books were still elitist, expensive, and not especially portable – serious literature was mostly found in hardback, and what was available in paperback might be easy to carry round, but was usually terrible to read. Until this point, paperbacks were the home of sensational fiction and adventurous but unliterary tales, or of reprints of titles that had already been in print for many decades.

Lane's vision was to reinvent the book just enough for a new age – keeping the best of the familiarity that readers and buyers were used to, but making changes for a modern readership. He would publish good literature from modern writers, printed on quality paper, in a small and light format, showcased with thoughtful typesetting and design, and, crucially, with an overarching brand – Penguin Books – that readers could recognise, even if they didn't know the author. The price point also had to be perfect – the price of a packet of cigarettes – and kept low by large print runs and publishing out-of-copyright titles, with no royalties to pay.* These books had to be as mobile as their new market: away from static, unapproachable elitist book stores, and into shops like Woolworths – or why not a book vending machine on railway station platforms? Lane championed good text design and good writing, allied with mass production and distribution. This combination proved to be a winning one on a scale that Lane probably never dared dream of. Four days after the launch of the first ten Penguin paperbacks, 150,000 had been sold. One million were sold inside four months, and by 1946, a hundred million paperbacks had been bought. Allen Lane was a disrupter, as George Orwell described: 'Penguin books are splendid value for sixpence, so splendid that if the other publishers had any sense they would combine against them and suppress them.'

The success of Penguin's paperbacks and the adoption of its model of quality mass-market publishing by others (particularly the Pocket Books list in America) breathed new life into the book just at the moment it most needed it. As with Gutenberg's printing press, this bookish revolution didn't happen in a vacuum. Allen Lane and Penguin took advantage of a confluence of progress that smoothed the way: the 'new reading public' had been identified and established, and the mechanics of production and promotion had been industrialised.

The book's ability to adapt to worldwide events was proven again during the Second World War. Millions of books were distributed by the US military to its soldiers, a reminder of the changes to reading habits that the First World War had brought about earlier in the

---

* Penguin doubled down on making money during the Second World War by selling advertising space on its covers.

century. 'Books are weapons in the war of ideas' was the slogan of the Council on Books in Wartime. Originally, librarians had collected donated books for soldiers to read, but most were unsuitable either in subject, or because they were heavy hardbacks – not ideal when you were packing to go to war – which led to the creation of Armed Services Editions paperbacks. These reprints of popular works were designed to fit into a cargo pocket, with one newspaper describing how 'the hunger for these books, evidenced by the way they are read to tatters, is astounding even to the Army and Navy officers and the book-trade officials'. Adventure, biography, aviation, classics, cartoons, contemporary history, mysteries, fantasies and drama along with other genres were all well represented. These editions were printed on light paper, and, unusually, across four horizontal columns – which was thought to help the eyes of the war-weary reader. Cheap (6 cents a copy on average), colourful and, most importantly, dealing with topics the average soldier wanted to read about, between 1943 and 1947 more than 122 million books were distributed.

After the war, the book seemed to have reached its zenith. It was a tried, tested and tweaked product that had made itself ubiquitous. At the same time as gaining from economies of scale and mature production, it had also cultivated a reputation for being more than the sum of its papery parts: for helping us showcase to the world who we were, or wanted to be. And in an age of increasing individualisation, this combination seemed unbeatable.

Once upon a download

In 1949, Spanish patent number 190,698 was issued to Ángela Ruiz Robles. Born in 1895, she worked for most of her life as an educator, at a time and in a country where only 25 per cent of women could read or write. Yet as well as being a wife, mother and teacher, Ruiz Robles was also the inventor of the precursor to the e-book: a 'Mechanical Encyclopaedia' that used compressed air to move spools and spindles to show text and pictures. This is a description of her invention: 'All the components are replaceable. When closed, it is the same size as an ordinary book, and easy to handle. For authors and publishers, it greatly reduces production costs, for it does not require either paste or binding.' Even at the height of its reach, the next challenge to the book was incubating.

Ángela Ruiz Robles was a visionary – her invention was a complete reimagining of everything we thought we knew about the book. It wasn't like Gutenberg's press or Allen Lane's foresight in taking an established process or product and refining it for a new audience. Ruiz Robles lived in a world and a time where most people agreed that the book did its job perfectly. Books were the default way of storing information, and it was difficult to think how they could be improved. But Ruiz Robles had the imagination to dream of a new form of an old friend, so ahead of her time that the technology to realise her vision didn't exist, and wouldn't for several more decades.

Between Ruiz Robles and the e-books we're now used to came the gradual, then rapid, digitisation of literature. In 1971, spurred on by advances in computing, Project Gutenberg got underway to 'provide as many e-books in as many formats as possible for the entire world to read in as many languages as possible', as its 2004 mission statement explained. These 'e-books' were simply digitised versions of a text; useful perhaps for academics, but ultimately limited: you couldn't carry round your unwieldy home computer on your commute so you could get lost in a good story on the way home. In 1998, however, the first e-reader as we would recognise it was launched. The Rocket reader stored up to ten books but at a prohibitive cost of $499; a novelty accessible only to few.

Over the next decade, more and more e-readers were developed, with each one proving more efficient and cheaper than the last. The Rocket was followed by the EveryBook, the Millennium eBook, and the Cybook. The emergence of the e-reader and e-book inspired both awe and terror in traditional publishers. It was an existential threat, a once-in-a-millennium step change – one that threatened to modify every single part of the book supply chain: from how writers published their books, to how they were bought, to how readers and writers connected. It affected everything: supply, distribution, bookselling. And George Orwell would have had to concede that even if publishers worked together, they would never be able to suppress this new technology. Its advantages were both too obvious and too great for that.

The early fears of traditional publishers were understandable: the music industry had already been destabilised by digital piracy, and the same threat hung over their business model, with the potential for content to be distributed free online. The 2006 launch of the Sony Reader was a turning point, introducing readers to a paper-like screen that was attractive to read. With publishers realising that this new format was here to stay, and a way of accessing a new market of readers, they began to work together towards one standard e-book format. This pragmatic shift was crucial, transforming the e-book from an unmanageable threat into a controllable, and highly profitable, new distribution channel that could be strategically embraced.

Sales of e-readers were further enhanced by the arrival of the Amazon Kindle in 2007. Just a year later, the CEO of Penguin Group, John Makinson, noted that '[e-readers] have become mainstream in the sense that they are a genuine consumer product for which there is real appetite', and in 2009 the *Guardian* noted that Dan Brown's *The Lost Symbol* would be available not just as a hardback, but also as an e-book, with traditional publishers commenting that although e-book sales were small, they were growing quickly.

So, by the mid-2000s, the e-reader had evolved to become a supremely portable reading device that could store many thousands of texts, with lower production and retail costs for both publishers and readers. Now, it can interact with text in real time – searching, clipping and highlighting words – and do all this while concealing what we're reading from others (a marked shift away from the idea of a book as an extension of the reader's personality in the mid-twentieth century). As space (and privacy) are increasingly commodified, a reading device that assures privacy and needs neither bookstores nor bookshelves is a plus.

And the e-reader has changed us, too. The digitisation of text has altered forever how we interact with words. I don't know what form you are reading this book in – a physical copy, or on an e-reader, or listening to it as an audiobook. And I don't know how your reading habits have evolved over the last few years. But I know how mine have. When I was young, I read everything I could, everywhere I could – but always a book; there was nothing else. Increasingly, though, I feel as if my brain has been rewired: my attention span is shorter, I'm used to scanning text at speed instead of properly engaging with it. While

I often berate myself about this, I'm aware that it's not *just* laziness, but one of the effects of living in a screen age. Smartphones, laptops and e-readers have altered not just what we read, but how and what information we retain. It's a real and growing threat, both to the cognitive powers of humans (research shows that readers who read print have a better comprehension of what's on the page), but also to the future of the physical book. Academics have noticed that students are increasingly less willing to engage with classic literature because of its length and complexity – these texts require 'deep-reading', rather than skimming. Will Self describes how 'I remain a voracious reader, but . . . with the advent of bi-directional digital media, I've become more of a snacker than a hearty literary eater. I still read codices, but a tendency to read multiple texts concurrently that was well-advanced before e-books, has now become near-pathological: I really am reading about 100 books at the same time.' Us fellow voracious bi-directional multiple snackers can relate.

The Hitchhiker's Guide to the Machine-Learning Galaxy

The author Nicholson Baker once wrote of the book: 'We've come up with a beautifully browsable invention that needs no electricity and exists in a readable form no matter what happens.' But while physical books do decay, not even e-books are immortal. File corruption, format obsolescence and data loss are to e-books what fire, water damage and falling behind the bookcase are to printed books.

And books, despite their romantic appeal, rely on deforestation and consume significant amounts of paper, water and energy. We probably don't think much about this when we're engrossed in a good novel, but books come with a large production and distribution footprint, and publishers are only slowly shifting towards more sustainable practices. Print-on-demand allows for better prediction and control of print runs, while the use of eco-friendly inks, improved paper recycling, and typographic innovations like thinner paper or designs that fit more text per page without sacrificing readability have all driven some change – but print remains a fundamentally destructive and energy-heavy way of telling a story. That's not something the first oral storytellers would have worried about.

From an environmental point of view, we might have expected that e-books would help improve the carbon footprint of publishing. But while like any innovative product they saw explosive growth in their early years – unsurprising given their starting point was zero – by the early 2020s, print sales had rallied and climbed again, increasing by 10–14 per cent in English-speaking markets. It's clear that while readers might guiltily acknowledge that physical books are an indulgence, it's not one we're prepared to give up, despite the advances of the e-reader. It turns out that we cling tightly to our luxuries, especially when we feel under threat. In the US in 2021, just over 15 per cent of readers chose an e-book to read from, with 36 per cent sticking with hardback, and 29 per cent paperback. Printed books saw a particular resurgence during the Covid pandemic, with 213 million of them being purchased in 2021 in the UK. Amazon, the dominant book retailer in the print market, sold three times as many print books as e-books in 2023. Notably, the expectation that e-book sales would flourish with digital-native younger readers has not come to pass. In fact, Kindles and other e-readers are more popular with older readers – possibly because they offer features like adjustable text size – and appeal to demographics that simply read more.

Gen Z has been unexpectedly driving print book sales, with this demographic keen to purchase 'trophy copies' of genre fiction, often to display proudly on their shelves or on social media. It may seem counter-intuitive, but the tactile appeal of books, combined with digital fatigue and the visual culture of platforms like TikTok, has fuelled physical book sales to record highs in the UK and US, with Gen Z buying print books for 80 per cent of purchases between 2021 and 2022. After all, downloading an e-book doesn't quite have the same anticipatory joy as visiting a bookshop, or holding a book in your hands.

And that desire to own books has also bolstered independent bookshops. In 2016, there were 867 independent bookshops in the UK; by 2022, after six straight years of growth, that number had risen to 1,072. These indies are the canaries in the coalmine of the book trade. Unlike big chains that diversify into cafés and giftware, small bookstores tend to stick to books alone – making their growth an even stronger indicator of print's enduring power.

Publishers have learnt to lean into the dual-format world of e-books, audiobooks and physical books. They now often release a new book simultaneously in all three formats, giving extra revenue streams and reaching new audiences. But this multi-format world brings with it a challenge we thought we'd solved in the early twentieth century: oversupply. There are plenty of readers – but millions of books. And the barrier to publishing has nearly vanished. With a Wi-Fi connection and a laptop, anyone can write and upload a book overnight. In fact, in 2007 there were 3,804 self-published titles on Amazon; by 2023, that number exploded to 1.4 million. That same year, Amazon began limiting self-published authors to just three books per day. Yes, per day.

When asked about the future of the novel, Italian writer Italo

Calvino replied with a question: 'Is it possible to tell stories that are not novels?' His point still resonates: the future of storytelling doesn't hinge on format. Audiobooks, podcasts, films, and digital editions offer alternate ways to experience stories. As our media consumption shifts, we may stop asking 'Have you read . . . ?' and instead ask: 'Do you know the story of . . . ?'

While the number of books being published in the twenty-first century suggests that there are more readers out there than ever and that the publishing business must be in good health, looking beyond the figures tells us a very different story. A 2021 *New York Times* article about book sales during the Covid pandemic highlighted that roughly 98 per cent of the books released in 2020 sold fewer than 5,000 copies. The only books really selling in big numbers were those by celebrities and established authors.

And this was further confirmed in 2022 in the US, where a court case was brought by the Department of Justice to try to stop the merger of Penguin Random House with fellow publisher Simon & Schuster, on the grounds that it would create a monopoly (the merger was indeed blocked). While the outcome of the trial didn't tell us much about the future of the book, the details of the case did. In an article ominously headed 'No One Buys Books' journalist Elle Griffin, who read through *The Trial*, a 1,194-page book about the case, reported an exchange in court with the CEO of Penguin Random House in the US, which highlighted that in the four preceding years, roughly fifty authors were responsible for selling more than 500,000 copies. The DOJ, as part of the court case, looked at 58,000 titles published in a year, and discovered that 90 per cent sold fewer than 2,000 copies. Even more depressingly if you're a writer, 50 per cent sold fewer than a dozen copies. So, a tiny number of writers are selling an enormous number of books, and the rest are struggling to make a living. In 2022, the Society of Authors published a report which confirmed this: authors had seen a 60 per cent drop in income since 2006, suggesting more and more authors are failing to earn back their advances and make any money at all. Simultaneously, publishers are reducing advances, with their already thin margins being squeezed further by online retailers with immense negotiating power.

Threats to the book are piling up like overdue library fines. Imagine you could pay one fee a month, and in return access all the books you could ever want, as consumers already do with Spotify for music and Netflix for television. For now, you can't do that with books, because none of the 'big five' publishers* have agreed to this type of business model. In *The Trial*, the CEO of Penguin Random House US responds to the question of why books can't be bought on Kindle Unlimited by saying: 'We think it's going to destroy the publishing industry.'

So how do publishers make any money at all? Mostly through their backlist: through classic long-lived titles – those we read as children, or in school, or that have been around forever. To this they can occasionally add (every ten years or so) a huge commercial best-seller that will provide them with enough income to keep going. Publishers have realised that they can't prevail over alternative entertainment like Netflix or other streaming services: instead, they have decided to copy Hollywood by spending huge amounts on a very small number of books, at least one of which they hope will become a best-seller. This explains, at least in part, why three-quarters of all the advances

* This is the collective name for Penguin Random House, HarperCollins, Hachette, Simon & Schuster and Macmillan – the biggest publishers globally.

that publishers pay out go to celebrity writers: they are safe bets in a risky business.

And it is risky: at heart, publishers are gamblers, and mostly, their bets don't pay off. Like all professional punters, they try and hedge their exposure to risk, in the hope that something will win through. So they publish more and more books, to test the market and not miss out on new trends. And, while the number of things you *could* read increases, the revenue generated has dropped. In 2004 in the US the publishing industry made $23.72 billion in revenue. In 2023, that figure was $12.6 billion. That's right. In twenty years, the book industry has lost two-thirds of its value. The digital age means that the barrier for entry to write and publish a book is lower than ever – but so is the financial reward an author can expect.* On the upside, authors can now be their own self-publishers, and some genres – romance in particular – have seen the majority of authors move to self-publishing online. William Blake would have liked that bit, although being responsible for writing, editing, producing (in electronic form, mostly), marketing and selling your own titles could also be seen as a time-consuming and not necessarily welcome expansion of the role of the author.

404: foresight not found

While the Penguin Random House/Simon & Schuster merger was a threat to books because it risked creating a monopoly, with adverse

* That reward can also be affected by digital piracy: in 2019, *Forbes* reported that in the US, $300 million was lost due to it. A 2023 study indicated that in Italy, more than a quarter of the value of the overall market was being lost to e-book piracy.

effects for writers (via downward pressure on advances) and readers (via upward pressure on book prices), previously the biggest existential threat to writers and publishers was consolidation of book retailers – Barnes & Noble in the US, particularly – and then online retailers like Amazon creating cartels and aggressively driving down income for authors and publishers alike. Now, the threat to books has pivoted once again, and reached extinction-level proportions: AI and words generated by a non-human are the front line of the battle for the soul of books.

AI may generate coherent prose and mimic literary styles with impressive technical skill, but it will never truly match human novelists in creating works of profound resonance and authentic emotional depth. The greatest novels emerge from lived experience – the quiet desperation of unrequited love, the complex grief of loss, the nuanced joy of personal triumph – feelings an AI can only simulate rather than genuinely understand. Human writers create from an internal wellspring of contradictions, traumas and epiphanies that shape their unique perspective, drawing upon childhoods spent watching parents argue across dinner tables, lovers met and lost, or the specific quality of light through a hospital window. These experiences forge the empathy necessary to craft characters whose inconsistencies and desires feel genuinely alive rather than algorithmically optimised. A novel is not merely a sequence of well-arranged words but is the culmination of a consciousness grappling with what it means to exist – complete with the messy, irrational impulses and inexplicable motivations that make us recognisably human. Until AI experiences life's heartbreaks and wonders first-hand, rather than processing them as data points, the soul of great literature will remain distinctly, irreplaceably human.

Full disclosure: this last paragraph was written by my friendly local

AI chatbot, Claude. I requested a paragraph that summarises why AI will never be able to write novels like a human, and this was the result. It's alarmingly human-passing, and took seconds to produce. The power and potential uses of AI is inspiring, and alarming.

For most authors, the biggest current threat from AI is 'scraping' – when books are fed to generative AI models to 'train' them. In 2023 in the US, seventeen authors worked with the Authors Guild to file a lawsuit alleging that OpenAI violated copyright law when it fed books to its models. The companies behind these models countered by arguing that what they are doing is 'fair usage' – no different to someone reading a book to improve their own writing. The lawsuit alleged that chatbots can now produce 'derivative works' that mimic an author's writing – with profound implications for creative industries, stating: 'The success and profitability of OpenAI are predicated on mass copyright infringement without a word of permission from or a nickel of compensation to copyright owners.'

Currently, there is no clear consensus on who will win this battle. Experts are split as to whether the complaints of authors will be held up in court. After all, if a chatbot ingests someone else's work, but produces something substantially distinct, is that any different to me digesting a book and allowing it to influence my own writing? Humans are of course far slower than chatbots at ingesting, digesting and regurgitating words – is it just a matter of speed and scale?

For a minority of well-known authors, the danger is even more pronounced: 'AI that can reproduce content similar to what it ingested poses an existential threat to the writing profession and to the publishing industry – if it's unchecked,' says Mary Rasenberger, CEO of the Authors Guild. Rasenberger continues: 'If you start inundating the market with these AI-generated books, it's going to be that much harder for publishers to invest in authors. Particularly if you allow AI to generate books in the style of John Grisham or George R. R. Martin or Elin Hilderbrand and actually steal sales from those authors.'

Generative AI can produce huge amounts of content because it is so cheap to create – the words it uses are stolen from real live authors. Unlike these actual pen-wielders, AI has no mortgage to pay or children to feed. The idea of the 2017 lawsuit was to force tech companies to acknowledge the thousands of human hours that had gone into writing the books that were ingested by a machine. And the question of who should renumerate writers for their words is currently undecided. Should books be licensed before they are used to 'train' machines? But who would regulate that? And how would it work, when most writers are freelancers, with no group negotiating power?

Another danger for authors comes from stories entirely generated by AI, or 'assisted' in creation by it. Instead of a carefully crafted story that might take many hundreds of hours to create, readers can now request and then buy a story fed to them by a data-crunching machine – choosing to personalise these novels by asking for characters with names and features they can choose themselves.

Even traditional publishers are keeping their options open. Although the copyright pages of many books now contain disclaimers expressly forbidding use of an author's words to train large language models on, and no major publisher has publicly expressed a wish to have AI actually write books, as always with a constantly evolving landscape, the position is not clear-cut. The CEO of Penguin Random House, Nihar Malaviya, while acknowledging that a publisher's first obligation is to protect the intellectual property of its authors, states that PRH wants to use technology to publish more books, but crucially, without hiring more staff. And AI is already used extensively by most publishers to produce marketing copy, classify content with meta-data, and to fact-check and detect plagiarism.

A literary agent interviewed by *Esquire* for a 2024 article on the future of AI in publishing summarised that the biggest threat for authors (and publishers) is not necessarily that they will be entirely replaced by AI, but rather that the financial margins that they live on will be ever more squeezed by a flood of free or cheap content that shows no sign of letting up, gradually devaluing all our words. The speed that AI moves at and the lag between that and legislation to protect an author's words, along with reluctance by traditional publishers to come down firmly on one side or the other, means, said the agent, that 'I don't think authors fully understand the ramifications of generative AI. I think they are confused and upset, but they don't know what to do about those feelings.' Trithemius might have empathised. It's no wonder. Rasenberger worries that 'The books that I fear losing are the kinds that make us think and understand each other.' If a book takes a human ten years to write, but with no financial reward at the end of it, what aspiring writer would ever make the decision to embark on sharing their story? The concern is that the voices we most need to hear are precisely the ones that will be lost to us in the future.

Digital time is many orders of magnitude faster than real time. Although the traditional book might have seen off the threat of the e-book, or at least found a way to co-exist with it, the next challenge is already hurtling towards it, before we've even finished the last chapter. Now books are competing not just with digital forms of selling stories, but also with digital ways of *creating* them. In 2022 a writer called Tim Boucher set out to 'craft a series of unique, captivating ebooks merging dystopian pulp sci-fi with compelling AI world-building'. He has now published ninety-seven 'AI lore books' of between 2,000 and 5,000 words, sometimes in as little as three hours. Between August 2022 and May 2023, he sold 574 books and made roughly $2,000, explaining that the works 'all cross-reference each other, creating a web of interconnected narratives that constantly draw readers in and encourage them to explore further'. Is this Harry Stephen Keeler's 'web-work' dream become reality – the ability to create an infinite number of interconnected plots across an infinite number of stories? With this speed of production and ease to get to market, authors who spend months and years honing their prose may feel a shiver run down their traditional hardback spines at what lies ahead.

Perhaps if we had left the market to itself in the early twentieth century, instead of artificially constructing one, the book's reckoning would have come much sooner. Physical books as they existed between 1550 and 2050 may well return to their beginnings: rare, written only by the well-off, read by the elite. But there's a difference between the physical format of the book and the story within it. The promise of digitisation is that it allows disintermediation: authors – storytellers – can now go directly to their readers. Who needs a traditional publisher standing in the way when you don't need their financial backing to market and print books? If you have built your brand online, then your readers are already there, waiting for you, without a middleman to dilute your words, or your income. We're already seeing that specific genres of writing – romance and fantasy primarily – are more likely to be self-published than traditionally published.

In 2023 a murder mystery called *Death of an Author* was published. It was 95 per cent computer-generated, overseen by journalist Stephen Marche. In an article for *Slate* magazine, it was described as having a 'better than average' prose style. Marche noted that:

> if you make bad art with a new tool, you just haven't figured out how to use the tool yet . . . what you need is to have it write something about a murder scene in the style of Chinese nature poetry, then make it active, then make it conversational, then Select All and put it in the style of Ernest Hemingway.* That gets you something interesting.

Where Marche struggled with his digital assistant was in getting it to work out the machinations of plot. The machine was unable to grasp the idea that one thing could happen, which would then lead to another, and then on to a third. Instead, Marche had to work the plot out in advance and hand-feed it to the machine. This feels counter-intuitive, but of course, for a mystery plot to work, it must often rely on misdirection.† As the *Slate* article noted: 'Such deceptions require a theory of mind, the ability to anticipate what a reader is thinking and how she can be tricked. No AI can do that – at least not yet.'

As well as posing a threat to individual authors, AI brings broader concerns. Large language models, which generate the content, are rear-view mirrors of storytelling. They imitate writing produced by humans, and that imitation text – *almost* human, but not quite – is then used to train the next iteration. Gradually (yet quickly) the quality of the text degrades and becomes less and less authentically

* Interestingly, there's a Hemingway app, Hemingway Editor, which allows you to make your writing more 'concise and correct' – and like Hemingway's. Perhaps his style of writing lends itself to ChatGPT.

† There's an echo here of the G. K. Chesterton concept we encountered in Chapter 2; that authors are under an 'implied contract' to connect those things in a story that appear to have no connection. That's not something AI could understand or deliver.

human – leading to what some computer scientists call 'model collapse'. Unless new and authentic stories are used to 'refresh' LLMs, AI will very soon be reduced to churning out . . . garbage. One version of hell is to live in an age where you will never run out of free, accessible content to read – but none of it will be any good.

Stories rely on a complex and multi-dimensional creativity that springs from our shared experiences and emotions. It's why they have always been so necessary to us. They are how we understand each other and try to make sense of the world we live in. A good story can be many things, but readers have always been drawn to tales of the unexpected. The tangle in the tale, the contorted plot, the late reveal, are what makes our investment in words worthwhile. And because these desires are very human, it takes other humans to be able to fulfil them. AI lacks this human context and intuition – indeed, it is based on anticipating what word will follow another word. Who wants a predictable story?

AI is generated by statistical models of likely words and terms, which makes its output banal and predictable. While AI is already able to write 'best-sellers' (online you can find AI writing tools that 'generate book ideas, enhance character development, write grammatically correct sentences, overcome writer's block, and write books with unprecedented speed' – I wish I'd known before I embarked on this book), it will never be able to create using the 'human' ingredients that make up great literature. Surprise, passion, eccentricity, nuance, the unexpected and emotion – shock, horror, joy, misery and everything in between – all these feelings are the exclusive preserve of living, breathing writers. But as with the e-reader promoting us to think more about the value of the book, there's the possibility that novels 'written' by AI will help us appreciate this human element even more. Does writing by a flesh-and-blood human stand out in sharp relief against the standardised and cliché-heavy prose of an AI? As readers, we'd like to think so.

In an interview in 2023, literary agent Andrew Wylie posited that authors who write commercial fiction (broadly, those books that rely on plot rather than writing style to attract readers) were susceptible to AI: 'Because the books on it are written without any particular gift in the nature of their expression. Stephen King is susceptible to artificial intelligence. Danielle Steel is even more susceptible to artificial intelligence. The worse the writing, the more susceptible it is' – while, said Wylie, literary novels and their authors had less to fear, because AI was incapable of writing in the same way that literary novelists do. But of course, the advances that AI makes are so fast that we can't possibly know for sure how long these distinctions will remain in place.

The best writing is often difficult or uncomfortable and takes a reader on an unexpected journey. As author Anita Felicelli writes, 'An algorithm trained on well-known books can't find what's both moving and surprising . . . But it will figure out three-act structure, cliffhanger endings for chapters and what events will titillate readers faster to maintain reader attention.' Like a pinball machine, an AI can give us a dopamine hit of word salad that will almost immediately wear off – unlike words written by a real person that have a chance of resonating and staying with us forever.

It's not just the novel that has had its funeral rites read. The title of Stephen Marche's ChatGPT-written novel, *Death of an Author*, echoed the title of an essay by Roland Barthes written in 1967, which proclaimed the 'death of the author'. But, as the twentieth century has unfolded into the twenty-first, the 'author' is probably more important than ever. The most successful authors now are brands, names promoted online by themselves, and there and in physical space by their publishers. An author brand is an essential shortcut for readers. We want a name on the cover that we recognise, not a story written by machine, because the name gives us an assurance of what we're getting. 'Written by AI' is unlikely to appear on the front cover of books any time soon; indeed, in 2025, publisher Faber included a 'Human Written' sticker on the cover of novelist Sarah Hall's tenth book.

An author's name brings with it human connection: we might feel that a writer is important to us because we share things in common with them, or we've read an interview or intriguing backstory about them that makes us want to know more. These are some of the things that make us eagerly await an author's new book: it's not *just* about the writing, but about their story as people we can relate or aspire to. It's why we have blurbs on a book, publicity tours and interviews. We want to know the story behind the story. And digitisation of stories has created a whole new level of externalities for authors to explore. Blogs, websites, conferences and close relationships with some fans mean more ways of monetising and publicising a story than Gutenberg or Allen Lane could ever imagine. Far from being dead, the author is more alive than ever – interacting online and in person with their readers in ways that would have astonished early novelists.

During the Covid-19 pandemic we saw a surge in the curated bookcase used as a backdrop for Zoom calls. Unlike an e-reader, which tells us precisely nothing interesting about a person, these books were displayed and prized as things of beauty that we have an emotional connection to and that tell visitors (and viewers) something about us, an external manifestation of our inner lives (the X feed Bookcase Credibility – 'What you say is not as important as the bookcase behind you' – was set up to interpret the meaning of these bookshelves: 'Liam Fox's bold grab at credibility is somewhat undermined by the hardback copy of *The Da Vinci Code*' versus 'Rachel Reeves has taken no chances here. Everything is bookcase. No gap has been left where credibility might leak away. Utilising three dimensions, sending a bookcase charging at us along a wall, leaves us no sanctuary. We are overwhelmed, swamped by credibility'). At the same time, we might rely on an e-reader for convenience or listen to an audiobook for a completely new experience of a story.

The book as an object has always had its own story, and that will never change. Readers have long been fascinated by how it came to be, and what will happen to it next. We are uncertain what the future of the book looks like, which makes us fearful, but we know there will be some continuity with the past. Because of what it can do and what it means for us, the book is much more than the sum of its parts. It always has been. Perhaps we'll see a future where physical books return ever closer to the beautifully illustrated style of Gutenberg's Bibles, expanding the clear water between themselves and digital book forms.

The gift of good literature is that it creates empathy between writer and reader, and then between reader and world. That's what is missing from AI, no matter how embedded in our storytelling it becomes. The beauty of being a writer is that your words – your thoughts – can live on long after you; for as long as readers can find you. Periods of invisibility for a writer are backlit by rediscovery: by new markets, new readers, new approaches. The durability and brilliance of the book has made words rediscoverable over and over again for new and diverse audiences. And these new readers of old books breathe life into how we approach a text, in ways we may never have previously considered.

This chapter might be called 'Bad Endings', but 'stories' never end.

An individual one might reach a conclusion, but the next generation of storytellers will build on what is already there, just as today's stories weave in elements of yesterday's. We're moving towards a time when a word will never be forgotten – and hence can never be rediscovered. All stories will be stored digitally, and forever. The reading horizon will be limitless. There will be no end, bad or otherwise.

Acknowledgements

In a *Paris Review* article on Acknowledgements, Anna North writes 'at the end of a really great book, how wonderful to recognize that it was written not by a monolith or a beam of white light or the manifestation of the goddess Athena, but by a living, breathing person who remembered to thank her agent.' You'll have to decide if this is a 'really great book', and I don't have an agent, but that's no excuse for not saying thank you.

I'm incredibly grateful to my editor, Louisa Dunnigan, who asked me to write this book. She has worked with me on it from proposal to finished manuscript, and at every step of the way her enthusiasm and sharp eye have made these words far better than they were at the start. Thanks also to Zara Sehr Ashraf for getting the manuscript safely into production (and for tenacious work on the jacket quotes), along with her colleagues Emily Frisella and Georgina Difford. The delightful chapter illustrations were drawn by Steve Coventry-Panton. And thank you to the wider team at Profile Books, especially Alex Elam, for their support.

Patrick Taylor did an exemplary copy-edit and saved me from myself on several occasions. The proof reader S. J. Forder was the 'patient and trained mind' described by Charles Dickens that followed me around and elevated the text further.

I was fortunate to receive a grant from the Society of Authors when I was writing – they do a great job of supporting authors wondering how they can carve out time and space to write.

Thanks also to my Penguin Press publishing family, who are all funny, wise, entertaining and very good at what they do. In particular, I'm grateful to Richard Duguid (Richard also found time to supply the index for this book), Ruth Pietroni and Anna Tuck for the shuffleboard, pints, and all-round support.

Louise Willder was a brilliant and sage sounding-board on all sorts of issues, but especially on difficult second books. Her incisive eye and cheerleading helped keep me going when it got tough.

John Seaton was his usual enthusiastic self when it came to reading early drafts, and ever supportive. I'm always grateful for his generously shared knowledge. Thanks also to Wendy Tse Shakespeare for putting sensitivity readers in publishing into context.

Ever since *How Words Get Good* was published, my brother Jonathan Lee has been reminding me that I didn't include him in the Acknowledgements there. I'm rectifying that here, with thanks to all my family and the Saunders family.

This book is dedicated to Grant Saunders, who is the perfectionist creative to my slap-dash enthusiasm. Between us I think we've found a healthy middle way.

Selected Bibliography

Martin Amis, *The War Against Cliché: Essays and Reviews, 1971–2000* (London: Jonathan Cape, 2001)

Roland Barthes, 'The Death of the Author' [1967], in *Image – Music – Text*, trans. Stephen Heath (New York: Hill and Wang, 1977)

Alex Beam, *The Feud: Vladimir Nabokov, Edmund Wilson, and the End of a Beautiful Friendship* (New York: Pantheon, 2016)

Richard Bradford, *Literary Rivals: Feuds and Antagonisms in the World of Books* (London: Robson Press, 2016)

Richard Cohen, *How to Write Like Tolstoy* (London: Oneworld, 2016)

Oliver Darkshire, *Once Upon a Tome: The Misadventures of a Rare Bookseller* (London: Bantam, 2022)

Geri Della Rocca de Candal, Anthony Grafton and Paolo Sachet (eds.), *Printing and Misprinting: A Companion to Mistakes and In-House Corrections in Renaissance Europe (1450–1650)* (Oxford: Oxford University Press, 2023)

Martin Edwards, *The Life of Crime: Detecting the History of Mysteries and Their Creators* (London: Collins Crime Club, 2022)

Peter Finn and Petra Couvée, *The Zhivago Affair: The Kremlin, The CIA, and the Battle Over a Forbidden Book* (London: Vintage, 2015)

Alice W. Flaherty, *The Midnight Disease: The Drive to Write, Writer's Block, and the Creative Brain* (Boston and New York: Houghton Mifflin, 2004)

Anthony Grafton, *Inky Fingers: The Making of Books in Early Modern Europe* (Cambridge, MA: Harvard University Press, 2020)

Michael Heyward, *The Ern Malley Affair* (London: Faber & Faber, 1993)

Holbrook Jackson, *The Anatomy of Bibliomania* (New York: Farrar, Straus and Giroux, 1950)

Melissa Katsoulis, *Telling Tales: A History of Literary Hoaxes* (London: Constable, 2009)

Martin Latham, *The Bookseller's Tale* (London: Particular Books, 2020)

C. S. Lewis, *An Experiment in Criticism* (Cambridge: Cambridge University Press, 1961)

Jeremy Lewis, *Penguin Special: The Life and Times of Allen Lane* (London: Viking, 2005)

Jack Loudan, *O Rare Amanda!: The Life of Amanda McKittrick Ros* (London: Chatto & Windus, 1954)

Stephen Marche, *On Writing and Failure* (London: Sort of Books, 2023)

Javier Marías, *Written Lives* (London: Penguin Classics, 2016)

Mark O'Connell, *Epic Fail: Bad Art, Viral Fame, and the History of the Worst Thing Ever* (The Millions, 2013)

Susan Orlean, *The Library Book* (London: Atlantic, 2019)

George Orwell, 'Good Bad Books' (November 1945), available at orwellfoundation.com/the-orwell-foundation/orwell/essays-and-other-works/good-bad-books

J. P. Romney and Rebecca Romney, *Printer's Error: Irreverent Stories from Book History* (New York: HarperCollins, 2017)

Emma Smith, *Portable Magic: A History of Books and Their Readers* (London: Allen Lane, 2022)

Adam Smyth, *The Book-Makers: A History of the Book in 18 Remarkable Lives* (London: Bodley Head, 2024)

Graham Tarrant, *For the Love of Books: Stories of Literary Lives, Banned Books, Author Feuds, Extraordinary Characters, and More* (London: Summersdale, 2018)

Notes

Introduction

'the "loudest" dressed man in the state': Mark Twain, 'My First Literary Venture', in *Mark Twain's Sketches, New and Old* (Hartford, CT: American Publishing Company, 1875), americanliterature.com/author/mark-twain/short-story/my-first-literary-venture

In among the printers' terms for disaster: John Southward, *Dictionary of Typography and Its Accessory Arts* (London: Powell, 1875), archive.org/details/dictionaryoftypooosoutuoft

Bad Times

'may just clear the front of the lower case': A. A. Stewart, *Type Cases and Composing-Room Furniture* (Chicago: United Typothetae of America, 1918), gutenberg.org/files/31704/31704-h/31704-h.htm

"'In the short time it took him to turn those pages"': Isaac Asimov, 'Galley Slave', in *The Complete Robot* (New York: Doubleday, 1982)

'In 2014 a manuscript from the thirteenth century': https://textandcanon.org/recovering-an-erasedgospel/

'submit yourselves to your owl husbands': https://www.churchpop.com/12-hilariously-bad-misprints-bible/

Print shops were often signposted with a red devil: Seanetta Allsass, '"Printer's Devil": A Reformation-Era Fiery Figurehead Once Denoted This Location as a Print Shop', Atlas Obscura, 1 March 2021, atlasobscura.com/places/stonegate-devil

In 1543 a German printer: Anthony Grafton, 'The Correctors: Meet the Editors of Early Modern Book Publishing', *Lapham's Quarterly*, 10 June 2020, laphamsquarterly.org/roundtable/correctors

'They do everything solely for the use of money': Hieronymus Hornschuch, *Orthotypographia* [1608], ed. and trans. Philip Gaskell and Patricia Bradford (Cambridge: University Library, 1972)

actors would pass round a draft of the play: 'How Did Actors Learn Their Lines?', *Let's Talk Shakespeare* podcast (2015), shakespeare.org.uk/explore-shakespeare/podcasts/lets-talk-shakespeare/how-did-actors-learn-their-lines

Pope was one of the first: https://timespencil.org/exhibits/show/rise-of-shakespeare-ii-sum-sha/collated-and-corrected-by-the-

from the sixteenth century onwards error was celebrated: Adrienne LaFrance, 'A Corrected History of the Typo', *The Atlantic*, 26 June 2014, theatlantic.com/technology/archive/2014/06/a-corrected-history-of-the-typo/373396

the publishers of Winston Churchill's The Gathering Storm: Charles Foster, 'Winston Churchill and the Poop of France', Plenty of Taste blog, 31 December 2016, plentyoftasteblog.com/2016/12/31/winston-churchill-and-the-poop-of-france

This was a family trait: https://www.theguardian.com/books/2020/jan/27/stephen-joyce-last-direct-descendant-of-jamesjoyce-dies-aged-87

In 2010 American author Jonathan Franzen: Rowenna Davis and Alison Flood, 'Jonathan Franzen's Book *Freedom* Suffers UK

Recall', *Guardian*, 1 October 2010, theguardian.com/books/2010/oct/01/jonathan-franzen-freedom-uk-recall; 'Jonathan Franzen Book Shelved Over Printing Error', BBC News, 1 October 2010, bbc.co.uk/news/entertainment-arts-11451600

The dream of harnessing technology to eliminate error: Dave Van Everen, 'The History of OCR', Veryfi, 19 May 2023, veryfi.com/ocr-api-platform/history-of-ocr/; Martin Edmonds, 'A Brief History of Optical Character Recognition (OCR)', Pitney Bowes, 1 September 2022, pitneybowes.com/uk/blog/brief-history-of-ocr.html

Bad Taste

Margaret Atwood tells us that we need: https://www.theguardian.com/books/2010/feb/22/margaret-atwood-rules-for-writers

Kurt Vonnegut advises that: https://www.writingclasses.com/toolbox/tips-masters/kurtvonnegut-8-basics-of-creative-writing

Nineteenth-century German novelist Gustav Freytag: Sean Glatch, 'The 5 Elements of Dramatic Structure: Understanding Freytag's Pyramid', Writers.com, 31 May 2024, writers.com/freytags-pyramid

'great thoughts, strong emotions, certain figures of thought and speech': 'Longinus', in Vincent B. Leitch (ed.), *The Norton Anthology of Theory and Criticism* (New York: Norton, 2001), p. 136

'A comick incident loaths tragic strains': Horace, *Ars Poetica*, gutenberg.org/ebooks/9175

He would begin by interrogating his words: George Orwell, 'Politics and the English Language', *Horizon* (April 1946), orwellfoundation.com/the-orwell-foundation/orwell/essays-and-other-works/politics-and-the-english-language

the first 'best' books list was drawn up in 1886: 'Lubbock's List: The Original "Must-Read" List', Pioneer Library, 18 September 2019, olddeadguys.com/2019/09/18/lubbocks-list-the-original-must-read-list/; authorama.com/pleasures-of-life-7.html

'there is nothing better than the thorough analysis': Samuel McChord Crothers, 'The Hundred Worst Books', *The Atlantic*, May 1909, cdn.theatlantic.com/media/archives/1909/05/103-5/129556481.pdf

stories that have 'no plot, just vibes': Caelan McMichael, 'Who Needs Plot When You Have Vibes?', *Elle*, 18 September 2023, elle.com/culture/books/a45127506/no-plot-just-vibes-books

'Keeler is the master of the ludicrous': Georges T. Dodds, '*The White Circle* and *Y. Cheung Business Detective*: A Review', SF Site (2001), sfsite.com/12b/wc118.htm

'The perfect Keeler character': William Poundstone, 'Harry Stephen Keeler' (2007), home.williampoundstone.net/Keeler/Home.html

'every absurd complication turns out to make blissfully perfect sense': Francis M. Nevins Jr, 'The Wild and Woolly World of Harry Stephen Keeler: Part Two', *Journal of Popular Culture* 4:2 (September 1970), pp. 410–18

'In his own wacko way he worked desperately': Francis M. Nevins, 'First You Read, Then You Write', mysteryfile.com/blog/?p=65036

'We are drawn to the unescapable conclusion': https://www.nytimes.com/1942/03/08/archives/thebottle-with-the-green-wax-seal-by-harry-stephenkeeler-319-pp.html

Anthony Burgess said that: from *Homage to QWERTYUIOP: Selected Journalism 1978–1985*, Hutchinson, 1986.

From first publication in 1925 onwards: Megan Garber, 'To Its Earliest Reviewers, *Gatsby* Was Anything but Great', *The Atlantic*, 10 April 2015, theatlantic.com/entertainment/archive/2015/04/to-early-reviewers-the-great-gatsby-was-not-so-great/390252

'For it must be remembered that at the time': Daniel Riccuito, 'The Greatest Bad Writer in America: Harry Stephen Keeler', The

Chiseler, 4 December 2024, thechiseler.org/home/the-greatest-bad-writer-in-america-harry-stephen-keeler

Purple prose does nothing for a reader: Lucy Hope, 'What Is Purple Prose? Everything You Need to Know', Jericho Writers, jerichowriters.com/what-is-purple-prose

Dan Brown's most recent: https://www.theguardian.com/books/2025/sep/09/thesecret-of-secrets-by-dan-brown-review-weaponsgrade-nonsense-from-beginning-to-end

'the million and one who thirst for aught': Miles Corwin, 'Words to Remember', *Smithsonian*, June 2009, smithsonianmag.com/arts-culture/words-to-remember-133116350

reviewer Thomas Beer opined that her writing: Michael Dirda, 'What's the Worst Novel Ever? It Might Be This 19th-Century Train Wreck', *Washington Post*, 22 August 2018, washingtonpost.com/entertainment/books/whats-the-worst-novel-ever-it-might-be-a-19th-century-novel-youve-never-heard-of/2018/08/21/702d50b2-a494-11e8-a656-943eefab5daf_story.html

In a 2024 article on McKittrick Ros: Andrew Doyle, 'History's "Worst Novelist," or Artful Troll?', *Washington Post*, 10 September 2024, washingtonpost.com/opinions/2024/09/10/amanda-ros-worlds-worst-novelist

the academic journal Philosophy and Literature: 'The World's Worst Writing', *Guardian*, 25 December 1999, theguardian.com/books/1999/dec/24/news

The 2015 winner of the Bad Sex Award: Nicola Slawson, 'Morrissey Wins Bad Sex Award for Love Scenes in Debut Novel *List of the Lost*', *Guardian*, 1 December 2015, theguardian.com/books/2015/dec/01/morrissey-wins-bad-sex-award-fiction-debut-novel-list-of-the-lost

'Every character in List of the Lost': Michael Hann, 'Morrissey:

What We Learned About Him from *List of the Lost*', *Guardian*, 24 September 2015, theguardian.com/music/musicblog/2015/sep/24/morrissey-what-we-learned-about-him-from-list-of-the-lost

'more self-indulgent and tedious': Ludovic Hunter-Tilney, '"List of the Lost", by Morrissey', *Financial Times*, 2 October 2015, ft.com/content/fd2536c8-681b-11e5-a57f-21b88f7d973f

'a leaden festival of self-pity': Adam Sherwin, '*List of the Lost* by Morrissey, First Read: Debut Novel Is a Leaden Festival of Self-Pity', *Independent*, 24 September 2015, independent.co.uk/arts-entertainment/books/reviews/list-of-the-lost-by-morrissey-first-read-debut-novel-is-a-leaden-festival-of-selfpity-10515977.html

'bad sixth-form James Joyce impersonation': Ed Cumming, '*List of the Lost* by Morrissey Review – the Publishers Should Be Ashamed of Themselves', *Guardian*, 4 October 2015, theguardian.com/books/2015/oct/04/list-of-the-lost-morrissey-review-publishers-ashamed

Bad Takes

'a baby playing with a pair of shears': Richard Whiteing, 'Bowdler Bowdlerised', *The English Review* (August 1916), pp. 100–11

An Index on Censorship poll in 2024: Katie Dancey-Downs, 'Banned: School Librarians Shushed Over LGBT+ Books', Index on Censorship, 19 August 2024, indexoncensorship.org/2024/08/banned-school-librarians-shushed-over-lgbt-books

this trend mirrors the US: Nadra Nittle, 'Book Bans in Schools Jumped 33 Percent Last Year', The 19th News, 6 October 2023, 19thnews.org/2023/10/book-bans-in-schools-up-33-percent-2023

in the United States in 2022: 'American Library Association Reports Record Number of Demands to Censor Library Books and

Materials in 2022', American Library Association, 22 March 2023, ala.org/news/press-releases/2023/03/record-book-bans-2022

Uncle Tom's Cabin *escaped*: 'Vatican Censors' Secrets Soon Only a Click Away', *Business Recorder*, 30 September 2004, brecorder.com/news/3086364

The Index never listed Marx, Freud or Darwin: Tom Heneghan, 'Secrets Behind the Forbidden Books', *America*, 7 February 2005, americamagazine.org/issue/517/article/secrets-behind-forbidden-books

A Boston professor called in defence of the book: Stephen E. Cotton and Sanford J. Ungar, '"Fanny Hill" Given Her Day in Court', *Harvard Crimson*, 29 May 1964, thecrimson.com/article/1964/5/29/fanny-hill-given-her-day-in

In 2017 the Mail on Sunday: Dr Judith Hawley, 'I Didn't "Ban" *Fanny Hill* Because of Trigger Warnings – I Don't Teach It at All', *Guardian*, 15 August 2017, theguardian.com/books/2017/aug/15/fanny-hill-ban-university-trigger-warnings-judith-hawley

was not shared by Jeanette Winterson: Hephzibah Anderson, '*The Well of Loneliness*: The Book That Could Corrupt a Nation', BBC Culture, 22 November 2022, bbc.co.uk/culture/article/20221121-the-well-of-loneliness-the-most-corrosive-book-ever

with Lawrence writing to his literary agent: Mollie Panter-Downes, 'The Lady at the Old Bailey', *New Yorker*, 11 November 1960, newyorker.com/magazine/1960/11/19/the-lady-at-the-old-bailey

Madame Bovary *was legally available to buy in the UK*: 'Cover Your Eyes! Five Bestselling Books the Censors Didn't Want You to Read', BBC Radio 4, bbc.co.uk/programmes/articles/5r4mF3kPcNYm37dSxCtw8Pq/cover-your-eyes-five-bestselling-books-the-censors-didnt-want-you-to-read

One of the authors they approached was Enid Blyton: Moira C. Robinson, 'Popular Fiction and Publishing, 1960s–1990s', Master's thesis, University of Birmingham (September 2001), core.ac.uk/download/200371184.pdf, p. 141

the defence of Lady Chatterley *was successful*: Emily Temple, 'Why Exactly Is This Book Obscene? (Skip to the Dirty Bits)', Literary Hub, 22 November 2017, lithub.com/why-exactly-is-this-book-obscene-skip-to-the-dirty-bits

the British government intervened to prevent the sale: 'University of Bristol Acquires "Significantly Important" Copy of *Lady Chatterley's Lover*', University of Bristol, 20 September 2019, bristol.ac.uk/news/2019/september/lady-chatterley-.html; Hannah Lowery, 'Sixty Years Since Lady C – The "Lady Chatterley's Lover" Trial and the Penguin Book Archive', Special Collections blog, University of Bristol Library, 30 October 2020

In an article to commemorate the fiftieth anniversary: Geoffrey Robertson QC, 'The Trial of *Lady Chatterley's Lover*', *Guardian*, 22 October 2010, theguardian.com/books/2010/oct/22/dh-lawrence-lady-chatterley-trial

'My moral defense of the book is the book itself': Maria Popova, 'A Lolitigation Lament: Nabokov on Censorship and Solidarity', The Marginalian, 24 September 2014, themarginalian.org/2014/09/24/lolitigation-nabokov-censorship

Much of the outrage of the citizens of Boston: Wayne A. Wiegand, 'Part of Our Lives: A People's History of the American Public Library', Literary Hub, 9 October 2015, lithub.com/part-of-our-lives-a-peoples-history-of-the-american-public-library

A 1952 article in the Harvard Crimson: Ronald P. Kriss, 'Widener "Inferno" Guards Choice Collection of Erotica, Miscellany', *Harvard Crimson*, 25 April 1952, thecrimson.com/article/1952/4/25/widener-inferno-guards-choice-collection-of

who described himself as a 'prize prude': https://www.theguardian.com/books/2008/feb/24/features.review

The poet Anna Akhmatova: https://lithub.com/writing-poetry-under-stalin-samizdat-and-memorization

The state (via the Orthodox Church) retained control: Noah R. Zerbe, 'History of Censorship in Russia', EBSCO (2022), ebsco.com/research-starters/politics-and-government/history-censorship-russia

The New York Times *wrote*: Lewis Nichols, 'In and Out of Books', *The New York Times*, November 2, 1958.

Khruschev, who once described: https://www.standard.co.uk/comment/comment/sovietspite-for-dr-zhivago-repeated-by-today-s-tyrantsa4288081.htmld

there were 5,000 censors at work: 'Glavlit & State Censorship', Poster Plakat, posterplakat.com/soviet-poster-history/glavlit-state-censorship

the case of David Irving versus Penguin Books and Deborah Lipstadt: Sanchia Berg, 'The True Story Behind Denying the Holocaust', BBC News, 28 January 2017, bbc.co.uk/news/entertainment-arts-38758249

a case brought by Mineko Iwasaki: Calvin Sims, 'Arts Abroad; A Geisha, a Successful Novel and a Lawsuit', *The New York Times*, 19 June 2001, nytimes.com/2001/06/19/books/arts-abroad-a-geisha-a-successful-novel-and-a-lawsuit.html

In 2015 the Supreme Court in Britain: Ian Cobain and Robert Booth, 'Pianist James Rhodes Wins Right to Publish Autobiography Telling of Abuse', *Guardian*, 20 May 2015, theguardian.com/music/2015/may/20/concert-pianist-james-rhodes-wins-right-to-publish-autobiography

In 2020 a novel called American Dirt: Constance Grady, 'The Controversy Over the New Immigration Novel *American Dirt*, Explained', *Vox*, 30 January 2020, vox.com/culture/2020/1/22/21075629/american-dirt-controversy-explained-jeanine-cummins-oprah-flatiron

American Dirt *was attacked for its inauthenticity*: André Wheeler, '*American Dirt*: Why Critics Are Calling Oprah's Book Club Pick Exploitative and Divisive', *Guardian*, 22 January 2020, theguardian.com/books/2020/jan/21/american-dirt-controversy-trauma-jeanine-cummins

In 2015 American poet Michael Derrick Hudson: Jane Hu, 'The "Yi-Fen Chou" Poetry Scandal Goes Beyond "Yellowface"', *Guardian*, 19 September 2015, theguardian.com/books/2015/sep/19/literary-history-yellowface-michael-derrick-hudson-ezra-pound; 'Michael Derrick Hudson's Problematic Turn as Yi-Fen Chou', Poetry Foundation, 8 September 2015, poetryfoundation.org/poetry-news/73498/michael-derrick-hudsons-problematic-turn-as-yi-fen-chou

Sherman Alexie, who selected the poem: 'Sherman Alexie Speaks Out on the *Best American Poetry* 2015', *Best American Poetry* blog, 7 September 2015, blog.bestamericanpoetry.com/the_best_american_poetry/2015/09/like-most-every-poet-i-have-viewed-the-publication-of-each-years-best-american-poetry-with-happiness-i-love-that-poem-je-1.html

increased focus on the sensitivity reader: Lucy Knight, 'Sensitivity Readers: What Publishing's Most Polarising Role Is Really About', *Guardian*, 15 March 2023, theguardian.com/books/2023/mar/15/sensitivity-readers-what-publishings-most-polarising-role-is-really-about; Zoe Dubno, 'The Rise of the "Sensitivity Reader"', *Spectator*, 10 July 2021, spectator.co.uk/article/the-rise-of-the-sensitivity-reader

her memoir had been 'sullied to suit their agenda': Kate Clanchy, 'How Sensitivity Readers Corrupt Literature: They Sullied My Memoir to Suit Their Agenda', UnHerd, 18 February 2022, unherd.com/2022/02/how-sensitivity-readers-corrupted-literature

Eventually Clanchy and her publisher agreed to part ways: Lucy Knight, 'Kate Clanchy "Parts Company" With Publisher After Discrimination Row', *Guardian*, 20 January 2022, theguardian.com/books/2022/jan/20/kate-clanchy-parts-company-from-publisher-after-discrimination-row; Alison Flood, 'Kate Clanchy's Controversial Memoir Reissued by Independent Publisher', *Guardian*, 1 February 2022, theguardian.com/books/2022/feb/01/kate-clanchy-independent-publisher-some-kids-i-taught

In a Guardian *article*: Gaby Hinsliff, 'The Book That Tore Publishing Apart: "Harm Has Been Done, and Now Everyone's Afraid"', *Guardian*, 18 June 2022, theguardian.com/books/2022/jun/18/the-book-that-tore-publishing-apart-harm-has-been-done-and-now-everyones-afraid

For example, conservatives in the US: https://www.theguardian.com/books/2023/apr/24/calls-toban-books-hit-highest-level-recorded-in-the-uscensorship

After reportedly paying him a $255,000 advance: Martin Belam, '"Unclear, Unfunny, Delete": Editor's Notes on Milo Yiannopoulos Book Revealed', *Guardian*, 28 December 2017, theguardian.com/books/2017/dec/28/unclear-unfunny-delete-editors-notes-on-milo-yiannopoulos-book-revealed

Hachette reversed its decision: Edward Helmore, 'Hachette Workers Stage Walkout to Protest Publication of Woody Allen Memoir', *Guardian*, 6 March 2020, theguardian.com/books/2020/mar/05/hachette-woody-allen-memoir-protest-ronan-farrow; Jennifer Schuessler and John Williams, '"Imagine This Were Your Sister," Ronan Farrow Tells Woody Allen's Publisher', *The New York Times*, 3 March 2020, nytimes.com/2020/03/03/books/woody-allen-ronan-farrow.html

In 2023, the most frequently challenged titles: 'Top 10 and Frequently

Challenged Books Archive', American Library Association, ala.org/bbooks/frequentlychallengedbooks/top10/archive

In 2024 a Chinese municipal official was expelled: Helen Davidson and Chi-hui Lin, 'China Cracks Down on Communist Party Officials for Reading Banned Books', *Guardian*, 13 October 2024, theguardian.com/world/2024/oct/12/china-communist-party-banned-books-rules-xi-jinping

School texts there must be 'age appropriate': Mike Trautmann, 'Iowa's Book Ban Battle: How Public Schools Removed Thousands of Books Over a New Law', *Des Moines Register*, 13 June 2024, desmoinesregister.com/story/news/education/2024/06/13/iowa-book-ban-battle-the-story-behind-sweeping-ban-george-orwell-margaret-atwood-john-green/74071601007

Iowa's books were assessed by ChatGPT: Arwa Mahdawi, 'Can't Decide Which Books to Ban? Leave It to ChatGPT!', *Guardian*, 22 August 2023, theguardian.com/commentisfree/2023/aug/22/cant-decide-which-books-to-ban-leave-it-to-chatgpt

Bad Apples

the Roman poet Martial used plaga: Andrei Tapalaga, 'The First Plagiarism Case in History', Medium, 1 March 2022, andrei-tapalaga.medium.com/the-first-plagiarism-case-in-history-af476f83ae82

Martial wrote a number of epigrams: topostext.org/work/677

'The Chair she sat in, like a burnished throne': Patrick Gillespie, 'The Writing and Art of Iambic Pentameter – II', PoemShape, 7 May 2013, poemshape.wordpress.com/tag/plutarch

Carson McCullers once complained: https://www.theatlantic.com/magazine/archive/2001/04/no-apologies-necessary/302176/

In 2022 the Australian author John Hughes: Anna Verney, 'Parts of John Hughes' Novel *The Dogs* Copied from *The Great Gatsby* and *Anna Karenina*', *Guardian*, 15 June 2022, theguardian.com/australia-news/2022/jun/15/parts-of-john-hughess-novel-the-dogs-copied-from-the-great-gatsby-and-anna-karenina

Hughes apologised, explaining that: John Hughes, 'I Am Not a Plagiarist – and Here's Why', *Guardian*, 16 June 2022, theguardian.com/books/2022/jun/16/john-hughes-i-am-not-a-plagiarist-and-heres-why; Kelly Burke, 'Literary Experts Find John Hughes' Plagiarism Defence Unconvincing', *Guardian*, 18 June 2022, theguardian.com/books/2022/jun/18/literary-experts-find-john-hughes-plagiarism-defence-unconvincing

In 2017, the Carnegie Library of Pittsburgh: Travis McDade, 'The Inside Story of the $8 Million Heist from the Carnegie Library', *Smithsonian*, September 2020, smithsonianmag.com/arts-culture/theft-carnegie-library-books-maps-artworks-180975506/

In Naples, the sixteenth-century Girolamini library: Alan Johnston, 'Naples' Girolamini: The Looting of a 16th Century Library', BBC News, 19 December 2013, bbc.co.uk/news/magazine-25403595

240 rare books were stolen from a warehouse: Marc Wortman, 'Cracking the Case of London's Elusive, Acrobatic Rare-Book Thieves', *Vanity Fair*, 25 March 2021, vanityfair.com/style/2021/03/the-case-of-the-purloined-books

A couple of Guardian *investigations*: Alison Flood and Sian Cain, 'Beatrix Potter-Pinching and Žižekian Swipes: The Strange World of Book Thefts', *Guardian*, 24 July 2017, theguardian.com/books/2017/jul/24/strange-world-of-book-thefts-beatrix-potter-zizek; Danuta Kean, 'Stolen Good Books: Why Canadian Thieves Outclass the British', *Guardian*, 9 January 2017, theguardian.com/books/booksblog/2017/jan/09/stolen-books-canadian-thieves-outclass-british-murakami

How to Shoplift Books *by artist David Horvitz*: editiontaube.de/artists-books/how-to-shoplift-books-5

As Horvitz notes: curamagazine.com/product/david-horvitz

a strange series of events: Reeves Wiedeman, 'The Talented Mr Bernardini: A Young Italian Is Accused of Pulling Off the Book World's Most Perplexing Crime. Who Is He?', *Vulture*, 17 August 2021, vulture.com/2022/02/filippo-bernardini-publishing-manuscripts-books-scam.html; Jonathan Bailey, 'Trying to Understand the Motives of "The Spine Collector"', Plagiarism Today, 15 March 2022, plagiarismtoday.com/2022/03/15/trying-to-understand-the-motives-of-the-spine-collector

Author Peter Baker wrote of his experience: Peter C. Baker, 'How It Felt to Have My Novel Stolen', *New Yorker*, 14 March 2022, newyorker.com/books/page-turner/how-it-felt-to-have-my-novel-stolen

the target of repeated attempts: 'Margaret Atwood Says Thieves Targeted *Handmaid's Tale* Sequel', BBC, 9 September 2019, bbc.com/news/entertainment-arts-49635236

His responses became personal, and unpleasant: Reeves Wiedeman and Lila Shapiro, 'The Spine Collector: For Years, a Mysterious Figure Has Been Stealing Books Before Their Release. Is It Espionage? Revenge? Or a Complete Waste of Time?', *Vulture*, 24 March 2023, vulture.com/2023/03/stealing-books-before-release-mystery.html

Court papers report Bernardini: Sarah Shaffi, 'Book Thief Who Stole More Than 1,000 Manuscripts "Wanted to Cherish Them Before Anyone Else"', *Guardian*, 13 March 2023, theguardian.com/books/2023/mar/13/book-manuscripts-thief-margaret-atwood-sally-rooney-ian-mcewan

'I wanted to keep them closely to my chest': Elizabeth A. Harris, 'No Prison Time for Book Thief', *The New York Times*,

25 March 2023, nytimes.com/2023/03/23/books/filippo-bernardini-unpublished-manuscripts-deported.html

'I had a burning desire': Dan Sheehan, 'Turn the Italian Manuscript Thief Loose', Literary Hub, 13 March 2023, lithub.com/turn-the-italian-manuscript-thief-loose

Marie Kondo, doyenne of tidying: Aaron Hicklin, 'Interview: Don't Mess With Marie: Tidying Up With Author and Netflix Star Marie Kondo', *Guardian*, 30 December 2018, theguardian.com/global/2018/dec/30/dont-mess-with-marie-tidying-up-with-author-netflix-star-marie-kondo

the comedian Barry Humphries: Peter Coleman, 'Barry Humphries Obituary', *Guardian*, 22 April 2023, theguardian.com/stage/2023/apr/22/barry-humphries-obituary

In 2025 Puffin Books: Sarah Manavis, 'Meet-cute at Mansfield Park: Can Modern Covers Turn Young Readers on to Jane Austen?', *Guardian*, 6 February 2025, theguardian.com/books/2025/feb/06/modern-covers-young-readers-jane-austen-booktok-puffin

The first use of the word came in 1802: Mark Purcell, 'The Book Disease', *Lapham's Quarterly*, 3 September 2019, laphamsquarterly.org/roundtable/book-disease

as explained by journalist Louis Menand: Louis Menand, 'Literary Hoaxes and the Ethics of Authorship', *New Yorker*, 3 December 2018, newyorker.com/magazine/2018/12/10/literary-hoaxes-and-the-ethics-of-authorship

American author James Frey: Edward Wyatt, 'Several Million Little Dollars', *The New York Times*, 12 March 2006, nytimes.com/2006/03/12/books/several-million-little-dollars.html

One fake book about the Holocaust: Alison Flood, 'Author of Fake Holocaust Memoir Ordered to Return $22.5m to Publisher', *Guardian*, 12 May 2014, theguardian.com/books/2014/may/12/author-fake-holocaust-memoir-to-return-22m; Blake Eskin, 'Crying

Wolf: Why Did It Take So Long for a Far-Fetched Holocaust Memoir to Be Debunked?', *Slate*, 29 February 2008, slate.com/culture/2008/02/why-did-it-take-so-long-for-a-far-fetched-holocaust-memoir-to-be-debunked.html

one of the most high-profile literary scandals: Lucy Knight, 'Inside the Salt Path Controversy: "Scandal Has Stalked Memoir Since the Genre Was Invented"', *Guardian*, 10 July 2025, theguardian.com/books/2025/jul/10/inside-the-salt-path-controversy-scandal-has-stalked-memoir-since-the-genre-was-invented

Bad Blood

he aimed to write 250 words every quarter of an hour: James Clear, 'The 15-Minute Routine Anthony Trollope Used to Write 40+ Books', jamesclear.com/anthony-trollope

Charles Dickens wrote roughly 2,000 words a day: Robert McCrum, 'The Best of Times to Write', *Guardian*, 27 October 2011, theguardian.com/books/booksblog/2011/oct/27/best-times-to-write

Hugo's wife described how he wrote: Marianna Hunt, 'Party Tricks and Naked Writing: The Eccentric Life of Victor Hugo', *Guardian*, 30 December 2018, theguardian.com/books/booksblog/2018/dec/30/party-tricks-and-naked-writing-the-eccentric-life-of-victor-hugo

American short story writer John Cheever: Caitlin Shetterly, 'Coffee, Booze, Undressing, Deprivation: How Writers Get in the Mood to Write', Literary Hub, 24 June 2024, lithub.com/coffee-booze-undressing-deprivation-how-writers-get-in-the-mood-to-write

D. H. Lawrence climbed mulberry trees naked: Diane Ackerman, 'O Muse! You Do Make Things Difficult!', *The New York Times*, 12 November 1989, archive.nytimes.com/www.nytimes.com/books/97/03/02/reviews/ackerman-poets.html

undisputed Queen of Romance Barbara Cartland: Jessie Gaynor, 'Here Are Some Good Facts About Barbara Cartland, Who Wrote 723 Novels', Literary Hub, 9 July 2019, lithub.com/here-are-some-good-facts-about-barbara-cartland-who-wrote-723-novels

Samuel Taylor Coleridge felt 'an indefinite indescribable Terror': 'Blocked', *New Yorker*, 6 June 2004, newyorker.com/magazine/2004/06/14/blocked

Patchett tried to overcome writerly procrastination: 'Ann Patchett on Grabbing Galleys and Getting Drafts Done', Literary Hub, 1 August 2023, lithub.com/ann-patchett-on-grabbing-galleys-and-getting-drafts-done

Bergler was dedicated to understanding: Maria Konnikova, 'How to Beat Writer's Block', *New Yorker*, 11 March 2016, newyorker.com/science/maria-konnikova/how-to-beat-writers-block

After the commercial and critical success of To Kill a Mockingbird: Casey Cep, 'The Real Story Behind Harper Lee's Lost True Crime Book', *Guardian*, 4 May 2019, theguardian.com/books/2019/may/04/and-the-missing-briefcase-the-real-story-behind-harper-lees-lost-true-book

his writer's block lasted for forty years: Jessica Winter, '"It's All in My Head": Did Truman Capote and Ralph Ellison Have Writer's Block – Or Were They Just Chronic Procrastinators?', *Slate*, 14 May 2008, slate.com/human-interest/2008/05/ralph-ellison-truman-capote-and-the-difference-between-writer-s-block-and-procrastination.html

More recently, George R. R. Martin: Michelle Dean, 'George RR Martin: When Writers Just Can't Finish Their Books', *Guardian*, 5 January 2016, theguardian.com/books/2016/jan/05/george-rr-martin-when-writers-cant-finish-books; Adrienne Westenfeld, 'When Are We Getting *The Winds of Winter*?', *Esquire*, 19 August

2024, esquire.com/entertainment/books/a39875481/george-rr-martin-winds-of-winter-finishing-update

In 1966 Truman Capote signed a contract: Alice Vincent, '*Answered Prayers*: The Mysterious Manuscript That Devastated Truman Capote', Penguin blog, 25 January 2021, penguin.co.uk/discover/articles/answered-prayers-the-mystery-manuscript-that-devastated-truman; Julie Miller, 'The Enduring Mystery of Truman Capote's *Answered Prayers*', *Vanity Fair*, 13 March 2024, vanityfair.com/hollywood/truman-capote-answered-prayers-book

'The simplest way to overcome this': 'On Writer's Block: Advice from Twelve Writers', *Paris Review*, 19 March 2018, theparisreview.org/blog/2018/03/19/advice-from-12-famous-authors-on-writers-block

'If she's feeling stuck on something': Erin McCarthy, 'How 5 Famous Authors Dealt With Writer's Block', *Mental Floss*, 25 January 2022, mentalfloss.com/article/654682/how-famous-authors-overcome-writers-block

'I thought I'd dried up completely': 'T. S. Eliot, The Art of Poetry No. 1', Interview by Donald Hall, *The Paris Review* 21, Spring–Summer 1959, theparisreview.org/interviews/4738/the-art-of-poetry-no-1-t-s-eliot

Marcel Proust was not a writer to back down: Emily Temple, '"Perhaps We're Being Dense." Rejection Letters Sent to Famous Writers', Literary Hub, 19 June 2019, lithub.com/perhaps-were-being-dense-rejection-letters-sent-to-famous-writers

T. S. Eliot, whose day job was as a director at Faber & Faber: Toby Faber, 'A Legendary Publishing House's Most Infamous Rejection Letters', Literary Hub, 12 September 2019, lithub.com/a-legendary-publishing-houses-most-infamous-rejection-letters/

John Kennedy Toole took his own life in 1969: Tom Bissell, 'The Uneasy Afterlife of "A Confederacy of Dunces"', *New Yorker*,

5 January 2021, newyorker.com/books/second-read/the-uneasy-afterlife-of-a-confederacy-of-dunces

A ninth-century leader in Byzantium: 'The First Book Reviewer', Medievalists.net, 11 January 2024, medievalists.net/2024/01/first-book-reviewer

We don't need to imagine how Marcel Proust felt: Sean Charles Hall, 'Blasé in the Face of Death', Dandyism.net, 12 February 2012, dandyism.net/2024/04/15/dueling-dandies

the novelist and critic Elizabeth Hardwick explained: Sarah Fay, 'Book Reviews: A Tortured History', *The Atlantic*, 25 April 2012, theatlantic.com/entertainment/archive/2012/04/book-reviews-a-tortured-history/256301

John Updike was a public (and prolific) reviewer: Mary Hawthorne, 'Remembering Updike: The Gospel According to John', *New Yorker*, 27 January 2009, newyorker.com/books/page-turner/remembering-updike-the-gospel-according-to-john

'I was hired as an assassin': Patricia Lockwood, 'Malfunctioning Sex Robot', *London Review of Books*, 10 October 2019, lrb.co.uk/the-paper/v41/n19/patricia-lockwood/malfunctioning-sex-robot

In 2024 author Cait Corrain: Ella Creamer and Lucy Knight, 'Publisher Drops Author for Using Fake Accounts to "Review-Bomb" Peers', *Guardian*, 13 December 2023, theguardian.com/books/2023/dec/13/cait-corrain-publisher-drops-author-fake-accounts-review-bomb; David Smith, '"It's Totally Unhinged": Is the Book World Turning Against Goodreads?', *Guardian*, 18 December 2023, theguardian.com/books/2023/dec/18/goodreads-review-bombing

Look at Ernest Hemingway and F. Scott Fitzgerald: Maria Popova, 'Hemingway's Tough-Love Letter of Advice to F. Scott Fitzgerald on Writing and Turning Suffering into Creative Fuel', The

Marginalian, 21 July 2016, themarginalian.org/2016/07/21/hemingway-f-scott-fitzgerald-letter-advice

the first recorded instance of a scatological insult: Tao Tao Holmes, 'Flyting Was Medieval England's Version of an Insult-Trading Rap Battle', Atlas Obscura, 14 January 2016, atlasobscura.com/articles/flyting-was-medieval-england-s-version-of-an-insult-trading-rap-battle

the Twitter spat was one thing: 'Camilla Long on *Aftermath* by Rachel Cusk', The Omnivore (2014), theomnivore.com/camilla-long-on-aftermath-by-rachel-cusk/; Alison Flood, 'Hatchet Job of the Year Goes to Assault on Rachel Cusk', *Guardian*, 12 February 2013, theguardian.com/books/2013/feb/12/hatchet-job-of-the-year-rachel-cusk

some writers, like Zadie Smith: Alison Flood, 'Zadie Smith Says Using Social Media Would Threaten Her Writing', *Guardian*, 21 September 2017, theguardian.com/books/2017/sep/21/zadie-smith-says-using-social-media-would-threaten-her-writing

Bad Endings

In 2021 a Bulgarian wine producer: 'Gutenberg GTO Turns Out the Wine', Print Business, 1 April 2021, printbusiness.co.uk/gutenberg-gto-turns-out-the-wine

The price of books dropped more than 60 per cent: Rachel Adler, 'The 19th Century Moral Panic Over . . . Paper Technology', *Slate*, 4 August 2017, slate.com/technology/2017/08/the-19th-century-moral-panic-over-paper-technology.html

in 2018 a bound manuscript of Donne's poems: Alison Flood, 'Unknown John Donne Manuscript Discovered in Suffolk', *Guardian*, 30 November 2018, theguardian.com/books/2018/nov/30/unknown-john-donne-manuscript-discovered-in-suffolk

Blake worked on what he called his 'illuminated printing': Victoria, 'William Blake's Illuminated Songs: Something between a Thing and a Thought', Medium, 24 May 2015, medium.com/art-stories/william-blake-s-illuminated-songs-something-between-a-thing-and-a-thought

the Doves Press, which he had co-founded in 1900: 'The Doves Type, Revisited: Robert Green Upgrades an Iconic Typeface', typeroom, 28 November 2022, typeroom.eu/the-doves-type-revisited-robert-green-upgrades-an-iconic-typeface

In Britain in the second half of the nineteenth century: Matthew Ingleby, 'Charles Dickens and the Push for Literacy in Victorian Britain', Queen Mary University of London, 10 June 2020, qmul.ac.uk/media/news/2020/hss/charles-dickens-and-the-push-for-literacy-in-victorian-britain.html

an unexpected by-product of the First World War: Alex Johnson, 'The Book List: The Literature That Gave Soldiers Solace in the Trenches', *Independent*, 1 May 2018, independent.co.uk/arts-entertainment/books/features/first-world-war-soldiers-book-list-read-trenches-first-world-war-a8330731.html

'Today accumulating printed books and shelving them': Ted Striphas, *The Late Age of Print: Everyday Book Culture from Consumerism to Control* (New York: Columbia University Press, 2009), p. 27, klangable.com/uploads/books/Striphas_complete.pdf

In 1933 William Lyon Phelps delivered a speech: 'William Lyon Phelps: The Pleasure of Books', The History Place – Great Speeches Collection, historyplace.com/speeches/phelps.htm

a PR man called Edward Bernays: Iris Mostegel, 'Edward Bernays: The Original Influencer', *History Today*, 6 February 2019, historytoday.com/miscellanies/original-influencer

Bernays decided to come up with a 'lethal epithet': Mike Selby, 'Booknotes: The Old Guard Versus the Upstarts', *Cranbrook Daily*

Townsman, 6 March 2015, cranbrooktownsman.com/opinion/booknotes-the-old-guard-versus-the-upstarts-5307363

he was busy setting up the Book Publishers Research Institute: Phil Kirby, 'The Strange History of the Bookshelf and a New Meaning of a Familiar Phrase', The Culture Vulture, 14 January 2012, theculturevulture.co.uk/conversations/speakerscorner/the-strange-history-of-the-bookshelf-and-a-new-meaning-of-a-familiar-phrase

Four days after the launch: Stuart Kells, 'The Penguin Books Story Laid Bare (Even the Naked Board Meetings)', *Guardian*, 27 October 2015, theguardian.com/books/2015/oct/27/the-story-of-penguin-books-laid-bare-naked-board-meetings-and-all

Millions of books were distributed by the US military: Yoni Appelbaum, 'Publishers Gave Away 122,951,031 Books During World War II', *The Atlantic*, 10 September 2014, theatlantic.com/business/archive/2014/09/publishers-gave-away-122951031-books-during-world-war-ii/379893

between 1943 and 1947 more than 122 million books: Natalie Russell, 'Fighting a War With Books', Huntington Verso blog, 22 May 2019, huntington.org/verso/fighting-war-books

Spanish patent number 190,698: Cindy Shmerler, 'Overlooked No More: Ángela Ruiz Robles, Inventor of an Early E-Reader', *The New York Times*, 11 November 2023, nytimes.com/2023/11/10/obituaries/angela-ruiz-robles-overlooked.html

'[e-readers] have become mainstream': Sarah Marsh and Georgina Prodhan, 'E-readers Face Tough Competition', Reuters, 20 October 2008, reuters.com/article/technology/e-readers-face-tough-competition-idUSTRE49I12H

in 2009 the Guardian *noted*: Katie Allen, 'E-readers Turn Heavy Textbooks into a Light Read – Just Like Dan Brown's Latest', *Guardian*, 10 September 2009, theguardian.com/business/2009/sep/10/sony-readers-boost-ebook-market

It's a real and growing threat: https://www.theguardian.com/commentisfree/2018/aug/25/skim-reading-new-normal-maryanne-wolf

Will Self describes how: Will Self, 'The Death of the Shelf', *Prospect*, 21 May 2014, prospectmagazine.co.uk/essays/46354/the-death-of-the-shelf

typographic innovations like thinner paper: Christine Ro, 'Publishers Try Skinnier Books to Save Money and Emissions', BBC, 17 September 2024, bbc.com/news/articles/c24pqrvvll9o

In the US in 2021: Kate Whiting, 'Book Sales Are Up: This Is What We've Been Reading During the Pandemic', World Economic Forum, 26 May 2021, weforum.org/stories/2021/05/covid-19-book-sales-reading

213 million of them being purchased in 2021: 'UK Pandemic Reading Trends Revealed at the London Book Fair', London Book Fair, 6 April 2022, hub.londonbookfair.co.uk/uk-pandemic-reading-trends-revealed-at-the-london-book-fair

sold three times as many print books as e-books: 'Does Amazon Sell More Print Books or eBooks?', Just Kindle Books, 19 February 2024, justkindlebooks.com/article_jkb/does-amazon-sell-more-print-books-or-ebooks

Kindles and other e-readers are more popular with older readers: Brandie Weikle, 'E-readers Were Supposed to Kill Printed Books. Instead, They're Booming', CBC Radio, 17 December 2023, cbc.ca/radio/costofliving/print-books-thrive-despite-e-readers-1.7056731

digital fatigue and the visual culture of platforms like TikTok: Chloe Mac Donnell, '"Reading Is So Sexy": Gen Z Turns to Physical Books and Libraries', *Guardian*, 9 February 2024, theguardian.com/books/2024/feb/09/reading-is-so-sexy-gen-z-turns-to-physical-books-and-libraries

record highs in the UK and US: 'UK Publishing Reached a

New High in 2021', Publishers Association, 21 April 2022, publishers.org.uk/uk-publishing-reached-a-new-high-in-2021; 'AAP StatShot Annual Report for 2021', Association of American Publishers, 16 September 2022, publishers.org/news/aap-statshot-annual-report-for-2021-book-publishing-revenues-up-12-3-for-the-year-reaching-all-time-high-of-29-33-billion

In 2016, there were 867 independent bookshops: Zoe Wood, 'Indie Bookshop Numbers Hit 10-Year High in 2022 Defying Brutal UK Retail Year', *Guardian*, 6 January 2023, theguardian.com/books/2023/jan/06/indie-bookshop-numbers-hit-10-year-high-in-2022-defying-brutal-uk-retail-year

there were 200,000 books published annually in the UK: Richard Godwin, '"More Are Published Than Could Ever Succeed": Are There Too Many Books?', *Guardian*, 21 March 2025, theguardian.com/books/2025/mar/21/more-are-published-than-could-ever-succeed-are-there-too-many-books

A 2021 New York Times *article*: Alexandra Alter and Elizabeth A. Harris, 'What Snoop Dogg's Success Says About the Book Industry', *The New York Times*, 18 April 2021, nytimes.com/2021/04/18/books/book-sales-publishing-pandemic-coronavirus.html

journalist Elle Griffin, who read through The Trial: Elle Griffin, 'No One Buys Books', *The Elysian*, 22 April 2024, elysian.press/p/no-one-buys-books

authors had seen a 60 per cent drop: Martin Reed, 'A Profession Struggling to Sustain Itself', Society of Authors, 6 December 2022, societyofauthors.org/2022/12/06/a-profession-struggling-to-sustain-itself

In 2004 in the US the publishing industry: Jeff Alworth, 'The Death of Books', 26 April 2024, Beervana blog, beervanablog.com/beervana/2024/4/24/the-death-of-the-book-as-information-source

That reward can also be affected by digital piracy: Adam Rowe, 'U.S. Publishers Are Still Losing $300 Million Annually to Ebook Piracy', *Forbes*, 28 July 2019, forbes.com/sites/adamrowe1/2019/07/28/us-publishers-are-still-losing-300-million-annually-to-ebook-piracy; Porter Anderson, 'Piracy in Italy: Study Shows Book Industry Losing €705 Million Annually', Publishing Perspectives, 8 March 2024, publishingperspectives.com/2024/03/piracy-in-italy-study-shows-book-industry-losing-e705-million-annually

In 2023 in the US, seventeen authors: Alexandra Alter and Elizabeth A. Harris, 'Franzen, Grisham and Other Prominent Authors Sue OpenAI', *The New York Times*, 20 September 2023, nytimes.com/2023/09/20/books/authors-openai-lawsuit-chatgpt-copyright.html

'AI that can reproduce content similar to what it ingested': Rebecca Ackermann, 'Is AI the Bitter End – or the Lucrative Future – of Book Publishing?', *Esquire*, 9 July 2024, esquire.com/entertainment/books/a61485201/books-ai-lawsuits/

The CEO of Penguin Random House, Nihar Malaviya: Elizabeth A. Harris, 'The Most Powerful Person in Publishing Doesn't Like to Talk About Himself', *The New York Times*, 30 January 2024, nytimes.com/2024/01/30/books/penguin-random-house-nihar-malaviya.html

In 2022 a writer called Tim Boucher: Tim Boucher, 'I'm Making Thousands Using AI to Write Books', *Newsweek*, 15 May 2023, newsweek.com/ai-books-art-money-artificial-intelligence-1799923; Katyanna Quach, 'Sci-fi Author "Writes" 97 AI-Generated Tales in Nine Months', The Register, 22 May 2023, theregister.com/2023/05/22/ai_in_brief

In 2023 a murder mystery called Death of an Author: Laura Miller, 'The Robot Did It!: The Biggest Twist in the New Mystery Story "Written" by Artificial Intelligence? It's Pretty Good!', *Slate*, 24

April 2023, slate.com/culture/2023/04/ai-chatgpt-mystery-novel-death-author-stephen-marche.html

In an interview in 2023, literary agent Andrew Wylie: David Marchese, 'When Ruthless Cultural Elitism Is Exactly the Job', *The New York Times*, 10 November 2023, nytimes.com/interactive/2023/11/12/magazine/andrew-wylie-interview.html

As author Anita Felicelli writes: 'As a Writer I Don't Despair About AI – It Can't Replicate Our Imaginations', *Los Angeles Times*, 31 December 2023, latimes.com/opinion/story/2023-12-31/ai-books-writers-literature-robots-novels-lawsuits

publisher Faber included a 'Human Written' sticker: Melina Spanoudi, 'Faber Includes "Human Written" Stamp on Sarah Hall's *Helm* in Anti-AI Bid', *The Bookseller*, 18 June 2025, thebookseller.com/news/faber-includes-human-written-stamp-on-sarah-halls-helm-in-anti-ai-bid

Index

Achebe, Chinua, *Things Fall Apart*, 184
Akhmatova, Anna, 'Requiem', 114
AI, 139, 213–14, 215, 245–53
  ChatGPT, 128–9
  large language models, 133 and n, 169–70, 250–51
  OpenAI, 246
alcohol, and the commission of error, 24
Alcott, Louisa May, told she can't write, 184
Alexie, Sherman, 122
Allen, Woodie, 124
Amis, Martin
  on Truman Capote, 180
  The War Against Cliché, 49–50
Angry Penguins (journal), 164–9
Antiphanes, 54
Aristotle, 51
  on good writing (and goats), 48
  Poetics, 54
  on *The Very Hungry Caterpillar*, 53
Asimov, Isaac
  'Galley Slave', 12–13, 39–41
  on rejection, 191
Atwood, Margaret
  gets to grips with reality, 47
  The Handmaid's Tail and sequels, 128, 150–51
  paraphrasing Chaucer, 129
Austen, Jane
  considered by John Lubbock, 52
  published by Puffin Books, 154
  as tonic for the troops, 227

Bacon, Francis, 212
Bad Sex Award, 80–81
Baker, Nicholson, 239
Baker, Peter, and Bernardini, 150
Ballard, J. G., 188
banning/destruction of books, 85, 86–7, 89, 90–92, 100–106, 107–13
Barthes, Roland, 140, 252
Baum, L. Frank, *The Wonderful Wizard of Oz*, 54
Beckett, Samuel, improving *Finnegans Wake*, 35
Beecher Stowe, Harriet, *Uncle Tom's Cabin*, 88, 91
Beer, Thomas, on McKittrick Ros, 71
Belloc, Hilaire, errata slip in *The Last Days of the French Monarchy*, 29
Bellow, Saul, on rejection, 191

Bergler, Edmund, and writer's block, 177–8, 182, 186
Berkeley, William, 87
Bernadini, Filippo, 'spine collector', 149–50, 151–2
Bernays, Edward, assault on borrowers of books, 229–30
Bibles, errors in, 3, 16, 28
Blake, William, merging manuscript and print, 220–22
Blume, Judy, on writer's block, 181
Blyton, Enid, almost becoming an expert witness for *Lady Chatterley*, only to be confounded by her harrumphing husband,104n
book reviews, 191–201
Bookcase Credibility (X feed), 253–4
Bookstagram, 154
BookTok (TikTok community), 54–5, 154–5
borrowing books, 229–30
Boucher, Tim, 248–9
Bowdler, Thomas, 86
bowdlerisation, 86
Boyd, William, 214
Bradbury, Ray, on rejection, 189–90
Brown, Dan
  and his weapons-grade bollocks, 69
  The Lost Symbol as early e-book, 238
Bukovsky, Vladimir, 115
Bukowski, Charles, 75
Bullock, William, perfects the rotary press, 222
Bulwer-Lytton, Edward George, *Paul Clifford*, 82
Bulwer-Lytton Fiction Contest, 82–3
Burgess, Anthony, 63, 179
Burroughs, Edgar Rice, 188
Burroughs, William S., 50
  Naked Lunch, 106, 112–13
Butler, Judith, winning bad-writing award, 79–80
Byron, George Gordon
  antipathy towards Keats, 192–3
  and William McGonagall, 77

Calvino, Italo, 241–2
Camus, Albert
  'awful' (Nabokov), 201
  on bad writing, 74
'Cannibal's Bible', 16
Capote, Truman
  failing to finish *Answered Prayers*, 180
  Gore Vidal on, 206
  on Jack Kerouac, 205
Carey, Peter, *My Life as a Fake*, 168
Cartland, Barbara, daily output, 174–5
Cather, Willa, warming up her juices, 180
censorship, 85
  in China, 127–8
  and *Lady Chatterley* trial, 86, 103–6
  and LGBTQIA+ issues, 86, 127
  libraries and, 86, 89, 109–12, 109n, 125, 126–7
  and religion, 89, 90–94
  in Russia/Soviet Union, 113–18
  in Singapore, 98 and n
  in USA 88–9, 98–9, 107–13
  see also banning/destruction of books; self-censorship
Chandler, Raymond, *The Big Sleep*, 53
Chatterton, Thomas, hoaxer, 160–61
Chaucer, Geoffrey, *Canterbury Tales*, 109
Cheever, John, undressing, 173
Chesterton, G. K., 57, 250n
Churchill, Winston, inadvertently pooping on the French, 28–9
CIA, and *Doctor Zhivago*, 116–18

Clanchy, Kate, *Some Kids I Taught ...*, 123
Cleland, John, *Fanny Hill*, 97–9, 100
cliché
Martin Amis on, 49–50
Cobden-Sanderson, Thomas, and Doves Press, 223, 224–5
Cockerell, Sydney, trying to defuse the Doves Press dispute, 224–5
Coleridge, Samuel Taylor, 175
Collins, Wilkie, and Dickens, 77–8
Comstock Laws, 109
Conan Doyle, Arthur
and Moriarty's motivation, 63
un-retires Sherlock Holmes, 227
Connolly, Cyril, 66
Conrad, Joseph, 233
Copernicus, Nicolaus, *On the Revolutions of the Heavenly Spheres* and its cuckoo Preface, 19–20
copy-editing, 30, 31
copyright, 94, 95–6, 137–8, 138n, 246
Corrain, Cait, *Crown of Starlight* dropped, 199–200
'correctors', 22–4, 30, 31
see also proofreaders
Covid epidemic, influence on book production, 240, 242, 253–4
Cummins, Jeanine, *American Dirt*, 121
Cusk, Rachel, feuding with Camilla Long, 208–9

Dadaism, 56
Dahl, Roald, *The Witches*, 62
Dark, Sidney, sheds light on the 'New Reading Public', 232–3
Daunt, James, on book theft, 147
Dawson, Juno, *This Book Is Gay*, 127
De Wael, Monique (Misha Defonseca), *Misha*, 161
defamation, *see* libel
Defoe, Daniel, 95, 152, 162
Dekker, Thomas, 205–6
deus ex machina, 54
Diagram Prize for Oddest Book Title, 83
Dibdin, Thomas Frognall, *Bibliomania*, 157
Dickens, Charles
daily output, 173
Dombey and Sons, 77
infamous sentence in *Great Expectations*, 77
on piracy in the USA, 95–6
on printers' readers, 31
suspecting George Eliot of being a woman, 162–3
Wilkie Collins on, 77–8
Dictys Cretensis, 162
Didion, Joan, and writer's block, 180–81
Dionysius the Renegade, 159–60
Donne, John, 219–20
Douglas, James, and *the Well of Loneliness*, 100–101
Doyle, Andrew, on McKittrick Ros, 75
Dreiser, Theodore, fighting with Sinclair Lewis, 203
Dunbar, William, *flyting* with Walter Kennedy, 205
Dutton (publishers), 59

e-books, 39, 141, 153, 236–9, 241
economics of publishing, 242–4
Eliot, George, 162
Eliot, T. S., 136
annoying Graham Greene, 182
'not quite first rate' (Nabokov), 201
rejecting *Animal Farm*, 186–7
The Sacred Wood, 138
The Waste Land, 136, 138, 140
on writer's block, 181

Ellison, Ralph, on writer's block, 178
Emerson, Ralph Waldo, 5
environmental impact of book production, 239–40
erratum slips, errata lists, 28–9
'etaoin shrdlu', 33
Euphuists, 71 and n
Euripides, *Medea*, 53–4

Faber & Faber, 'Human Written' sticker, 253
Farrow, Dylan, 124
Faulkner, William
  As I Lay Dying compared unfavourably with cereal boxes, 200
  on characters, 63
  'ridiculous' (Nabokov), 201
  The Sound and the Fury, 34
  on writing, 180
Felicelli, Anita, on AI, 252
feuds, literary, 201–8
Fidentius (Roman poet), 136–7
First World War, influence on book production, 227
Fitzgerald, F. Scott
  feuding with Hemingway, 203–4
  The Great Gatsby, criticism of, 62, 195
  Tender Is the Night, Hemingway on, 204
  the turn to alcohol, 175–6
'Fool's Bible', 16
Forster, E. M., 103 and n
Foucault, Michel, *What Is an Author?*, 137
Franzen, Jonathan, and *Freedom* debacle, 36
Frey, James, *A Million Little Pieces*, 161

Gaiman, Neil, on H. S. Keeler, 60
Gascoigne, George, 51
Gen Z's approach to book-buying, 241
Girodias, Maurice, French publisher of *Lolita*, 106–7
Golding, William, *Lord of the Flies*, 54, 195–6
Goodreads, online reviewing site, 123, 193, 199–200
Goodwin, Hazel, 58
Gorky, Maxim, 115
Grafton, Anthony
  Inky Fingers, 30–31
  Printing and Misprinting, 27–8
Green, Robert, resurrector of Doves Type, 225
Greene, Graham
  daily output, 174
  drawing attention to *Lolita*, 107
  on plagiarism, 140
  writing poetry with T. S. Eliot looking over his shoulder, 181–2
Griffin, Elle, 'No One Buys Books', 242–3
Guardian (newspaper; *Grauniad*), 32
Gutenberg, Johnannes, 212–13, 214, 215, 217, 223

Hall, Radclyffe, *The Well of Loneliness*, 100–101, 101n
Halliwell, James Orchard, 156
Hardwick, Elizabeth, on reviewers, 196 and n
Hardy, Thomas
  mastery of character development, 63
  The Mayor of Casterbridge, 61
HarperCollins, and *Freedom* debacle, 36–7
Harris, Max, and *Angry Penguins*, 164, 167–9
Heller, Joseph, *Catch-22* rejected, 188

Hemingway, Ernest
and AI, 250n
A Farewell to Arms, 203–4
feuding with Fitzgerald, 203–4
For Whom the Bell Tolls, 204
on parody, 8
on rejection, 184–5
sharpening pencils, 180
The Sun Also Rises, 185
The Torrents of Spring, 185
Henry VIII, 93
Heraclitus, 61
Herodotus, *Histories*, Photius on, 193–4
Hesse, Hermann, 5, 214
Heyward, Michael, *The Ern Malley Affair*, 164–5
Hitler, Adolf, *Mein Kampf*, 91
hoaxes, literary, 159–64
Hoffman, Abbie, *Steal This Book*, 146
Horace
Ars Poetica, 48, 50
and 'purple prose', 65
Hornschuch, Hieronymus, *Orthotypographia*, 23–4, 31
Horvitz, David, *How to Shoplift Books*, 148
Hsu, Hua, 204
Hubbard, James M., Boston librarian, 110–11
Hudson, Michael Derrick, 122
Hughes, John, *The Dogs* accused of plagiarism, 138–40
Hugo, Victor, 173, 212
Humblot, Marrc, rejecting *Swann's Way*, 186
Humphries, Barry, 153
Hunt, Leigh, and his overheating temples, 155
Huxley, Aldous, on McKittrick Ros, 71
Index Librorum Prohibitorum, 90–92
Inklings, The, 72
International Imitation Hemingway Competition, 83

Jackson, Holbrook, *The Anatomy of Bibliomania*, 157–9
James, Henry, 195
Jerome, Jerome K., *Three Men in a Boat*, 65–6
John of Wales, 14
John the Evangelist, 14
Johnson, George M., *All Boys Aren't Blue*, 127
Johnson, Samuel, 154
Dictionary, 30, 32, 137
as proofreader, 30
Johnson, Steven, 212
Jonson, Ben, 137
feuding with Gabriel Spenser, 203 and n
on John Donne, 219
and 'The War of the Theatres', 205–6
Joyce, James
Finnegans Wake, 35–6
Ulysses, 34–5, 128
Joyce, Stephen, 35n
'Judas Bible', 28

Keats, John,192–3
Keeler, Harry Stephen, 55–61, 64–5, 249
Kelmscott Press, 224
Kennedy, Walter, *flyting* with William Dunbar, 205
Kerouac, Jack, Capote on, 205
Khrushchev, Nikita, 118
King, Stephen, *Carrie* rejected, 189
King James Bible, 16
Kipling, Rudyard, 188

Kobabe, Maia, *Gender Queer*, 125, 127
Kobek, Jarett, *I Hate the Internet*, 120–21
Koch, Theodore, 227
Kondo, Marie, not really understanding what books are, 152–3
Kuang, R. F., *Yellowface*, 121–2

Lane, Allen, founder of Penguin Books, 103, 233–4
Lawrence, D. H.
  on the 'censor-moron', 100
  'execrable' (Nabokov), 201
  Lady Chatterley's Lover, 86, 98, 101–2, 103–6
  naked in a mulberry tree, 173
  Sons and Lovers disparaged while unread, 200
Lee, Harper
  Go Set a Watchman, 178
  To Kill a Mockingbird, 135, 178
  on writing as heartbreak, 178
legal ramifications of error, 22
Leitch, Vincent B., on Longinus, 48
Lewis, C. S., *An Experiment in Criticism*, 66–8
Lewis, Sinclair, 174n, 203
libel, 119, 120–21
libraries
  Carnegie libraries, 143 and n, 144
  Girolamini library, Naples, 144
  theft from, 142–6
  Trithemius' library, 218
  see also censorship: libraries and
Linotype printing, 222
literacy, and book sales, 226–7
Locke, John, 94–5
Lockwood, Patricia, hired to assassinate Updike, 198
Long, Camilla, feuding with Rachel Cusk, 207–8
Lorrain, Jean, duelling with Proust, 195
Loudan, Jack, biographer of McKittrick Ros, 75, 76, 77
Lubbock, John, 52
Luther, Martin, berating printers, 21–2

Macpherson, James, and Ossian hoax, 160
Mailer, Norman, feud with Gore Vidal, 206–7
Makinson, John, 238
Malavia, Nihar, 247
manuscript error and correction, 5, 14–16, 17
Marche, Stephen, *Death of an Author*, 249–50, 252
Marston, John, 205–6
Martial (Roman poet), and *plaga*, 134–5, 136–7, 140
Martin, George R. R., trying to finish *The Winds of Winter*, 178–9
Matthews, Thomas, duelling with Sheridan, 203
McAuley, James, hoaxing *Angry Penguins*, 164–9, 170
McCarthy, Cormack, 135–6
McChord Crothers (*sic*), Samuel, 'The Hundred Worst Books', 52
McCullers, Carson, accuses Harper Lee of 'poaching', 135
McGonagall, William, 76–7
McKittrick Ros, Amanda, 70–79
Mechanick Exercises, 30
Menand, Louis, 160
Mencken, H. L., 62
Metcalf, Keyes D., Harvard librarian, 111
Miller, Christopher, *Impostors*, 160

Miller, Henry, *Tropic of Cancer*, 98, 106
Milton, John, 126, 140
  Areopagitica, 94–5
Modernism, literary, and the potential for error, 34–6
More, Thomas, 93
Morris, William, 224
Morrissey, Steven Patrick, wins Bad Sex Award, 80–81
Morton, Thomas, *New England Canaan*, 108

Nabokov, Vladimir
  on censorship in Russia, 113
  and Edmund Wilson, 202–3
  feuds, 201–3
  Lolita, 106–7, 108n, 188
  Strong Opinions, 202
Nevins Jr, Francis M., on H. S. Keeler 57, 60
New England Watch and Ward Society, 108
New York Times
  on H. S. Keeler, 60
  last hot-metal edition, 33
Ng, Celeste, on *American Dirt*, 121
Nietzsche, Friedrich, 54
non-human correction of error
  Asimov's proofreading robot, 12–13, 39–41
  autocorrect, 37
  spellcheck, 37
'noonday devil', 173 and n

O'Connell, Mark, 51, 70, 73, 74
optical character recognition (OCR), 38
Orlean, Susan, 141
Orwell, George
  Animal Farm rejected, 186–7
  on Penguin Books, 234
  rules for writers, 48–9
Oulipo, 56
Ovid, *The Art of Love*, 90

Pain, Barry, reviewing *Irene Iddesleigh*, 70–72, 75, 79
Palimpsest (typesetter), 37
palimpsests, 29–30
papal infallibility, and the printed word, 22
Pasternak, Boris, *Doctor Zhivago*, 116–19
Patchett, Anne, on writer's block, 176
Peignot, Étienne-Gabriel, coins the word 'bibliomania', 157
Penguin Books, 102, 103–4, 105 and n
Penguin Random House/Simon & Schuster merger attempt, 242–3, 244–5
Phelps, William Lyon, 229, 231
Phillipps, Harriet, 156
Phillipps, Thomas, 155–6, 159
Photius, *Bibliotheca*, 193–4
Pirsig, Robert M., *Zen and the Art of Motorcycle Maintenance*, 184
plagiarism, 134–40, 203
Plath, Sylvia, 55
  on rejection slips, 189
  on writer's block, 182 and n
Plato, *The Republic*, 51
plot 53–61, 62
  Grace Paley on, 74
Plutarch, and *The Waste Land*, 136
Poe, Edgar Allan
  The Narrative of Arthur Gordon Pym, 163
  as reviewer, 194–5
poetry, bad/fake, 76, 78–9, 164–9
Pope, Alexander, revising Shakespeare, 26–7
Potter, Beatrix, books as easy prey for shoplifters, 147

Pound, Ezra
  'totally fake' (Nabokov), 201
Poundstone, William, on H. S. Keeler, 56–7
Pratchett, Terry, on writer's block, 182
printer's devil, 1, 19
Priore, Greg, librarian-thief, 143–4
Project Gutenberg, 38–9, 236–7
proofreaders, 30, 32
  see also 'correctors'
Proust, Marcel
  duelling with Jean Lorrain, 195
  Pleasures and Days, criticised, 195
  Sodom and Gomorrah, 34
  Swann's Way rejected and self-published, 186
Pseudo-Dionysius, 161–2
Pushkin, Alexander, *Eugene Onegin*

Radway, Janice, *A Feeling for Books*, 230
Rasenberger, Mary, on AI, 246–7, 248
rejection, of authors' submissions, 183–91
Rendell, Ruth, on Agatha Christie, 204–5
Robertson, Geoffrey, 106
Roth, Philip, on reviews, 200–201
Ruiz Robles, Ángela, and her 'Mechanical Encyclopaedia', 236
Rushdie, Salman, *The Satanic Verses*, 3

Salinger, J. D., *The Catcher in the Rye*, 88–9, 127
samizdat, 115–18
Second World War, influence on book production, 234–5

Self, Will, 208, 239
self-censorship, 87, 113
  see also censorship
self-publishing, 119
sensitivity readers, 88, 121–3
Seth, Vikram, *A Suitable Buy*, 33
Shakespeare, William
  Antony and Cleopatra, and *The Waste Land*, 136
  errors in editions of, 9–10, 25–7
  Hamlet, 61–2
  spelling of name, 25
  The Taming of the Screw, 33
  and 'The War of the Theatres' (possibly), 205
Shelley, Percy Bysshe, 51, 175, 192
Sheridan, Richard Brinsley, duelling, 203
Sidney, Philip, *Defence of Poesie*, 51
silverfish, bad news for books, 223 and n
Sinclair, Upton, *Oil!*, 112
Smith, Emma, *Portable Magic*, 93
Smith, Zadie, spurning social media, 208
Spenser, Gabriel, killed by Ben Jonson, 203 and n
Stationers' Company, as censors, 93–4, 95
Stein, Gertrude, 187
Steinbeck, John
  The Grapes of Wrath, 200
  Of Mice and Men, 127
  on writer's block, 180
Stevenson, Robert Louis, 184
Stewart, Harold, hoaxing *Angry Penguins*, 164–9, 170
Stockett, Kathryn, *The Help*, 184
Stravinsky, Igor, with a handy bon mot, 47
Striphas, Ted, 228

Tennyson, Alfred, recognising the imperfection of first editions, 154

Theobald, Lewis, kicking off with Alexender Pope, 26–7
Thomas, Angie, *The Hate U Give*, 125
Toole, John Kennedy, *A Confederacy of Dunces*, 190
Trithemius, Johannes, and the transition from manuscript to print, 216–19
Trollope, Anthony, 172–3
Twain, Mark
  on Gutenberg, 212
  on Mckittrick Ros, 71
  as 'printer's devil', 1–2
  on proofreaders, 31–2
Tyndale, William, 89
Tyson, Neil deGrasse, 37

Updike, John, on reviewing, 197–8

Vidal, Gore, feud with Norman Mailer, 206–7
Vonnegut, Kurt
  advocates sadism, 47–8
  thanks librarians, 126
Vorse, Mary Heaton, 174n

Walker, Emery, and Doves Press, 224–5
Webster, Noah, *American Dictionary of the English Language*, 32
Welles, Orson, and happy endings, 47
Wells, H. G., *War of the Worlds* rejected, 188
White, E. B., 181
'Wicked Bible', 3
widow, example of, 109
Wilde, Oscar, 11
Wilson, Edmund, on reviewers, 195–6
Winn, Raynor, *The Salt Path*, scrapes in as a footnote, 169n
Winterson, Jeanette, 101n
Wolfe, Tom, 206
Woolf, Virginia, 55, 232
writer's block, 171, 175–82
Wylie, Andrew, on AI, 252

Yiannopoulos, Milo, *Dangerous*, 124